treehouse™

HTML5
Foundations

Matt West

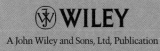

WILEY

A John Wiley and Sons, Ltd, Publication

This edition first published 2013

© 2013 Matthew West

Registered office

John Wiley & Sons Ltd, The Atrium, Southern Gate, Chichester, West Sussex, PO19 8SQ, United Kingdom

For details of our global editorial offices, for customer services and for information about how to apply for permission to reuse the copyright material in this book please see our website at www.wiley.com.

A catalogue record for this book is available from the British Library.

ISBN 978-1-118-35655-5 (paperback); ISBN 978-1-118-43268-6 (ebook); 978-1-118-43270-9 (ebook); 978-1-118-43269-3 (ebook)

Set in Chaparral Pro Light 10/12.5 by Indianapolis Composition Services

Printed in the U.S. at Command Web Missouri

About the Author

MATT WEST is a developer and entrepreneur who has a keen fascination with exploring new ways that technology can be used to make our lives simpler. Currently residing just outside Northampton, England, Matt fell into web development after getting involved in a number of open-source projects in his spare time.

Matt currently runs Developer City, a small web development agency that specializes in creating innovative web applications for clients all around the world.

Matt writes a blog called Coding Skyscrapers (`http://codingskyscrapers.com`) and can be found as @MattAntWest on Twitter.

Publisher's Acknowledgements

Some of the people who helped bring this book to market include the following:

Editorial and Production

VP Consumer and Technology Publishing Director: Michelle Leete

Associate Director–Book Content Management: Martin Tribe

Associate Publisher: Chris Webb

Assistant Editor: Ellie Scott

Development Editor: Sara Shlaer

Copy Editor: Debbye Butler

Technical Editor: Nick Elliott

Editorial Manager: Jodi Jensen

Senior Project Editor: Sara Shlaer

Editorial Assistant: Leslie Saxman

Marketing

Associate Marketing Director: Louise Breinholt

Marketing Manager: Lorna Mein

Senior Marketing Executive: Kate Parrett

Composition Services

Compositor: Indianapolis Composition Services

Proofreader: Wordsmith Editorial

Indexer: BIM Indexing & Proofreading Services

For my father.

Acknowledgments

There may be a single name on the cover of this book, but if the past six months has taught me anything, it is that writing a book is truly a team effort. I am forever grateful for the support and guidance given by so many throughout this process.

To Sara Shlaer, for her solid feedback, patience, and sharp editing skills.

To Nick Elliot, for his incredible eye-for-detail and honest feedback throughout.

To Debbye Butler, for guiding my transition to US English (and correcting the many mistakes that I made along the way.)

To Ellie Scott, for her help in keeping the legal department happy and her general support throughout.

To Chris Webb, for his help in conceiving the direction for this book and for giving me the opportunity to write it in the first place.

To all those at Wiley (and beyond) whom I didn't have the privilege of working with personally, but whom I know worked hard to make this book a reality.

To Ryan Carson, for putting his trust in a stranger and for creating a company that is changing the lives of people all over the world.

To the Treehouse team—particularly Jim Hoskins, Nick Pettit and Michael Poley—for providing support whenever it was needed.

To all those within the web industry who share their thoughts, knowledge, and ideas; their inspiration has been invaluable throughout this process.

To my family and friends, for keeping me reasonably sane over the past six months.

Thank you.

Contents

part 1: Creating Web Pages with HTML5

part 4: Advanced HTML5 Technologies

Introduction

SOMETIMES IT'S DIFFICULT to remember a time before the World Wide Web. A time before we could find information about anything we desired by simply typing a few words into a search box on our computers, and these days even our mobile phones.

The web has come a long way since its humble origins in the research labs of academics. It has grown to be the single most valuable resource for information that the world has ever known. In doing so, it has created countless billionaires, sparked revolutions within countries throughout the world, and transformed education and science. The United Nations has even proposed that access to the Internet should be a basic human right.

HTML5 is the next step in the history of the web; it is the future. The new technologies introduced by HTML5 enable developers to create websites that are smarter, faster, and more secure than they have ever been before. The best thing about the Internet is that it is an open platform; anyone can build his or her own website. The barriers to entry in this industry are surprisingly low—and that's awesome.

The community surrounding the web industry is the best in the world. Of course, I may be slightly biased, but I really believe that statement is true. I don't know of any other industry where so many people in the community come together to help each other and push the web forward in new and innovative ways. Every day, I wake up and feel privileged to be part of it all. Now it is time for you to join us.

Who Should Read This Book?

This book is for anyone who wants to learn how to create his or her own website and how to use HTML5's exciting new technologies.

The book doesn't assume that you have any experience with programming in HTML, CSS, JavaScript, or any other language for that matter. If you do, that's a bonus, but you will learn everything you need to know to start building awesome websites with HTML5.

This is not a book to help you make the transition from older HTML standards. Everything is covered from the ground up in order to make sure that all the techniques you will learn are up to date. There are plenty of books for experienced developers—books that go deep into the inner workings of HTML5 technologies and have lengthy explanations on why technologies were developed in a certain way. This book is not one of them. Some parts require a bit of explanation, but for the most part, I won't bore you with the details.

If you already have some knowledge of web design, you will still find the content useful; after all, a lot has changed in HTML5. Some explanations in the early chapters may be a little more verbose than you require at times, so feel free to skip ahead if you find yourself reading about things you already know.

What You Will Learn

HTML5 encompasses a huge number of new technologies, loads more than could possibly be covered in a single book, and therefore I have chosen the most exciting and relevant technologies for you to learn about.

Part 1 of the book, **Creating Web Pages with HTML5**, takes you through the basics of building web pages. It starts by introducing you to the tools of the trade and taking you through creating your first web pages with HTML5. You will learn about HTML elements and how to structure your web pages, as well as how to link multiple pages together to create websites. You will also cover the importance of web standards, validating your code, and testing your websites in multiple web browsers.

In part 2, **Dealing with Data**, you dive straight into working with web forms to collect data from your visitors. You will learn how to code a form and the various types of inputs that are available to you. You will also learn about input validations and how using them can help to ensure the quality of the data you capture.

Next you will learn about microdata and how to mark up your content so that search engines and other computer programs can easily find important information in your web pages.

Accessibility is an important topic when it comes to creating web pages. Unfortunately, not all visitors can enjoy the same great experience when using your website. You will learn about building web pages that are screen reader friendly and how to create designs that can be used by people with visual or motor impairments.

In part 3, **Enhancing Web Pages with HTML5 and JavaScript**, you start to get into some really exciting stuff, looking at how to embed video and audio into your web pages and how to create custom controls for them with JavaScript. You will also look at the LocalStorage and SessionStorage APIs and learn how to use them to store data on a user's computer.

Part 4, **Advanced HTML5 Technologies**, takes you even deeper, with GeoLocation and the Canvas API. GeoLocation is one of the most exciting new web technologies. You learn all about the GeoLocation API and how you can use it to make your website smarter.

The Canvas API enables you to draw objects directly in the browser. You'll learn how to draw various shapes and paths and how you can use this technology in your projects today.

That's a lot of content for you to cover, and so throughout the book you will be applying all your newfound knowledge in creating a real-world website for a fast-food chain, "Joe's Pizza Co." The final product will be a fully functional HTML5 website complete with promotional video, booking form, and a page that visitors can use to find their nearest store (making good use of the GeoLocation API, of course).

How to Use This Book

There is no particular order in which you should read this book. I rarely read computer books from cover to cover, so it would be foolish of me to assume that you will. It is often much more enjoyable to jump around to the chapters that are most interesting to you, so feel free to do so. You can always backtrack to a previous chapter if there is something that you don't quite understand.

That said, if you are completely new to the world of web design I recommend reading through Part 1 first so that you can obtain the basic foundations needed to move forward. After that, the book is structured so that you can dip in and out of different chapters as you please. This way you can easily refer back to things in the future when you are building websites out in the wild.

Readers that have some knowledge of programming websites will find that many of the new HTML5 semantic elements can be found in among the "older" ones in the first few chapters, so stay alert! You don't want to miss anything.

Some chapters contain fairly large chunks of code for you to work with. If you don't want to sit and type it all in to your computer (like a highly trained code-monkey), you can easily download all the code examples from the book's website at `http://wiley.com/go/treehouse/html5foundations`. Once you have extracted the archive, you will find all the code examples neatly placed in separate folders for each chapter, with subfolders for the specific exercises as you follow along.

Throughout the book, you will build a website for the fast-food chain, "Joe's Pizza Co." You will gradually add more and more features to the website as you move through the content of the book and learn about the technologies that enable them. If you decide to skip a chapter, you can easily download the code for that chapter from the book's website to update your example files.

Using This Book with Treehouse

Just to be clear, you don't have to be a Treehouse member to use this book. However, the online videos at `teamtreehouse.com` do supplement the content quite nicely. When there is a video that covers the same content that is being covered in the book, you will see the

Video icon in the margin and a link to the relevant video. Viewing all the videos and completing badges is a good way of testing what you have learned in the book (and of showing off your new skills to others).

If you ever get stuck on a concept in the book, Treehouse has a great community of members who would be more than happy to help you. You can find them in the official Treehouse members group on Facebook.

Ready to go? Let's get started.

part 1

Creating Web Pages with HTML5

chapter one

Getting Started with HTML5

SO YOU'RE EAGER to start building a website? By the end of this chapter, you will have done just that!

You start by getting your computer primed for building websites. That means you're going to install a text editor and a lot of web browsers. I take you on a brief tour through some of the most popular text editors, web browsers, and developer tools so you can decide which ones you want to use.

Once you have your computer set up for building websites, you'll learn about HTML elements and attributes. These are the basic building blocks that make up web pages.

There are a few things that all good web developers should know. That said, toward the end of this chapter, you will learn how to validate the HTML code that you have been writing. You will also learn that your websites can sometimes behave differently depending on which browser they are being viewed in.

What is HTML?

Hyper Text Markup Language, or *HTML*, is the basic code that makes up the foundation of every website on the World Wide Web. HTML is used for marking up text and other page content, and for defining how a web page is structured.

A web page is made up of lots of content—text, images, even videos. Each of these pieces of content is marked up using HTML syntax (a collection of words and symbols that can be understood by computer programs). HTML is also used to describe the structure of the page, defining each of the different sections it may have (such as a header, content area, and footer).

HTML is used to define the page content and how it is structured, but it is *not* responsible for how the page actually looks—the color, borders, and positioning of elements. That is a job for Cascading Style Sheets, or CSS, which you will look at briefly later in this book. There is also one other language that is commonly used when building websites. *JavaScript* is a programming language that is used in conjunction with HTML and CSS to build interactive features for web pages. Later in this book you will be using JavaScript to build custom playback controls for a video.

HTML is always evolving. The latest revision of HTML is HTML5, the subject of this book. The official specification for HTML5 outlines a large number of new features that enable web developers to create websites that are faster and smarter than those they could build using older versions of HTML. These new features include LocalStorage (which enables developers to store data on the user's computer) and HTML5 Video (that enables video playback in your web browser without needing a plug-in like Flash) as well as new interactive elements, such as date pickers and sliders.

The term *HTML5* has become somewhat of a buzzword in recent years, used by clients, bosses, and developers alike to describe what is coming next in the journey of web technologies. Although this usage is common, it is not strictly accurate. HTML5 is just one part of a large number of standards that are collectively referred to as New Exciting Web Technologies (NEWT). Alongside HTML5, NEWT also encompasses things like WebGL (3D graphics in the browser) and GeoLocation (finding a user's location). Although GeoLocation is not strictly part of HTML5, you will learn about it later in this book because it is so cool that I just couldn't leave it out.

Setting Up Your Tools

Before you can start building your own web pages, you first need to set up some tools. You likely have at least one browser and possibly a text editor already installed on your computer, but you'll want to widen your range of browsers and you'll need to add some specialist developer tools, too.

Browsers

Many different web browsers are available, and it is important that you test your website in all of the most popular ones in order to make sure that your website looks and behaves as you want it to. I recommend installing the latest version of each of the following five browsers (if they are available for your operating system):

Google Chrome

Google's web browser, Chrome, is known for being both fast and secure. It also boasts great support for the latest HTML5 and CSS3 technologies. Chrome has some great developer tools that you will be using later in this book to interact with the web pages that you create. Google Chrome also updates itself automatically whenever a newer version is available. You can download the latest version of Chrome at `http://www.google.com/chrome`.

Mozilla Firefox

One of Firefox's greatest strengths is its vast extension library that contains loads of great tools, including the very popular Firebug developer tools, to help you build websites. The browser also has great support for the majority of HTML5 technologies. Firefox also has an automatic update feature, similar to that found in Google Chrome. Download the latest version at `http://www.mozilla.org/en-US/firefox/new/`.

Apple Safari

Apple's Safari browser is popular with Mac and Windows users alike. The built-in developer tools can also be useful when trying to diagnose a problem in a web page. Like Google Chrome, Safari also has great support for some of the latest HTML5 technologies. You can grab the latest version of Safari from `http://www.apple.com/safari/`.

Microsoft Internet Explorer

Internet Explorer (IE) is still one of the most popular browsers used today. Microsoft has released many versions of IE over the years, and it is worth noting that not all Windows operating systems will support the latest versions of IE. Windows XP, for example, does not support any versions of Internet Explorer past IE8. This means that Windows XP users will never get the latest HTML5 features without installing extra plug-ins or a different browser. Some older versions of the browser were plagued with bugs that meant that developers had to spend hours of extra time getting their web pages to display correctly. Fortunately, Microsoft has done a great job with the latest versions of IE (9 and 10) and has also managed to incorporate some of the latest HTML5 technologies. The latest version of IE will usually be downloaded when you perform Windows Updates; otherwise you can get it at `http://windows.microsoft.com/en-GB/internet-explorer/products/ie/home`.

Opera

Opera has been gaining in popularity in recent years, due in part to the success of its mobile browser. Opera software is a driving force in the development of the HTML5 specification, and has implemented a lot of HTML5 technologies in the latest versions of its browser. Like Chrome, Opera also has an auto-update feature. You can download the latest version of Opera at `http://www.opera.com/browser`.

Text Editors

Your text editor is your faithful sidekick. You will use it to write all your HTML, CSS, and JavaScript code. A good text editor can actually make you more productive and help you to quickly identify any errors that you may make while coding. In this section, I list four of the most popular text editors for Mac, Windows, and Linux, but many other alternatives are available.

- **Sublime Text 2** is rapidly gaining popularity among developers because of its flexibility and its great set of features. It is used in the latest Treehouse videos and offers loads of features, including themes, code completion, and snippets. Sublime Text 2 is not free, but many developers find that purchasing it is a good investment because it can help to increase your productivity. Currently, versions are available for Mac, Linux, and Windows. You can download Sublime Text 2 at http://www.sublimetext.com/2. Figure 1-1 shows Sublime Text 2 in action.

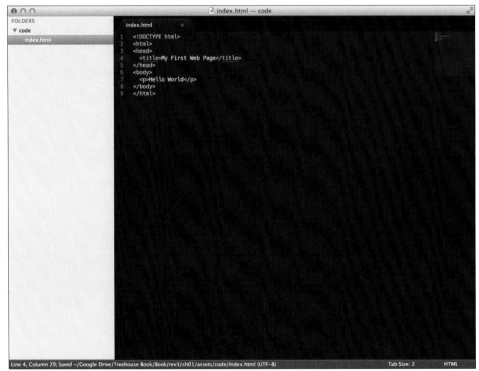

FIGURE 1-1 Editing an HTML document with Sublime Text 2.

- **TextWrangler** is a good general-purpose text editor that is available for the Mac. Unlike Sublime Text 2, TextWrangler is free. You can download it from http://www.barebones.com/products/TextWrangler/.

- **Notepad++** is a popular text editor for Windows developers, and the best bit is that it is completely free (as in beer). It supports many different programming languages, including the ones that you will be using in this book. Download Notepad++ at `http://notepad-plus-plus.org/download/v6.1.html`.

- **gedit** is a simple text editor that is available for all flavors of Linux that use the GNOME desktop environment (such as Ubuntu). It supports themes and syntax highlighting, and you can also find loads of great plug-ins online. Like Notepad++, gedit is free. You can download gedit at `http://gedit.en.softonic.com/download`.

You need a text editor to begin creating your website, so if you don't have one on your machine already, download one now and install it.

Developer Tools

Sometimes, when you are building a website you want to quickly manipulate the page styles or test some JavaScript without having to go back to your text editor to make the changes. This is where developer tools come in. All of the most popular web browsers either have developer tools built in or have extensions available that will give you similar functionality. You will find that you become most accustomed to the tools available in your browser of choice; however, it is useful to know how to access and use the developer tools in other browsers in case you have to look into a compatibility issue when testing your websites.

In this section, you learn how to access (and in some cases install) the developer tools for Chrome, Firefox, Safari, Opera, and Internet Explorer.

- **Chrome Developer Tools**—Access the Chrome developer tools from the Chrome browser by clicking on the little wrench to the right of the address bar and selecting the Developer Tools option from the Tools menu. Alternatively, you can right-click on an element on the screen and select Inspect Element from the context menu. Figure 1-2 shows the Google UK home page being inspected using the Chrome developer tools.

  The Chrome developer tools contain lots of features to help you interact with and monitor your web pages. The tools that you will be using the most for the examples in this book can be found in the Elements, Scripts, and Console tabs in the developer tools window. I use the Chrome developer tools throughout this book.

- **Firebug for Firefox**—Firebug does not come bundled with a fresh installation of Firefox, so with Firefox open, you need to download the latest version from `http://getfirebug.com`. Firebug is free to use.

  Once you have the Firebug extension installed, access it by choosing Tools➜Web Developer➜Firebug➜Open Firebug. As with the Chrome developer tools, you can also access Firebug by right-clicking an element on the page and selecting Inspect Element with Firebug from the context menu.

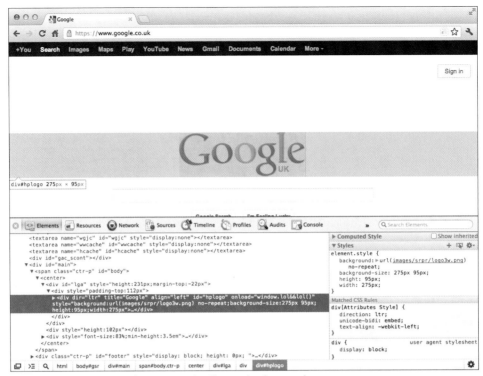

FIGURE 1-2 Inspecting a web page using the Chrome developer tools.

You can change the location of the Firebug tools panel by clicking the Firebug icon in the top-left corner and selecting an option from the Firebug UI Location menu.

- **Dragonfly for Opera**—Opera's Dragonfly developer tools are built directly into the browser so there are no extensions to install. You can access Dragonfly by going to Tools➜Advanced and selecting Opera Dragonfly.

  Dragonfly has many of the standard developer tools that you would expect from a modern browser. The Documents and Scripts tabs will be particularly useful when building the examples in this book. Note that the developer tools are updated automatically when new versions are released.

- **Web Inspector in Safari**—Safari's Web Inspector Developer Tools are similar to the developer tools found in Google Chrome. That's because they are both built upon the Web Inspector tools in WebKit.

  Before you can access the developer tools in Safari, you need to enable them. To do this, open the Preferences pane by pressing Ctrl plus the comma key in Windows or Command plus the comma key on a Mac. In the Preferences pane, click on the Advanced tab and select the checkbox labeled Show Develop Menu in Menu Bar. You should now see the Develop menu appear in the menu bar at the top of the screen. If you use Safari on Windows, you may need to display the menu bar by clicking the cog in the top-right corner and selecting Show menu bar. You can access all of Safari's developer tools, including Web Inspector, from the Developer drop-down menu.

Safari also has a number of other developer tools that enable you to easily turn off caching, images, styling, and JavaScript. These tools can be very useful when testing how a website will look and behave in less capable browsers.

- **IE Developer Tools**—Internet Explorer has a set of built-in developer tools that can be accessed through the Tools menu or by pressing F12 on your keyboard.

  The IE developer tools contain all the features that you would expect, including element, CSS, and JavaScript inspectors as well as a console. There are also a number of tools to help you test your website on older versions of IE. These tools are useful because some of the older versions of Internet Explorer had bugs that can affect how your web pages will be displayed to users. There is also a Validate menu that includes links to easily validate the page you are viewing using the W3C validator. You learn about web page validation later in this chapter.

Building Your First HTML5 Web Page

You're still here, and you have your tools set up. Great! Now it's time to start writing some real markup. In this section, you build your very first web page using HTML, in just three simple steps.

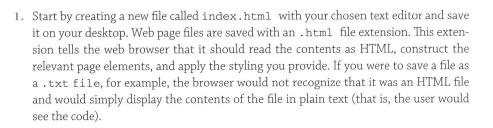

All download code files for the exercises in the book are available from the book's website at `http://www.wiley.com/go/treehouse/html5foundations`, and are grouped into folders by chapters. The code for this exercise can be found in the Chapter 1 folder, in folder 1.

1. Start by creating a new file called `index.html` with your chosen text editor and save it on your desktop. Web page files are saved with an `.html` file extension. This extension tells the web browser that it should read the contents as HTML, construct the relevant page elements, and apply the styling you provide. If you were to save a file as a `.txt file`, for example, the browser would not recognize that it was an HTML file and would simply display the contents of the file in plain text (that is, the user would see the code).

The home page of your website should always be named `index.html` because this is the file that the web server will look to return when somebody visits the root of your website. For example, if a visitor goes to `http://example.org`, the web server will look for an index file in the root directory of the website—that is, `http://example.org/index.html`. The *root* directory is the top-level folder in your web space.

2. Type the following code in your `index.html` file. (This code can also be downloaded from the book's companion website.)

```
<!DOCTYPE html>
<html>
<head>
  <title>My First Web Page</title>
</head>
<body>
  <p>Hello World</p>
</body>
</html>
```

3. Save your `index.html` file.

Now open the `index.html` file in your favorite web browser by double-clicking the file on your desktop. To open it in a browser other than the default one on your computer, right-click on the file and select a program from the Open With menu. This is how you will access your web page files for all the examples in this book.

You should see a page that looks like Figure 1-3.

FIGURE 1-3 Your first HTML5 web page.

If your web page doesn't look like the one in the figure, check that you typed all the code correctly. Make sure that you check the spelling of the words within the angle brackets, too.

That's it! You have successfully created your very first web page. It really wasn't as hard as you thought it would be, was it? I know, it's not very colorful or exciting, but that will come soon enough. First, let's explore this code a bit.

Constructing Elements

HTML web pages are made up of a number of *elements*; think of these as the components of a web page. Each element has a particular purpose; it might contain some text content, a heading, an image, or some information to be used by the browser. The code in your example includes three main elements: an `<html>` element, a `<head>` element, and a `<body>` element.

Those elements in turn contain some other elements, such as a `<title>` and a `<p>` (for paragraph) element. You learn more about each of those shortly.

In most cases, an element is made up of two tags, a start tag and an end tag. You may place some content between these tags that will be displayed on the web page—such as text, or even more elements. Each tag starts with a less-than sign (<) and ends with a greater-than sign (>). End tags also have a forward slash (/) immediately after the less-than sign so the browser can differentiate them from start tags and recognize the end of an element. Here is the `<title>` element from the page you just created:

`<title>``My First Web Page`**`</title>`**

Note the start and end tags (bolded here) with some text content in the middle.

Several elements do not have end tags. These are called *void* elements. A void element should not contain any content and therefore does not have an end tag. I point out these elements as the book progresses.

The `<html>` Element

Open your `index.html` file in your text editor again (if you've closed it) and take a look at the second line of the code, and the very last line:

```
<html>
...
</html>
```

The DOCTYPE Declaration

Take a look at the first line of the code:

```
<!DOCTYPE html>
```

The DOCTYPE is a small piece of code that should be placed at the start of each web page to indicate which standard the respective page complies with. The DOCTYPE in this example indicates the code is compliant with HTML5.

When you open a web page in your browser, the browser looks for a DOCTYPE declaration. It examines the DOCTYPE to decide whether the page is using modern web standards, such as HTML5, or if it was designed to work with older browsers. The browser then uses this information to determine how to interpret the code and display it on the screen.

These lines indicate the start and end of the `<html>` element. The `<html>` element is the root of an HTML document. This means that it should contain all your HTML code. The only code that should not be placed within this element is the DOCTYPE declaration (see sidebar). You can see that all the other elements (the `<head>` and `<body>`) are nested within the `<html>` element in your code.

Attributes

Start tags can also contain additional information by using *attributes*. These attributes contain a *value* (or a set of values) and are listed before the tag is closed with the > sign. Here's an example, the `<img>` element. The `<img>` element is used to add an image to your web page. Note that this is a void element so it has no end tag.

```
<img src="image.jpg" width="300" height="100"
    alt="A description of the image.">
```

This image element has four different attributes: `src`, `width`, `height`, and `alt`. Each of these attributes is assigned a value that passes some information to the browser. The value is placed within quotation marks. This example uses the `src` (source) attribute to tell the browser that the image that you want to display is the `image.jpg` file. You use the `width` attribute, with a value of `300`, to tell the browser that your image should be displayed 300 pixels wide, and the `height` attribute with a value of `100` to make it 100 pixels tall. The value of the `alt` attribute here provides some text that the browser might display if the image cannot be loaded. You learn more about the `<img>` element, as well as lots of other content elements, in Chapter 4.

The `<html>` element is often used to define the language of the content within the document. This is done by adding a `lang` attribute to the start tag that has a two-character language code as its value. (This applies only to the actual page content and not to the tag names; they should always be written in English.) The following example defines the content language as English by adding the `lang` attribute with the value `"en"`. (I highlight the new portion of the code with each new example so you can identify it easily.)

```
<html lang="en">
```

Ready to play with your code again? Let's define the content language for your web page.

The code for this exercise can be found in folder 2.

1. Open your `index.html` file in your text editor.

2. Now add the `lang` attribute to the `<html>` start tag and set its value to en.

   `<html `**`lang="en"`**`>`

3. Save the `index.html` file.

You can find a full list of two-character language codes under the 'ISO 639-1 Code' column on the following web page: `http://www.loc.gov/standards/iso639-2/php/code_ list.php`.

The `<head>` Element

The first element contained within the `<html>` element should be a `<head>` element. This element contains information about the page, such as the title. Here's the `<head>` element from the sample code:

```
<head>
  <title>My First Web Page</title>
</head>
```

Look back at the complete code sample. Note that the `<head>` is contained within the `<html>` element, between the start and end tags.

One of the most important elements in the `<head>` is the `<title>` element. The content of this element is used to set the title of your page in the browser and will appear at the top of your browser window or on a tab, as you can see in Figure 1-3. In your web page, you define the page title as `My First Web Page`.

Try updating the title of your web page:

The code for this exercise can be found in folder 3.

1. Open the `index.html` file in your text editor.

2. Update the text between the `<title>` tags to be `My Updated Page Title`.

3. Save the file.

Now if you open the `index.html` file in your web browser, you should see that the page title has changed. This is displayed either at the top of the browser or in the browser tab, depending on which browser you are using.

The <body> Element

After the <head> element comes a new element—the <body>. In this element, you place all the content that will be displayed in the browser window. The following code shows the <body> element from your web page.

```
<body>
  <p>Hello World</p>
</body>
```

You can have only one <body> element in a page.

The `Hello World` text here has been placed within a <p> (paragraph) element. This element is used for blocks of text. You look at this element in more detail in Chapter 4.

Try adding some new content to your web page:

The code for this exercise can be found in folder 4.

1. Open the `index.html` file in your web browser.

2. Add the following code underneath the existing <p> element.

   ```
   <p>HTML5 Rocks!</p>
   ```

3. Save the file.

Now open the `index.html` file in your web browser. You should see that the new text is displayed on the page, as shown in Figure 1-4. Easy, right?

FIGURE 1-4 Your web page with the new text you just added.

In this section, you learned how to create the underlying structure of a web page; however, none of these elements really controls the physical layout of the page. In Chapter 2, you learn about the elements used to create the visual sections of a web page.

You can see a full list of HTML5 elements in Appendix A.

Nesting Elements

The practice of placing one element within another is called *nesting*. Think of nesting as a big tree diagram. You start with one element (<body>); this element has a number of other elements nested within it (in your web page, the <p> elements). These elements then in turn have elements nested within them, and so on. This creates a huge tree of elements with a number of different levels.

The position of each of the elements within your code is important. Make sure that both the start and end tags of your element are nested within the same element. For example, you should never have a start tag within the <body> element and the end tag outside of it. This code would be invalid, but more importantly, it will sometimes cause your web page to be displayed incorrectly in a web browser.

Indenting elements that are nested within others (as you have done with the <p> elements in your web page) is useful to quickly identify the structure of your HTML code.

Validating Your Web Page

Validating your web pages allows you to be sure that your code is *standards-compliant*. This means that the code that you write follows the best practices and guidelines outlined in the relevant *web standards*.

Why Should You Validate?

Although validation is not mandatory, it is an important part of the development process. You should validate your code for a number of reasons:

- **Debugging your code**—Validation can be a useful way to find errors in your code that may be causing problems with how a page is being displayed in web browsers. For example, it is easy to miss an end tag in your code, resulting in problems with how browsers show the layout of the page. Using a validator can help you to find where end tags are missing or incorrectly placed, saving you a lot of time going painstakingly through each line of your code to check that you have used tags correctly.

- **Future-proofing your code**—Just because your code works in browsers today does not mean that it will work in the future. Browser makers generally implement technologies as they are defined in the relevant specifications, and these specifications are designed to ensure that technologies will be backwards compatible with older versions. This means that if you follow the web standards today, your code is more likely to work in the future because browser makers have a better idea of how your code is structured and what it is trying to do.

What Are Web Standards?

Web standards are specifications developed by organizations such as the W3C (World Wide Web Consortium) and WHATWG (Web Hypertext Application Technology Working Group)—developers sure like their acronyms! These specifications outline how browser makers should implement new technologies in their browsers and how developers should use these technologies.

The actual specifications are often very long and fairly dull to read. Luckily, however, there are concise versions of the HTML5 specification available for developers that cut out the more boring stuff aimed at browser makers. You can find the WHATWG web developer version of the HTML5 spec at `http://developers.whatwg.org/` and the W3C version at `http://dev.w3.org/html5/html-author/`.

Just to make things a little more confusing, the W3C and WHATWG both maintain separate versions of the HTML5 specification. These are mainly identical, but I have found that the WHATWG tends to adopt new technologies more quickly than the W3C does.

- **Best practices**—Valid code follows a set of best practices that have been designed by working groups, and so by learning to write valid code you are also learning the best practices for building web pages. This is especially important for people who are new to web development because often browsers will automatically correct mistakes that you have made in your code without telling you about them. This can lead you to believe that you are writing nice valid code when, in fact, you are making a lot of mistakes.

- **More maintainable web pages**—Writing code that conforms to a widely accepted set of standards makes it easier for multiple people to work on one project. Inevitably, everybody has his or her own, slightly different, programming style; by following web standards when writing code, you can ensure that your markup is consistent and easy for other people to understand.

- **It's just more professional**—If you are serious about creating quality sites, writing good valid code will show people that you know what you are doing. If you work in client services, it is also a great way of showing your clients that you are committed to building websites that are future-proof, maintainable, and standards-compliant. (***Pro Tip:*** Clients like those words; put them in your project proposals.)

Using validator.w3.org

Several code validators are available, but the exercises for this book use `http://validator.w3.org`.

Validator.w3.org is a free service maintained by the W3C that you can use to validate your HTML and CSS code against various web standards. You can run your code through the validator in a number of ways.

- Provide a link to a page on the web.

- Upload a file from your computer.

- Copy and paste your code directly into the browser.

The validator will attempt to identify what version of HTML the page is written in by looking at the DOCTYPE declaration at the top of the page. (See the sidebar on DOCTYPEs, earlier in this chapter.) This enables the validator to run your code against the relevant set of web standards. You can also explicitly tell the validator which standard you would like to test against by selecting one from the Document Type drop-down menu in the More Options section on the validator home page.

It's time to test the web page that you created earlier to see if it validates.

1. Open `http://validator.w3.org`.

2. Select the Validate by Direct Input method.

3. Copy and paste your code into the text box.

4. Click Check.

You should now see that your code passed validation as HTML5 (see Figure 1-5). Congratulations!

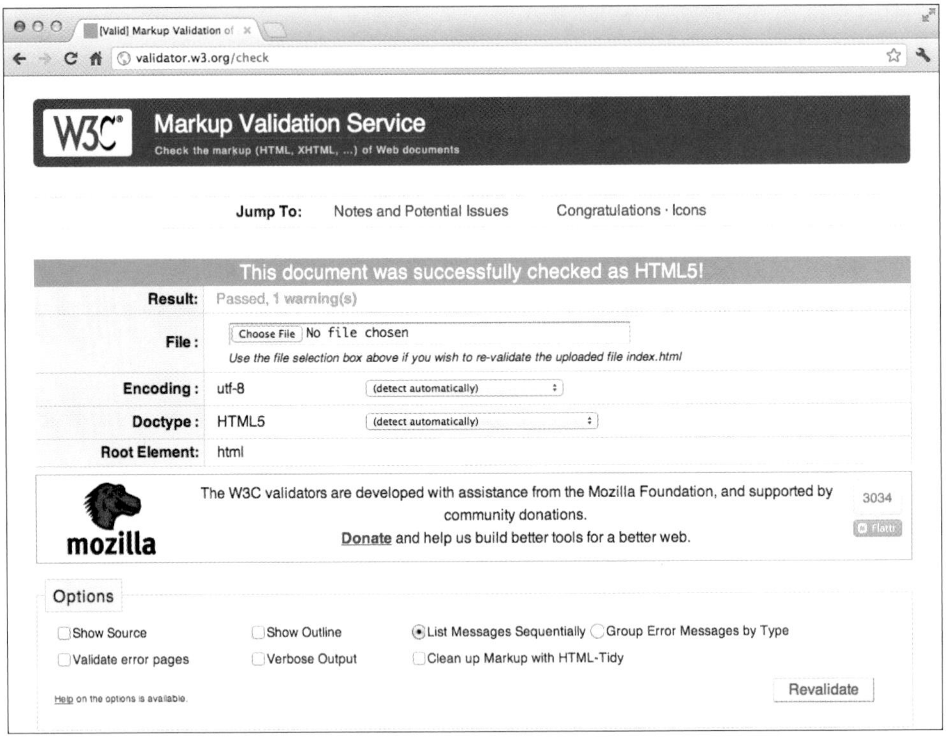

FIGURE 1-5 Your web page passed validation as HTML5.

Does Your Code Always Have to Validate?

Validation is a great tool for web developers, but it is just that, a tool. There will be times when it is not realistic to produce pages that pass validation. Sometimes there are small little *hacks* that you will have to write in order to get some browsers (read: IE) to play ball, and these will show up as errors when you come to validate your pages. Ideally you want your pages to have as few errors as possible, but even some of the most well-known websites don't pass validation. (Try running http://google.com or http://yahoo.com through the W3C validator.)

Just remember: Web standards are not strict rules. They are more like guidelines. Validation is a tool to help you produce better websites; it should never limit you.

All Browsers Are Not Created Equal

In an ideal world, you would be able to code a website and have it behave the same in all web browsers. Sadly, this is not the case. Cross-browser compatibility is an issue that all web developers have to tackle regularly, and often it can be a real pain and lead you to spending hours trying to work around a bug that is present in a browser.

To demonstrate this, take a look at Figures 1-6 and 1-7. These figures show the same HTML web page displayed in Google Chrome and Internet Explorer (using IE7 compatibility mode). Notice how the navigation links are inline in Google Chrome but appear in a list in Internet Explorer.

FIGURE 1-6 A simple HTML web page in Google Chrome.

FIGURE 1-7 The same HTML web page displayed in Internet Explorer (using IE7 compatibility mode).

It is important to remember that HTML5 is still very new, and therefore, not all browsers will support the technologies that you will learn to use in this book. Furthermore, your users will not always be running the latest versions of their web browsers. You would be surprised how many people are still using IE6 (which was released in 2001!). Business users are especially renowned for using outdated browsers, often because of the restrictions put in place by IT departments. I believe that over the next few years the problem of users running outdated browsers will largely be solved by the introduction of the automatic-update features present in many modern web browsers.

Even though some of your users may not be able to use the latest features of HTML5, you should not be scared of using those features in your websites. As long as the core functionality of your website will work in older browsers, you will be fine.

As you progress through the examples in this book, I walk you through the techniques needed to fix the most common cross-compatibility issues that you will encounter.

Summary

Congratulations; you are officially on your way to becoming an awesome HTML5 developer!

At the start of this chapter, I promised that you would build your first web page by this point, and you have. It may not be flashy, but you have now covered some of the core fundamentals of HTML.

A huge number of browsers and development tools are available to modern-day web developers, and you learned about some of the most popular. I encourage you to play around with each of these tools to find the set that you are most comfortable working with. The same goes for browsers. Mozilla Firefox and Google Chrome are often among the first to implement new web technologies, but find the one that you like most. You will probably discover it is the one with the best developer tools. Make sure that you have all the popular browsers installed because you will need to use them all in order to test that your web pages are cross-browser compatible and available to as many users as possible.

In Chapter 2, you learn how to structure your web pages in more depth and what each structural element is responsible for. You will also be introduced to Joe Balochio and his chain of pizza restaurants. Throughout this book, you will be creating a brand new website for Joe's business—a site that uses many of HTML5's fantastic new technologies.

chapter two

Structuring a Web Page

CHAPTER 1 EXPLAINED how to use elements and attributes to create a simple web page. As you progress through this chapter, you will learn about a number of elements used to create web page layouts, including the `<header>`, `<footer>`, and `<section>` elements.

You will also start working on the example website that you will continue to develop throughout this book, beginning by planning the pages of the website and then creating wireframes for the page layouts. The objective of this chapter is to convert these wireframes into web page templates using a collection of new HTML5 elements. In Chapters 3 and 4, you use these page templates to create all the pages for your website.

Creating Layout Templates

In this section, you start building a website for Joe's Pizza Co. Joe Balochio (the owner) wants a brand new website to help promote his chain of pizza restaurants. He tells you that he wants the website to look stylish and incorporate some design aspects inspired by his Italian roots. He wants a menu and information about the locations of all the different restaurants he operates. Joe would also love to have a page for news items so he can let his customers know about all the great things that his company does.

Now that you have learned how to add the page elements (`<html>`, `<head>`, and `<body>`) from Chapter 1, it's time to consider the sections that will make up the visible layout of your pages. When you create page layouts, you need a logical structure similar to the one described in the following list. (Note that it doesn't have to be *exactly* like this one.)

1. A header
2. Some navigation
3. Some page content
4. A footer

Figure 2-1 shows a screenshot of a page from the Treehouse website. Can you pick out each of these layout sections?

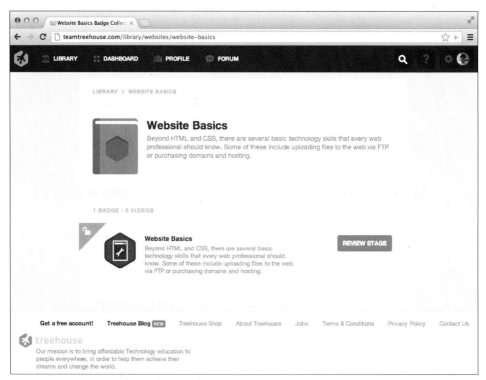

FIGURE 2-1 A page from the Treehouse website.

HTML5 includes a series of new elements that you can use to define each section. Some of these elements have semantic meaning, which can help to make your code easier to understand and help computer programs to identify the purpose of the content found within each element. I will be pointing out these semantic elements as you progress through this book.

Planning the Sitemap

The first task to complete when starting a new website project is to create a *sitemap*. This defines how many pages your website will have and what those pages will be. Starting from what Joe has requested, here is the sitemap for the website you are going to build:

1. Home
2. About
3. News
4. Menu
5. Locations
6. Sitemap

The Sitemap page here contains a list of links to all the other pages on the website.

For this particular website, a sitemap is not that important because you will have a small number of pages; still, this is a valuable resource for websites that have a lot of pages so it will be good practice for you to include it in the example.

Most websites are based on a few different *templates* that are used to create each page. These templates provide an empty shell that you can add content to in order to create new pages. Using templates enables you to keep all pages looking consistent throughout your website. You will create two templates for your website: one for the *home page* and one for the *content pages.* Content pages primarily contain text, so they need a slightly different layout from the home page.

Planning the Page Layouts

Before you start coding away, it's best to create a rough mock-up of how you want the pages to look. These mock-ups, often referred to as *wireframes,* use boxes to indicate the position of key elements, such as the navigation, content, and logo. In this section, you create a few quick wireframes for the home and content page templates.

All your web pages will have five common elements: a header, logo, navigation, main content area, and footer. You can use these key elements to create a quick wireframe for your pages.

Let's start with the home page template. Figure 2-2 shows a rough wireframe for the layout that I have put together.

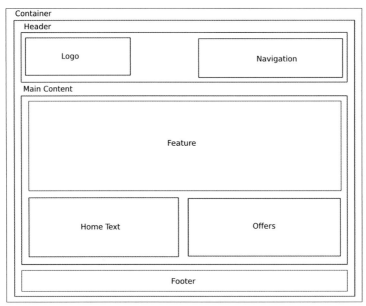

FIGURE 2-2 Wireframe of the home page layout.

This wireframe shows the position of all the main page sections: the header, which contains the logo and navigation; the main content area; and the footer. The home page will have three sections that contain the page content: a main feature to attract the viewers' attention, a text box for some initial information about the company, and a section for displaying special offers.

For the content page template, you will use a similar layout, changing only the main content area by replacing the three content sections with a single area for the page text. Figure 2-3 shows a rough wireframe of the content page.

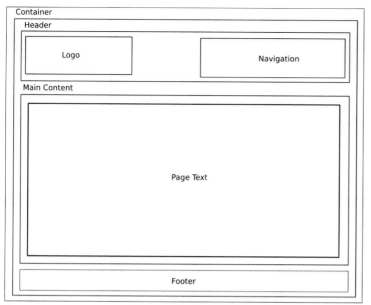

FIGURE 2-3 Wireframe of the content page layout.

Creating the Template Files

Now that you have a rough plan for how the page will look, it's time to create the template files. Remember, you need two templates for your website: a home page template and a content page template. In this section, you create new files for each of these. You will add the layouts to these files later in this chapter.

Creating the Home Page Template

First, you are going to create the template for the home page. Follow these steps to create this template.

You can download the code used here from the book's website and copy and paste it into your file if you aren't a fan of typing, or want to avoid typos that might cause the code to break. You can find the code in the `index.html` file in folder 1, under the download code for Chapter 2. All the code used in the example website is available at `http://www.wiley.com/go/treehouse/html5foundations`.

1. Create a new folder called `joes-pizza`.

2. In this folder, create a new file called `index.html`.

3. Add the following code to this file.

```
<!DOCTYPE html>
<html lang="en">
<head>
    <title>Joe's Pizza Co. - New York's Best Pizza</title>
</head>
<body>

</body>
</html>
```

4. Save the file.

Creating the Content Page Template

You have now created the base template for the home page. Next, you need to create a template file for the content pages. Follow these steps:

1. Create a new file in the `joes-pizza` folder called `about.html`.

2. Add the following code to this file.

```
<!DOCTYPE html>
<html lang="en">
<head>
    <title>About - Joe's Pizza Co./title>
</head>
<body>

</body>
</html>
```

3. Save the file.

You have now created the initial template files for the home and content page templates. As you progress through the rest of this chapter, you will learn about the elements used to add the visible page layout, adding to your templates as you go.

Notice that here you have actually started to create the About page. Because this page will have the same layout as the rest of the pages on your website (except the home page), you will be using it as your content page template. You will need to update the filenames and titles of any pages you create using this template. Don't worry, I'll remind you.

Adding a `<div>` Element to Each Template

The `<div>` element (short for *document divisions*) has historically been the most commonly used element for defining the sections of an HTML document, but with HTML5 it no longer plays such a big role. Best practice is to use the new HTML5 semantic elements (you will look at these soon) such as `<header>`, `<footer>`, `<nav>`, `<section>`, and `<article>` wherever possible, but there will be times when you just need an element to group a number of other elements together. This is where the `<div>` element comes in. The element itself is generic; it has no special semantic meaning.

You are going to use the `<div>` element to create a container for all of the page content. This will enable you to center all of this content using Cascading Style Sheets (CSS) later in this chapter.

The code for this exercise can be found in folder 2.

1. Open the `index.html` and `about.html` template files in your favorite text editor.

2. Add the following code to the `<body>` elements in each of the files.

```
<body>
    <!-- Page Container -->
    <div id="container">

    </div>
</body>
```

3. Save the `index.html` and `about.html` files.

I highlight the new element in bold text so that it is easier for you to identify within the extract of code. Don't worry about trying to make this text bold in your text editor.

You have then created a `<div>` element and given this element the ID `container`. This identifier will enable you to target this specific element using CSS. As you go through the rest of this section, place all the new elements within this container.

Now open your `index.html` file in your browser to see the sections you've just added. What, you can't see them?! This is because most HTML layout elements are "invisible" by default. You won't be able to see the sections in a browser until you add some content in them (or style them using CSS, as you learn later in this chapter).

To make sure that your new `<div>` element is, in fact, showing up correctly, you can use your browser's developer tools.

1. Open the `index.html` file in the web browser that has the developer tools you like to use. (If you don't have a favorite, I recommend Chrome.)

2. Now open your developer tools. You may find it easier to right-click on the page and select Inspect Element from the context menu (if this option is provided by your developer tools).

3. Make sure that you are viewing the tab that displays the page elements. This will be named Elements, HTML, or Documents, depending on which browser you are using.

4. In the main window of your developer tools, you should see a list of the HTML elements in your page, indented to match your page's structure (as shown in Figure 2-4). If your `<div>` is displayed here, everything is fine. If it isn't, you need to go back and check your code against what is in this book.

5. Close your developer tools.

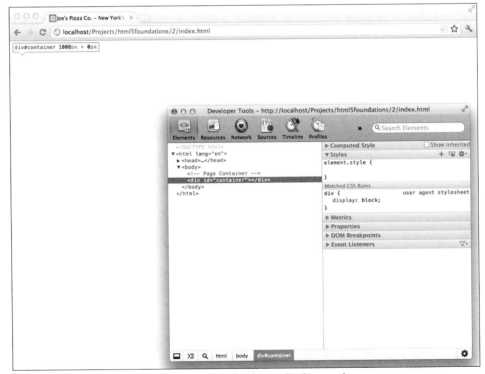

FIGURE 2-4 Inspecting your page elements using the Chrome developer tools.

Code Comments

The first bold line in the preceding code example is an example of a *code comment*. To start a code comment, you use the syntax `<!--` and to close a comment you use `-->`. Code comments will not be displayed by your browser but can be useful to you as a developer. You should use comments to document parts of your code, as notes to yourself or to others reading your code. I also like to use them to signal the start of new layout sections, as with the example in the preceding code sample:

```
<!-- Page Container -->
```

Adding a `<header>` Element to Each Template

Almost all web pages have a header section of some description. This section often contains information such as a company logo, slogan, and site navigation links. HTML5 introduces a new `<header>` element that you can use to define this section of your page's layout. You can use the `<header>` element more than once on a page, as you will see shortly when you learn about the `<article>` element.

The code for this exercise can be found in folder 3.

1. Open the `index.html` and `about.html` files in your text editor.

2. Add a `<header>` element to both of your page templates. This should be placed within the container that you just created.

```
<div id="container">
  <!-- Header -->
  <header>

  </header>
</div>
```

3. Save the files.

4. Open the files in your web browser.

5. Inspect the page using your developer tools to make sure that the new `<header>` is showing up within the container `<div>` (as shown in Figure 2-5).

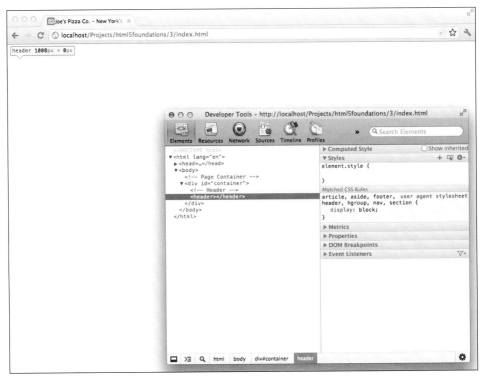

FIGURE 2-5 Inspecting the <header> element with the Chrome developer tools.

In your wireframes, your header contained two other elements: a logo and some navigation. You will look at adding the navigation in a moment, but first let's focus on the logo. For the logo, you will use a <div> element with the ID `logo`.

The code for this exercise can be found in folder 4.

1. Open the `index.html` and `about.html` files in your text editor.

2. Add a new <div> element for the logo to each template. This should be placed within the <header> element you just added.

```
<div id="container">
  <!-- Header -->
  <header>
    <!-- Logo -->
    <div id="logo">The Logo Goes Here</div>
```

```
      </header>
    </div>
```

3. Save the files.

I have added some dummy text so that the element can be more easily identified when you view the templates in your browser. Figure 2-6 shows the rendered `index.html` file with the new logo `<div>`.

The Logo Goes Here

FIGURE 2-6 The index.html file with the new logo <div> element, as displayed in Google Chrome.

That nearly completes the header; all that remains is to add some navigation. HTML5 introduces a new semantic element for that, too.

Adding a <nav> Element to Each Template

All websites need navigation links to enable users to easily move between different pages. HTML5 introduces the new <nav> element that enables you to indicate to computer programs exactly where these navigation links can be found on the page. This can be useful to users who rely on screen-reading software, for example, because the software can more accurately pinpoint the page navigation. That capability translates into the user being able to browse your website faster.

You can have more than one <nav> element on a page. Anywhere that you have a block of major navigation links is a candidate for using the <nav> element. You can also add other content to the <nav> element, such as headings or paragraphs of text. However, this content should be related to the links in some way.

You won't create the actual navigation links until Chapter 3; for now you are just creating space for them on the page.

The code for this exercise can be found in folder 5.

1. Open the `index.html` and `about.html` files in your text editor.

2. Add a new `<nav>` element under the logo, as shown in the following code.

```
<div id="container">
  <!-- Header -->
  <header>
    <!-- Logo -->
    <div id="logo">Logo</div>
    <!-- Navigation -->
    <nav>
      The Navigation Links Go Here
    </nav>
  </header>
</div>
```

3. Save the files.

4. Open the files in your web browser.

5. Use the developer tools to inspect the page and make sure that the new `<nav>` element is listed below the logo.

Again, I have added some dummy text to make this element more visible. Take a look at the templates in your browser. Figure 2-7 shows the home page, as displayed in Google Chrome.

FIGURE 2-7 The home page template, complete with <nav> element.

Adding <section> Elements

The `<section>` element should be used to represent a generic section of your web page. For example, you can use it to represent individual chapters in a document or the different sections of a home page (such as introduction, news, or contact information). Section elements usually contain a heading as their first piece of content.

For the templates that you are building, you will use a number of `<section>` elements to define the different parts of the main content. However, before you start adding these elements, you first need to create a new `<div>` element that will be used to group the main content sections together.

The code for this exercise can be found in folder 6.

1. Open the `index.html` and `about.html` files in your text editor.

2. Create a new `<div>` element below the `<header>` in your templates.

```
<div id="container">
  <!-- Header -->
  <header>...</header>

  <!-- Main Content -->
  <div></div>
</div>
```

3. Save the files.

4. Open the files in your web browser.

5. Inspect the page using your developer tools and make sure that this new `<div>` appears below the `<header>` element (as shown in Figure 2-8).

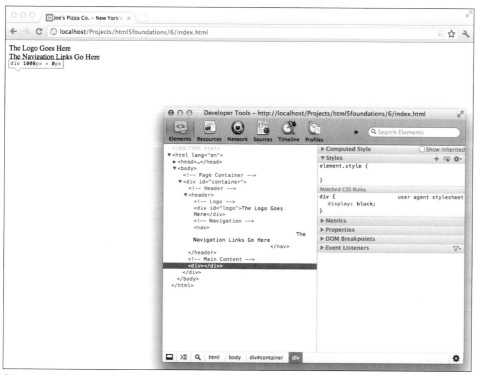

FIGURE 2-8 Inspecting the main content `<div>` with the Chrome developer tools.

The ellipsis within the `<header>` element is used to signify that there is content within the element. I want to keep these code extracts as concise as possible, so using this enables me to avoid repeating the entire code in each successive example.

Up until this point, the home and content page templates have been nearly identical. However, if you refer back to the original wireframes you created earlier in this chapter, you will see that the main content area for the templates is different, so you need to add different code for this section in your two template files.

Adding a `<section>` Element to the Content Page Template

The content page template contains only one big space for the page text. For this, you will use a single `<section>` element.

The code for this exercise can be found in folder 7.

1. Open the `about.html` file in your text editor.

2. Add a new `<section>` element within the `<div>` that you just created in the content page template. You should give this new element an ID of `page-text`.

```
<div id="container">
  <!-- Header -->
  <header>...</header>
  <!-- Main Content -->
  <div>
    <!-- Page Text -->
    <section id="page-text">
      The good stuff goes here!
    </section>
  </div>
</div>
```

3. Save the file.

4. Open the `about.html` file in your web browser.

5. Inspect the page using your developer tools and make sure that this new `<section>` appears within the main content `<div>`.

Open the content page template in your web browser. You should see that the page text section is now displayed, as shown in Figure 2-9.

FIGURE 2-9 The content page template with the new page text section.

Adding `<section>` Elements to the Home Page Template

The home page layout is a little more complex because it has three separate content sections: one for a main feature banner, one for some information about the company, and one for special offers. You will use a `<section>` element for each of these.

> The code for this exercise can be found in folder 8.

1. Open the `index.html` file in your text editor.

2. Add a `<section>` element within the main content `<div>` and give it an ID of `feature`.

```
<!-- Main Content -->
<div>
  <!-- Feature -->
  <section id="feature">
    The Main Feature Banner Goes Here
  </section>
</div>
```

3. Now add another `<section>` element below that one, this time with the ID of `home-text`.

```
<!-- Main Content -->
<div>
  <!-- Feature -->
  <section id="feature">...</section>

  <!-- Home Text -->
  <section id="home-text">
    The Company Information Goes Here
  </section>
</div>
```

4. Finally, add a third `<section>` element with the ID of `offers`.

```
<!-- Main Content -->
<div>
  <!-- Feature -->
  <section id="feature">...</section>

  <!-- Home Text -->
  <section id="home-text">...</section>

  <!-- Special Offers -->
  <section id="offers">
    The Special Offers Go Here
  </section>
</div>
```

5. Save the file.

6. Open the `index.html` file in your web browser.

7. Inspect the page using your developer tools and make sure that these `<section>` elements are displayed in the following order: feature, home text, special offers. Figure 2-10 shows how the page should look.

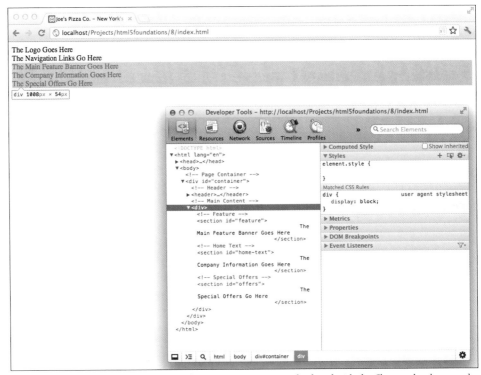

FIGURE 2-10 The home page template with new content sections, displayed with the Chrome developer tools.

Here you have given each of these new elements an ID so that they can be easily selected for styling with CSS.

Adding a `<footer>` Element to Each Template

Another new element in HTML5 is the `<footer>` element. This element typically contains content like the copyright notices and links that are found at the bottom of web pages. Like the `<header>` and `<nav>` elements, you can have more than one `<footer>` element on a page.

The code for this exercise can be found in folder 9.

1. Open the `index.html` and `about.html` files in your text editor.

2. Add a `<footer>` element to each of your page templates. You should place this under the main content `<div>`.

```
<div id="container">
  <!-- Header -->
  <header>...</header>

  <!-- Main Content -->
  <div>...</div>

  <!-- Footer -->
  <footer>
    The Boring Legal Stuff Goes Here
  </footer>
</div>
```

3. Save the files.

Success! Now you have created the main layout for both the home and content page templates. Figures 2-11 and 2-12 show how your templates should now look.

FIGURE 2-11 The home page template.

FIGURE 2-12 The content page template.

The last element that you are going to look at is the `<article>` element. You will be using this in your website—but not just yet.

Using the `<article>` Element

The new `<article>` element is used to represent a self-contained section of a web page. A good example of this is a blog post. You can use the `<article>` element to wrap each of the separate posts that are displayed on a blog home page, for example. The idea behind the `<article>` element is that if you removed all other content on the page, the content within the article element should still make sense standing alone.

The `<article>` element can also have a `<header>` and a `<footer>` element nested within it. In the following example, the article title is placed within the `<header>` element and the author's name is placed within the `<footer>` element.

```
<article>
  <header>
    An Example Article
  </header>
  <div>
    Some text content that makes up the body of the article.
  </div>
  <footer>
    By Joe Balochio.
  </footer>
</article>
```

The `<section>` and `<article>` elements are fairly similar, and it's easy to get confused about when to use one over the other. A simple rule is that you should use the `<article>` element if it would make sense for the content to be syndicated in something like an RSS feed. If your content doesn't meet this rule, use a `<section>` element instead.

So far in this chapter, you have been working on building the parts of your page templates that users will actually see. In the next section, you learn how to embed information in your templates that is solely for use by web browsers and other computer programs—the under-the-covers stuff.

Extending the \<head\> with Metadata

Chapter 1 explained the \<head\> element and how it can be used to specify information about the page, such as the page title. You can provide a lot of other information to computer programs in the \<head\>, using the \<meta\> element. In this section, you learn some uses of the \<meta\> element, adding metadata to your page templates as you go.

Working with \<meta\> Elements

The \<meta\> element is used to define metadata such as a description about the page, keywords, or the page's author. Here's an example:

```
<meta name="description" content="This is a description about
                                  the page">
```

To define this information, you use the two attributes shown in the example above: the name attribute and the content attribute. The content attribute is used to provide some information about the page (for example, a short description). You then use the name attribute to tell computer programs the purpose of this information. If the content is a description of the page, for example, you would set the value of the name attribute to description.

The \<meta\> element is an example of a *void* element and therefore has no end tag.

In this code exercise, you add metadata to the \<head\> in your page templates that will provide computer programs with a description of the page, related keywords, and the name of the author.

The code for this exercise can be found in folder 10.

1. Open the index.html file in your text editor.

2. Add the following <meta> elements to the <head>. They should be placed below the <title> element.

```
<head>
  <title>...</title>

  <meta name="description"
       content="Joe's Pizza is the home of the best pizzas in
                all of New York City.">
  <meta name="keywords"
       content="pizzas,joes pizza,garlic bread,pepperoni">
  <meta name="author" content="YOUR NAME">
</head>
```

3. Save the index.html file.

4. Open the index.html file in your web browser.

5. Use the developer tools to inspect these new <meta> elements and make sure that they all show up properly. You may need to expand the <head> element (by clicking the small triangle next to the start tag) to see the elements within it.

6. Now add these same three <meta> elements to your about.html file. Be sure to update the value of the content attributes to reflect the content of the page.

7. Save the about.html file.

Note that when the page is now viewed in a browser, you do not see any change from the previous version. Again, metadata is not displayed as content, but is simply information to be used by computer programs.

Metadata and Search Engine Optimization

Search engines sometimes use the description from the metadata as the text that appears below the link to the page when presenting your web page in search results. In the past, some search engines also used the keywords when ranking web pages but found that many people would abuse this practice by stuffing lots of keywords into the meta element to help their pages rank higher for certain searches. For this reason, most search engines no longer consider this information to be reliable and therefore do not use it for ranking purposes. It is still considered good practice to define keywords, however.

Make sure that the content for your meta descriptions and keywords is relevant to each individual page. Avoid using the same content for all of your pages. This is a best practice for search engine optimization (SEO).

Notice how keywords are separated by commas but do not have spaces after the commas.

Defining the Character Encoding

A principal use of the `<meta>` element is to define the character encoding of the page. Like the DOCTYPE, this element has been greatly simplified in HTML5:

```
<meta charset="utf-8">
```

The `charset` attribute on this `<meta>` element tells the browser how it should interpret the characters in the document. Unless you have a very special use case, you should use UTF-8 here. In the following exercise, you define the character encoding in your page templates.

The code for this exercise can be found in folder 11.

1. Open the `index.html` and `about.html` files in your text editor.

2. Define the character encoding by adding the following `<meta>` element to the `<head>`. The character encoding should always be the first element within the `<head>`.

```
<head>
    <meta charset="utf-8">
    <title>...</title>
    ...
</head>
```

3. Save the files.

That completes your page templates! In Chapter 4, you use these templates to create each page on your website.

Styling the Page with CSS

Cascading Style Sheets, or *CSS*, is a language used to describe how the web browser should present HTML elements and their content. You can use CSS to control the visual aspects of your web page, including element position, background colors and images, borders, fonts, and many more design aspects. The following example shows a brief extract of CSS code.

```
section {
    font-size: 14px;
    color: #CC0000;
}
```

This code is an example of a CSS style rule that sets the size of all text within <section> elements to 14 pixels and colors it red. The first part of a CSS rule selects the elements that the style should be applied to, and the code within the curly braces describes the styles.

Colors in CSS are defined using either a hexadecimal or RGB notation that defines the amount of red, green, and blue that should be used in order to produce the desired color. #CC0000 is the code for red.

HTML and CSS have always been very tightly coupled. Most developers who know HTML will also be knowledgeable about CSS and vice versa. I strongly urge you to learn CSS if you want to build professional web pages.

The aim of this book is to teach you about HTML5. CSS is an equally large topic, but I don't cover it in this book. There are, however, many great books on the subject, particularly the latest standard, CSS3. I definitely recommend that you pick up a copy of *CSS3 Foundations* by Ian Lunn (John Wiley & Sons, 2013), which is also part of the Treehouse series. The Treehouse website also has a number of great videos covering CSS. Try starting with the videos for *CSS Foundations*; you can find them at `http://teamtreehouse.com/library/websites/css-foundations.`

Linking CSS to Your HTML

Web pages with complex designs often have hundreds of lines of CSS code, which can get pretty hard to manage after a while. Luckily, you can create separate stylesheet files to help break up your CSS code and make it more manageable. For instance, some developers find it easier to split the code responsible for the page layout and the code responsible for branding and colors into separate files.

To create an external stylesheet, you simply need to create a file in your text editor that uses the `.css` file extension.

Once you have your CSS code in its own stylesheet file, you need to link it to your web page so that the browser knows how to find it. You do this using the `<link>` element.

```
<link rel="stylesheet" href="style.css">
```

The link element uses two attributes to point the browser to your separate resources, such as stylesheets: the `rel` and `href` attributes. The `rel` attribute describes the relationship of the file that you are linking. The `href` attribute tells the browser where it can locate the stylesheet file. In the previous example, the resource is a stylesheet, so the `rel` attribute will have the value `stylesheet`, and the `href attribute` points to a file named `style.css`.

Now that you have a basic understanding of what CSS does, you need to link a stylesheet to your page templates to make them a bit easier on the eye.

The code for this exercise can be found in folder 12.

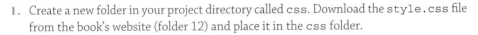

1. Create a new folder in your project directory called `css`. Download the `style.css` file from the book's website (folder 12) and place it in the `css` folder.

2. Create a new folder called `img` in your project directory. Download the image files from the book's website (folder 12, `img` folder) and place them in your new `img` folder. There should be two files: `bodyBg.png` and `featureBg.png`. These files are referenced in the CSS code.

3. Open the `index.html` and `about.html` files in your text editor.

4. Add the following `<link>` element to the `<head>` of your page templates.

```
<head>
  <meta charset="utf-8">
  <title>...</title>

  <link rel="stylesheet" href="css/style.css">

  ...
</head>
```

5. Save the files.

Now open the page templates in your web browser; you should see that there has been quite a transformation. It's just like magic!

Figures 2-13 and 2-14 show how your page templates should look with the new CSS styling.

FIGURE 2-13 The home page template, with CSS.
Pizza image reproduced by permission of William Rogers

You can use multiple `<link>` elements to reference multiple stylesheets. However, it is considered a good practice to minimize the number of external files that your web page needs. The reason? The more external files that you have, the longer the page takes to load.

Relative and Absolute Paths

As you build up your HTML pages, you will need to reference external files such as CSS stylesheets, images, JavaScript files, or even other pages within your website. You use *relative* and *absolute* paths to tell the browser where it can locate these files. Figure 2-15 shows a sample directory structure that I will be using when explaining how these different types of paths work.

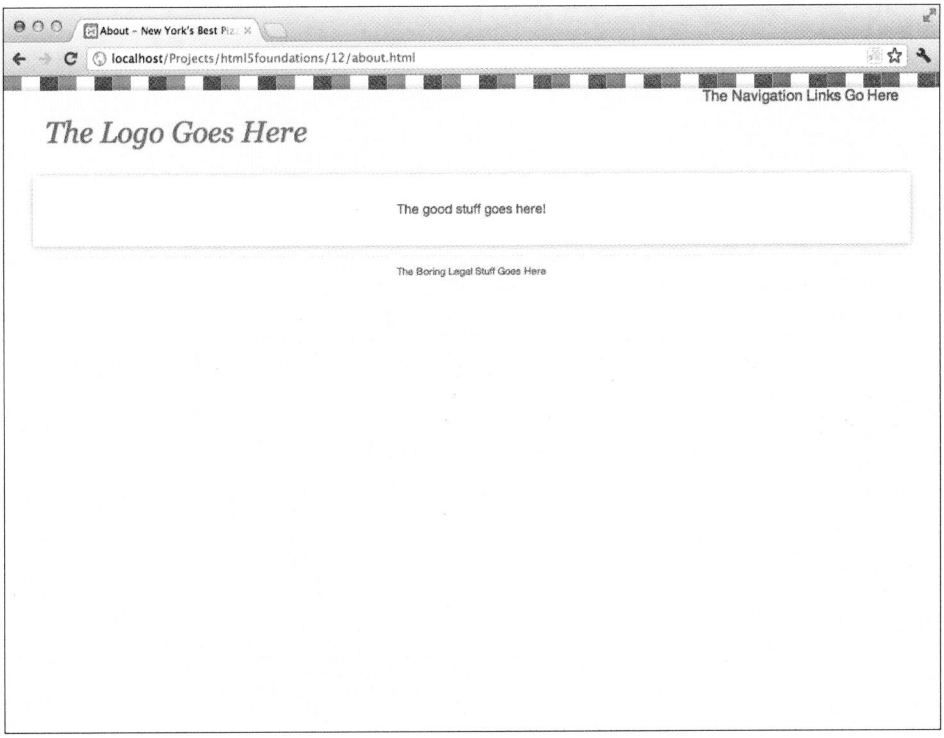

About – New York's Best Piz
localhost/Projects/html5foundations/12/about.html
The Navigation Links Go Here
The Logo Goes Here
The good stuff goes here!
The Boring Legal Stuff Goes Here

FIGURE 2-14 The content page template, with CSS.

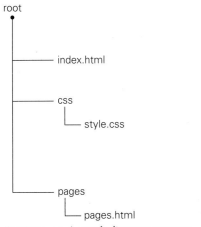

root
index.html
css
style.css
pages
pages.html

FIGURE 2-15 A sample directory structure.

Relative paths refer to the location of the desired file relative to the location of the current page. For example, if your stylesheet is contained within a folder named `css` that is in the same folder as the current HTML document, you could use the following path to link to the file:

```
href="css/style.css"
```

In this path, you specify that the CSS file is located in the `css` folder and that the file name is `style.css`.

Refer to the file structure shown in Figure 2-15. Suppose your current file is `page.html`, and you want to show the path to the same stylesheet. You can traverse folders using double periods, as in the following example:

```
href="../css/style.css"
```

This example refers to the `style.css` file in the `css` folder above the current file, `page.html`. You start at the `page.html` file, go up one folder (using `../`), enter the `css` folder, and finally, select the `style.css` file.

Absolute paths refer to the specific location of a file starting from the root directory. For the purpose of web page links, the root is the top-level directory, for example:

```
http://example.com/
```

You could use either of the following as an absolute path to refer to your stylesheet:

```
href="/css/style.css"
```

or

```
href="http://example.com/css/style.css"
```

Both paths point to the same file.

Summary

You learned about a number of HTML elements, including some that are brand new in HTML5. Most of these new HTML5 elements have semantic meaning and should be used for some applications and not for others. This can be confusing, but in this chapter, you used them correctly to build the layouts of your page templates.

HTML documents include a lot of information that is not directly presented to the user. You learned how to use the `<meta>` element to embed information within your web pages that can be used by web browsers, search engines, and other computer programs.

Finally, you learned how CSS is used to describe how elements can be styled by the web browser. You even hooked up a stylesheet to the example website to make it much more pleasing to the eye.

In Chapter 3, you learn about the HTML elements used for marking up content in your web pages. You look at how headings work, as well as learning about lists, tables, images, and captions. You continue working on the website for Joe's Pizza Co. This time you will add some content to each page and create some navigation so that visitors can easily browse through the website.

chapter three
Creating the Page Templates

IN THIS CHAPTER, you are going to continue to work on the page templates that you have been creating in Chapters 1 and 2. You will learn about several new HTML elements, such as heading elements, links, and lists. Once you are comfortable with these new elements, you will use them to complete your page templates, ready for adding the content, which you'll do in Chapter 4.

Adding a Logo

In this section, you learn about HTML heading elements and how they differ from the standard text in your web pages. Once you have grasped the concept of headings, you will use one to create the logo for your page templates.

Understanding Headings

Just as you use different levels of headings in a book to help you understand the structure of the content, in HTML, you can use the <h1>, <h2>, <h3>, <h4>, <h5>, and <h6> elements to mark up headings and signify their relative importance on the page. The number in the element name represents the rank of the heading element, with 1 being the highest rank and 6 the lowest. Heading elements with the same tag have equal rank. For example, you could mark up the title of a book as follows:

```
<h1>Venture Deals</h1>
<h2>Be Smarter Than Your Lawyer and Venture Capitalist</h2>
```

You use the `<h1>` element for the main title of the book and the `<h2>` element for the sub-title, signifying their respective importance.

Headings also create implied subsections of the content, just as you would use a subheading to indicate the start of a new section if you were writing an essay. In HTML, all content that appears after a heading is interpreted as being related to that heading. This creates a content hierarchy (sometimes referred to as the *document outline*). The following code is an example of a short piece of text that uses headings to define sections.

```
<h1>HTML5 Rocks</h1>
<p>
  HTML5 is the latest version of the Hypertext Markup Language.
  It includes loads of cool stuff like Video and Audio elements.
</p>
<h2>The Video Element</h2>
<p>
  The video element allows developers to embed videos within web
  pages without the need for third-party plug-ins like Flash.
</p>
<h2>The Audio Element</h2>
<p>
  Similar to the video element, the audio element also allows
  developers to embed audio without the need for third-party
  plug-ins.
</p>
```

Recall from Chapter 1 that the `<p>` element is used for blocks of text, comparable to a paragraph within a text document. You learn more about using `<p>` elements later in Chapter 4.

The implied hierarchy of this content is a top-level section, *HTML5 Rocks,* with two second-level sections beneath, *The Video Element* and *The Audio Element*. The two `<h2>` elements are given equal rank and therefore both appear as "children" of the `<h1>` element. Figure 3-1 shows how this text would be presented in the browser. Note how the two `<h2>` elements are displayed in smaller text than the `<h1>` element, indicating their relative importance.

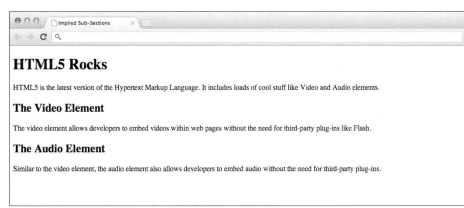

HTML5 Rocks

HTML5 is the latest version of the Hypertext Markup Language. It includes loads of cool stuff like Video and Audio elements.

The Video Element

The video element allows developers to embed videos within web pages without the need for third-party plug-ins like Flash.

The Audio Element

Similar to the video element, the audio element also allows developers to embed audio without the need for third-party plug-ins.

FIGURE 3-1 Page hierarchy.

Where is the code that tells the browser to use a larger font for the <h1> elements and a smaller font for the <h2> elements? It's in the Cascading Style Sheet (CSS)! Web browsers include a default set of basic styles in a *user agent stylesheet*.

For a quick review of HTML heading elements, check out Nick Pettit's video on Treehouse at http://teamtreehouse.com/library/websites/html/text/paragraphs-and-headlines.

Using a Heading for the Logo

The logo for Joe's Pizza Co. is very simple—only text—so you can just use an <h1> element that contains the company name. This text will then be styled by the CSS that you included at the end of Chapter 2.

The code for the exercises in this chapter can be downloaded from the book's website at http://wiley.com/go/treehouse/html5foundations. This code is in folder 1 of the Chapter 3 download code.

Follow these steps to create the logo:

1. Open the index.html file from your project folder in a text editor.

2. Find the <div> element that has the ID of logo. This <div> element is located in the header of your page layout. It looks like this:

```
<div id="logo">The Logo Goes Here</div>
```

3. Replace the dummy text inside the `<div>` with a new `<h1>` heading element that contains the text **Joe's Pizza Co.** (including the period). Your logo `<div>` should now look like the following:

```
<div id="logo">
    <h1>Joe's Pizza Co.</h1>
</div>
```

4. Save the `index.html` file.

5. Repeat this process for your content page template that is stored in the `about.html` file.

Open the home page in your browser. Figure 3-2 shows how your home page should look with the new logo.

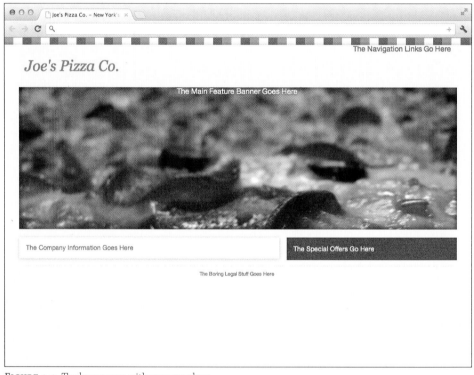

FIGURE 3-2 The home page with your new logo.
Pizza image reproduced by permission of William Rogers

 Remember that the top border and pizza image are being applied by the CSS!

Adding Navigation

Okay great, so now you have the logo sorted. It's time to create the navigation so that users can easily flow between the different pages in your website. Without good navigation, your users won't make it past the home page.

Before you can build this navigation, you first need to know how HTML links and lists work. The first two parts of this section focus on explaining just that.

Links

Hyperlinks are arguably one of the most important HTML elements. They represent a connection between two documents on the web, or to another part of the same document. By linking to other content on the web, you are signaling that you think the content may be of interest to someone who is reading your web page. The following sections address the elements you can use to include links on your web pages.

In this book, I use the terms *hyperlink* and *link* interchangeably. The term *link* is more commonly used.

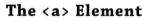

The <a> Element

Hyperlinks in HTML are created using the <a> element. As well as linking to other pages on the web, you can also use the <a> element to link to parts of the current page.

Let's first look at how you can use the <a> element to create links to other pages on the web. To link to other pages, you must specify the path to the target page using the href attribute. This path can either be an absolute or relative path (see Chapter 2 for more information about paths). Consider the following example:

```
<a href="http://google.com">Google</a>
```

Here we define a hyperlink to the Google home page, using an absolute path, and some anchor text. The anchor text is what is actually displayed to the user. This enables you to swap the long and ugly URL for something a bit more user friendly. A number of other attributes are also available on the <a> element; you look at these in the next section.

As well as using the <a> element to link to other web pages, you can also use it to link to content within the same web page. When a user clicks on the link, she will be taken to the relevant element on the page. Using links in this way is useful when you have very large web pages; it allows users to quickly reach the section that they are interested in without having to scroll for a long time to get there. To create these links, you place an ID on the element that you would like to link to and then place that same ID (prefixed with a # sign) in the `href` attribute of your link, as in the following example.

```
<h1 id="hello">Hello World</h1>
<p>
   . . .
</p>
<h2>Goodbye World</h2>
<p>
   . . .
</p>
<a href="#hello">Back to Hello World</a>
```

In this example, you define a `<h1>` element with the ID `hello`; this is the part of the page that you are linking to. The `<a>` element you have defined is a link to the position of that element in the document. Note that the content of the `href` attribute starts with a # and then the ID of the element you are linking to.

Link Attributes

The `<a>` element has a number of available attributes. These are described in the following sections.

The href Attribute

Every `<a>` element will usually include at least one attribute—commonly the `href` attribute. The `href` attribute should contain a valid URL that points to the file that you are linking to. If the file is on the same domain, this may be a relative path (`about.html`) or it may be an absolute path (`http://example.com/about.html`).

If you are linking to a particular element within a document, you may also use the ID of that element prefixed with a pound sign (#), as shown in the preceding code example.

The title Attribute

The `title` attribute is used to provide a description of the link. If you hover over the link with your mouse cursor, the title text will be displayed in a tooltip.

```
<a href="http://google.com" title="The Google search
  engine">Google</a>
```

Using the `title` attribute also makes your web pages more accessible to users that rely on assistive technologies such as screen readers. These programs can read aloud the contents of the `title` attribute to give the user more information about the page you are linking to.

The rel Attribute

The `rel` attribute is used for defining the relationship of the current page to the page that is being linked to. For example, `rel="author"` indicates that the linked page includes information about the author of the current page. You will look more at the different link types that are available in the "Link Types" section coming up shortly.

The target Attribute

The `target` attribute is used to instruct the browser *how* it should follow a link. If you want the browser to open the link in a new window/tab, use `_blank` as the target.

```
<a href="http://google.com" target="_blank">Google</a>
```

Clicking on this link would open the Google home page in a new tab. Using `_self` will instruct the browser to open the link in the current window. Most browsers will open links in the current window by default unless you specify otherwise.

The download Attribute

You can use the `download` attribute to tell the browser that it should prompt the user to download a file and not display the file in the browser window. This is particularly useful when you want to provide a download link for an HTML, CSS, or JavaScript file that browsers would normally display. The `download` attribute is a new addition in HTML5 and therefore browser support is currently limited.

You don't need to specify any content for the `download` attribute; its presence is enough to trigger a download. The following example shows how you could use this attribute to provide a download link to a JavaScript file.

```
<a href="script.js" download>Download my JavaScript file</a>
```

By default the browser will save the file using the same filename as the file on the web server. You can, however, change this behavior by defining a different name for the file in the content of the `download` attribute:

```
<a href="script.js" download="myscript.js">Download my JavaScript
  file</a>
```

Here I have set the filename of the downloaded file to `myscript.js`.

The ping Attribute

The `ping` attribute is used to define a URL (or a set of URLs separated by spaces) that should be notified when a user follows the link. This is useful for applications such as visitor tracking and analytics.

```
<a href="http://google.com" ping="http://example.com/click/google">
  Google
</a>
```

The ping attribute is also a new addition in HTML5 and therefore browser support for this attribute is currently limited.

Link Types

You can use a number of different link types to specify the relationship between the current page and the page that you are linking to. You specify this relationship using the `rel` attribute. Most links that you create probably will not specify a type, but you should try to use them where it is appropriate.

Table 3-1 shows the most commonly used link types, and their meanings, that are available for hyperlinks. For a full list of link types, check out `http://microformats.org/wiki/existing-rel-values`.

Table 3-1   Link Types

Link Type	Purpose
alternate	Links to alternative representations of a document. Use `alternate` to link to a copy of the page that is in a different language, for example.
author	Links to a page about the author of the document or article.
bookmark	Specifies a permalink (permanent link) to the nearest section. This type can be used when linking to posts in a blog.
help	Links to a page that contains help information relevant to the content of the current page.
license	Links to a page that contains a copyright license relevant to the content of the current page.
next	Links to the next page in a series of pages.
nofollow	Used to represent that the author of the current page does not endorse the page that is being linked to. This is commonly used by large websites such as news organizations when linking to smaller websites in news stories. Specifying this type of relationship also prevents search engine crawlers from following the link, hence the name `nofollow`.
prefetch	Instructs the browser that it is likely that the user will click this link so it should fetch the page in advance to help speed up browsing.
prev	Links to the previous page in a series of pages.
search	Links to a resource that can be used to search through the current page or related pages.
tag	Specifies a tag that is related to the contents of the current document. This is commonly used on blogs where posts might be tagged with certain keywords.

Hyperlinks can have multiple link types, separated by spaces.

Here are a few examples of <a> elements that use some of these link types.

```
<a href="http://myblog.example.com" rel="nofollow">Ben's Blog</a>
<a href="help.html" rel="help">Help Documentation</a>
<a href="author.html" rel="author">About the author</a>
```

For a quick refresher on how to create links, check out this Treehouse video:
http://teamtreehouse.com/library/websites/html/links/anchors.

Lists

When writing content for your web pages, you may find it useful to use lists. HTML has several elements that you can use to create lists and list items. In this section, you focus on the two main types of itemized lists: unordered lists and ordered lists. You will be using an unordered list later on to create the structure for the navigation.

Unordered Lists

The name gives it away but in an unordered list, the order of the list's items is not important. If you were to change the order of the list items, it would not affect the meaning of the list at all. An example of this would be a shopping list of ingredients needed for a recipe. You can change the order of the ingredients in the shopping list, but it does not change the fact that you still need to buy all of them.

Unordered lists are defined using the <ul> element, as shown in the following example code.

```
<ul>
  <li>Plain flour</li>
  <li>Salt</li>
  <li>Eggs</li>
  <li>Milk</li>
  <li>Butter</li>
</ul>
```

Here we have used a separate <li> (list item) element for each of the ingredients that are needed to make pancakes.

Most browsers will display unordered lists using bullet points, as shown in Figure 3-3. This styling can be changed using CSS.

FIGURE 3-3 An unordered list.

Ordered Lists

Unlike unordered lists, ordered lists require that their list items be displayed in a certain order. Modifying the order could greatly change the meaning of the list. For example, the steps in a recipe should follow a certain order; otherwise, your cooking could take a turn for the worse.

Ordered lists are defined using the <ol> element and contain one or more <li> elements.

```
<ol>
  <li>
    Sift the flour into a mixing bowl.
  </li>
  <li>
    Make a well into the center of the flour and break the eggs
    into it.
  </li>
  <li>
    Whisk the flour and eggs.
  </li>
  <li>
    Gradually add the milk and water whilst whisking until you have
    a smooth batter.
  </li>
  <li>
    Melt the butter into a frying pan.
  </li>
  <li>
    Add a small amount of batter into the pan, just enough to cover
    the base of the pan.
  </li>
  <li>
    Cook for about a minute.
  </li>
  <li>
```

```
   Flip the pancake over and cook the other side for about 10
   seconds.
</li>
<li>
   Serve the pancake with sugar and lemon.
</li>
</ol>
```

This example shows the steps for making pancakes. As these steps need to be completed in order, it is best to use an `<ol>` element. You don't have to manually add in the numbers for each of the list items; the browser will do this for you, as you can see in Figure 3-4.

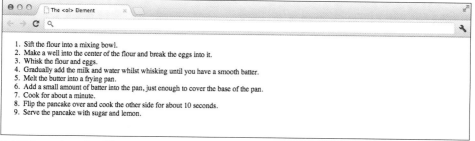

FIGURE 3-4 An ordered list.

For a quick recap on unordered and ordered lists, check out Nick Pettit's video on Treehouse: `http://teamtreehouse.com/library/websites/html/lists/html-lists-ordered-and-unordered`.

Building the Navigation

Now that you know how to use links and lists, it's time to create some navigation that will enable users to easily flow between the different pages in your website.

The code for this exercise can be found in folder 2.

Follow these instructions to create the site navigation.

1. Open the `index.html` file.

2. Locate the `<nav>` element that you created in Chapter 2.

3. Within this <nav> element, create a new <ul> element:

```
<nav>
  <ul>

  </ul>
</nav>
```

4. Next you need to add links to each page in your website. First create a new <li> element within the <ul> element for each of your pages, excluding the sitemap. (You should have five.)

5. Create a new link using the <a> element within each of these list items.

6. Set the anchor text for these links to the pages of your website: Home, About, News, Menu, and Locations. Here is an example of the home page link.

```
<li><a href="">Home</a></li>
```

7. Set the href attribute of these links to point to the pages in your website: index. html, about.html, news.html, menu.html, and locations.html.

```
<li><a href="index.html">Home</a></li>
```

8. Now add a title attribute to each <a> element and give it some content that describes the page you are linking to. I have provided some examples:

> Joe's Pizza Co.
>
> Find out more about Joe's Pizza Co.
>
> Latest news about Joe's Pizza Co.
>
> The restaurant menu for Joe's Pizza Co.
>
> Joe's Pizza Co. restaurant locations.

9. It's nice for users to be able to quickly identify the page that they are currently on when they look at the navigation. To make this possible for them, you need to add a class attribute to the link that points to the current page and set the value of this attribute to active.

```
<li><a href="index.html" title="..."
class="active">Home</a></li>
```

The stylesheet you added in Chapter 2 includes some code that will style the active link slightly differently to make it stand out.

10. Save the index.html file.

11. Copy the navigation that you just created into your about.html.

12. Move the class attribute that will apply the active styling to the about link.

13. Save the about.html file.

Here is how your navigation should look in your index.html file. If you are having problems, try copying this code from the index.html file that can be downloaded from the book's website.

```
<nav>
  <ul>
    <li>
      <a href="index.html" title="Joe's Pizza Co." class="active">
        Home
      </a>
    </li>
    <li>
      <a href="about.html"
         title="Find out more about Joe's Pizza Co.">
        About
      </a>
    </li>
    <li>
      <a href="news.html"
         title="Latest News about Joe's Pizza Co.">
        News
      </a>
    </li>
    <li>
      <a href="menu.html"
         title="The restaurant menu for Joe's Pizza Co.">
        Menu
      </a>
    </li>
    <li>
      <a href="locations.html"
         title="Joe's Pizza Co. restaurant locations.">
        Locations
      </a>
    </li>
  </ul>
</nav>
```

Figure 3-5 shows how your new navigation should look in your browser, with the links at the top right of the page. Notice that the Home link is a different color from the others, as it has the active class applied to it.

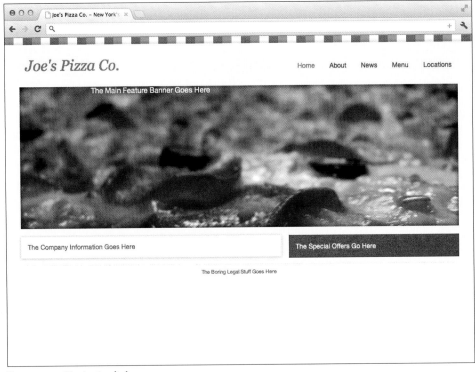

FIGURE 3-5 Navigation links.
Pizza image reproduced by permission of William Rogers

 Notice that the Sitemap link is missing from the navigation list. You will place that link in the footer of the page.

Adding Footer Content

Your page templates are very nearly complete! All that you have to do now is to add the footer content. Here you are going to be introduced to a new element, <small>, to mark up the legal text. You will also add in that link to the Sitemap page.

The <small> Print

The purpose of the <small> element has changed in HTML5. Previously, the element was used for presentational purposes (it made text smaller); however, it is now used to define short side comments such as legal disclaimers and copyrights, as shown in the example code below.

```
<small>Copyright 2012 Joe's Pizza Co.</small>
```

The <small> element should only be used for short passages of text. You should not use it to wrap all the text that makes up a website's privacy policy, for example. In that case, the text is the main content on the page and not a side comment.

Adding Links and Legal to the Footer

You may have noticed that you skipped over a page in your navigation, the sitemap. Instead of putting a link to this page in the navigation, it is often best to include it in the footer of the page. Why? Because it doesn't need the same exposure as the other pages.

The page footer should also contain the page copyright information. In this case, we are going to put the copyright text within a <small> element to give it a greater semantic meaning.

The code for this exercise can be found in folder 3.

To create the footer section for your pages, follow these instructions.

1. Open the index.html file.

2. Locate the <footer> element that you created in Chapter 2.

3. Create a new <small> element within the <footer>, using the text in the following code extract.

   ```
   <small>&copy; 2012 Joe's Pizza Co. All Rights Reserved</small>
   ```

4. Now create a new link to the sitemap.html file using an <a> element.

   ```
   <a href="sitemap.html">Sitemap</a>
   ```

5. Add a title attribute to this new link with the following text: Links to all the pages on this website.

6. Add a hyphen between the <small> and <a> elements with a space on the right and left of this hyphen. This is just because it looks good.

7. Save the `index.html`.

8. Copy the contents of the `<footer>` element into the `about.html` file.

9. Save the `about.html` file.

The following code shows how your `<footer>` element should now look.

```
<footer>
  <small>&copy; 2012 Joe's Pizza Co. All Rights Reserved</small>
  -
  <a href="sitemap.html"
     title="Links to all the pages on this website">Sitemap</a>
</footer>
```

Figure 3-6 shows how your home page should look with the new footer.

FIGURE 3-6 The home page with new footer content.
Pizza image reproduced by permission of William Rogers

HTML Codes

Note the use of © in the copyright line in the preceding code. This set of characters will display on your page as the copyright symbol. Special characters such as £, © and ™ must be written using special HTML codes. There are well over a hundred HTML codes available that allow you to add symbols to your web pages. A full list of these codes can be found at http://ascii.cl/htmlcodes.htm.

Global Attributes

In addition to the specialized attributes that you have looked at so far, every HTML element has a set of attributes that can be applied to it. These are known as *global* attributes.

In this section, you learn about the global attributes that you will find most useful when creating web pages. You saw a few of these attributes in examples earlier in this chapter and in the previous two chapters.

The id Attribute

The id attribute can be used to assign a unique ID to an element. This can make it easier to select the element using CSS or JavaScript.

An ID can be as small as one character long and should only be used for one element on a page. You should always try to make your IDs descriptive as this will make your code easier for others to understand. If you need to place the same identifier on multiple elements, you should use a class, described in the following section.

```
<section id="bio">...</section>
```

This example code would create a new <section> element that has the ID bio. You could then style this element by targeting it using this ID.

The class Attribute

The class attribute is similar to the id attribute in that it can be used to place an identifier on an element so that you can easily select it with CSS or JavaScript. The difference is that you can use the same class on multiple elements. This can be useful if you want to be able to target a set of list items, or a number of paragraph elements, for example.

```
<ol>
  <li>one</li>
  <li class="even">two</li>
  <li>three</li>
  <li class="even">four</li>
  <li>five</li>
</ol>
```

In this example, you have added the class even to alternate list items. This means that you could target just these list items in CSS to create a nice alternating background pattern to help users differentiate the rows.

The hidden Attribute

The hidden attribute can be used to instruct the browser to not display an element that is not relevant to the current state of the page.

For example, you might want to hide some page content from users who are not signed in. You could use JavaScript (you will be introduced to this in Chapter 11) to monitor whether a user has successfully logged in and show/hide the content appropriately. To hide the element, you set the attribute to true; to show it, you would set it to false.

```
<p hidden="true">Only signed in users can see this content.</p>
```

Note that the hidden attribute is a new addition in HTML5 and therefore browser support for this attribute is currently limited.

The title Attribute

You have already encountered the title attribute when you learned about links, but I want to cover it in a little more detail. The title attribute can be used to supply a description of the element's content. If you specify a title attribute, its contents will be displayed when users hover their mouse over the element for a few seconds.

```
<a href="http://google.com" title="The Google Search
  Engine">Google</a>
```

In this example, when users hover their mouse over the link, they see the value of the title attribute displayed in a tooltip. This is shown in Figure 3-7.

FIGURE 3-7 A tooltip displaying the value of the title attribute.

It may sound obvious, but remember that these tooltips will not work on mobile devices.

The lang Attribute

You encountered the lang attribute in Chapter 1, where you used it on the <html> element to set the language of the whole page to English. The lang attribute can be applied to any element in order to specify the language of its contents. The following example sets the language of the page as English, but also includes a paragraph of German text ("de" for Deutsche).

```
<!DOCTYPE html>
<html lang="en">
<head>
  <meta charset="utf-8">
  <title>Language Test</title>
</head>
<body>
  <p>HTML5 is awesome.</p>
  <p lang="de">HTML5 ist super.</p>
</body>
</html>
```

Summary

Awesome! Your page templates are now complete.

In this chapter, you have learned about a number of new HTML elements. This includes learning how to use heading elements in order to create a hierarchy for your page content.

Hyperlinks make up the backbone of the web. In this chapter, you learned how you can add links to your web pages that navigate to both external web pages and sections within the current web page.

You have also been introduced to HTML lists and learned the difference between unordered and ordered lists. These list elements can come in very handy for structuring navigation, as you found out when building the navigation section for your page templates.

Finally, you have applied all that you have learned in this chapter in order to finish your page templates. In Chapter 4, you will use these page templates to create each page in your website.

chapter four
Creating the Web Pages

IN CHAPTER 3, you focused on finishing off the page templates. Now you are going to put these page templates to use to create each of the pages for your website.

You are going to learn about several new HTML elements as you progress through this chapter. You will build on what you learned about heading elements in Chapter 3 and will learn how to properly group multiple heading elements together.

Text content will make up the majority of the content for the About page on your website. You will learn about a few new elements that you can use to mark up text (such as `<abbr>` and `<blockquote>`), as well as taking a deeper look at the paragraph element. (Appendix A includes a number of other text elements that I couldn't fit into this chapter.)

By the end of this chapter, you will have created all the pages for your website and added content to each of them. As you progress through the rest of this book you will optimize these pages using HTML5.

Adding Content to the Home Page

The home page is the first page that most people will see when visiting your website, so let's start there. In this section, you'll learn about an HTML element called `<hgroup>`; this is a new addition in HTML5.

73

Completing the Main Feature with Headings and <hgroup>

The <hgroup> element is used in instances where you need to group multiple levels of heading elements. You could use the <hgroup> element to group together the main title and subtitle of a book.

```
<hgroup>
  <h1>Venture Deals</h1>
  <h2>Be Smarter Than Your Lawyer and Venture Capitalist</h2>
</hgroup>
```

When you have two or more heading elements within a <hgroup> element, only the heading with the highest priority is taken into account by search engines and other algorithm-based programs when they examine the document outline. (All heading elements will still be displayed on the screen by your web browser.)

Now let's use the <hgroup> element and two heading elements to complete the main feature section on the home page.

The code for this exercise can be found in the download code for Chapter 4, folder 1.

Follow these steps:

1. Open the index.html file.

2. Locate the <section> element in your code that has the ID feature.

3. Delete the dummy text that you added to this element in Chapter 2 ("The Main Feature Banner Goes Here").

4. Create a new <hgroup> element within the <section> element.

5. Create a new <h1> element within the <hgroup> element.

6. Add the following text to this new <h1> element: New York's Best Pizza

7. Create a new <h2> element underneath the <h1> that you just created.

8. Add the following text to this new <h2> element: joe's pepperoni special

9. Save the index.html file.

The code for your main feature section should look like this:

```
<!-- Feature -->
<section id="feature">
  <hgroup>
    <h1>New York's Best Pizza</h1>
    <h2>joe's pepperoni special</h2>
  </hgroup>
</section>
```

Now take a look at the index.html file in your web browser; you will see that the main feature now has a main heading and a subtitle, as shown in Figure 4-1.

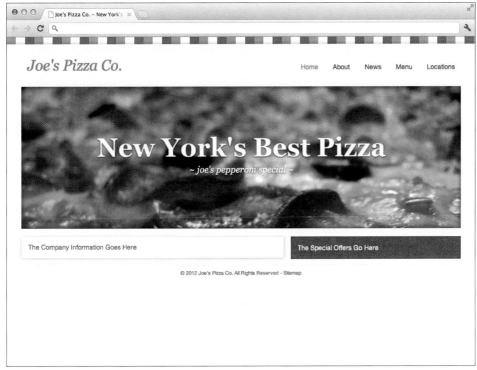

FIGURE 4-1 The home page with a completed main feature section.
Pizza image reproduced by permission of William Rogers

Adding the Home Page Text

You now have the main feature section sorted, so let's move on to the home page text. Most websites have a body of text on the home page to give the user a brief overview of the business. For this, you are going to need another heading and a couple of paragraph elements.

Paragraphs

You got a brief introduction to the <p> element in Chapter 1. The paragraph element is used to group text in the same way that you would use paragraphs in normal writing. Most browsers will apply some default styling to <p> elements to add a margin above and below the text. Here is an example of using the <p> element to mark up a passage of text.

```
<h1>Treehouse</h1>
<p>Our mission is to bring affordable Technology education to
  people everywhere, in order to help them achieve their dreams and
  change the world.<p>
```

Use the <p> element only if there is not a more specific element, such as a heading element, available for marking up the content.

Adding Text to the Home Page

Now it's time to add more content to the home page. You can see the code for this exercise on the book's companion website, but I recommend you try practicing your coding skills by working through the following steps before looking at the file.

The code for this exercise can be found in folder 2.

1. Open the index.html in your project folder.

2. Locate the <section> element in your code that has the ID home-text.

3. Delete the dummy text that you added to this element in Chapter 3.

4. Create a new <h1> element within this <section> element.

5. Add the following text to this new <h1> element: Welcome to Joe's Pizza Co.

6. Add the following text below the new <h1> element. Note the use of <p> elements here and the link in the second paragraph.

```
<p>
  We pride ourselves on serving up the best pizzas in New York
  City. Come and visit one of our family-friendly restaurants
  and take a look at our wide range of authentic Italian
  pizzas. We can also deliver direct to your door with our
  speedy takeaway service.
</p>
```

```
<p>
   Please take a look at the <a href="locations.
   html">Locations</a> page for more information about where you
   can find our fantastic restaurants.
</p>
```

7. Save the index.html file.

Your code for the home text section should now look like the following:

```
<!-- Home Text -->
<section id="home-text">
  <h1>Welcome to Joe's Pizza Co.</h1>
  <p>
    We pride ourselves on serving up the best pizzas in New York
  City. Come and visit one of our family-friendly restaurants and
  take a look at our wide range of authentic Italian pizzas. We can
  also deliver direct to your door with our speedy takeaway
  service.
  </p>
  <p>
    Please take a look at the <a href="locations.html">Locations</
  a> page for more information about where you can find our
  fantastic restaurants.
  </p>
</section>
```

Figure 4-2 shows how the home page should look in your browser at this stage. Wow, it's really shaping up!

The CSS style sheet that you added to the page at the end of Chapter 2 has taken care of applying separate styling to the heading elements in the main feature and home text sections. This is why they appear different even though they use the same elements.

There's just one more section to finish on the home page, the special offers. I show you how to do this next.

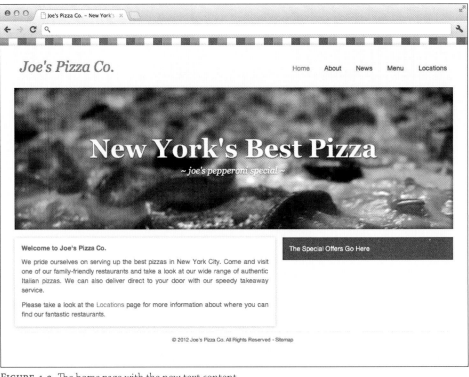

FIGURE 4-2 The home page with the new text content.
Pizza image reproduced by permission of William Rogers

Adding the Special Offers

The final section on the home page is the special offers. In this section, you are going to call on what you learned about HTML lists in Chapter 3 so you can create a list of special offers.

 The code for this exercise can be found in folder 3.

Follow these instructions to add this section to the home page.

1. Open the index.html file.

2. Locate the <section> element with the ID offers.

3. Create a new <h1> element with the text: Special Offers.

4. Create a new <ul> element below the heading that will contain the list of offers.

5. Create an <li> element for the first offer and add to it the offer text: 10% Off All Pizzas When You Eat In!

6. Create a `<li>` element for the second offer and add to it the offer text: `20% Off Joe's Pepperoni Special with the promo code NYBESTPIZZA`.

7. Save the `index.html` file.

Your code should look like this:

```
<!-- Special Offers -->
<section id="offers">
  <h1>Special Offers</h1>
  <ul>
    <li>10% Off All Pizzas When You Eat In!</li>
    <li>20% Off Joe's Pepperoni Special with the promo code
    NYBESTPIZZA</li>
  </ul>
</section>
```

That concludes the content for the home page. View the page in your browser; you should see something like Figure 4-3. It's starting to look like a real website!

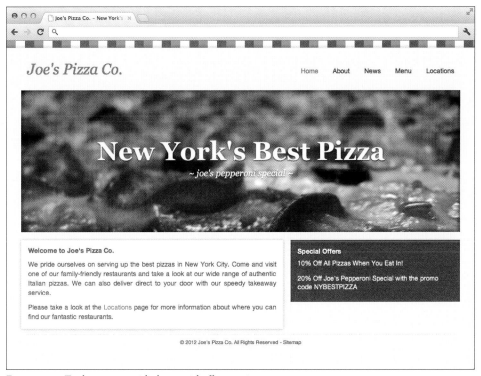

FIGURE 4-3 The home page with the special offers section.
Pizza image reproduced by permission of William Rogers

Adding Content to the About Page

The About page will contain mainly text content, but even text can be marked up using special HTML elements in order to provide greater semantic meaning to computer programs. In this section, you first learn how to mark up quotations and abbreviations in your text. You will then put these new skills to use by adding some text content to the About page.

Quotes

The `<blockquote>` element is used when quoting a block of text from another source. The element has an optional `cite` attribute that you can use to add a URL to the source of the quotation. If you choose to use the `cite` attribute, its contents must be a valid URL.

```
<blockquote cite="http://example.com/quotes">
  To cite, or not to cite, that is the question.
</blockquote>
```

The contents of the `cite` attribute will not be displayed to users but can be used by computer programs. To make the source more accessible to the user, you could link to it using the `<a>` element that learned about in Chapter 3.

You can also mark up a quotation within a block of text using the `<q>` element. A good example of this would be if you were writing a news article and wanted to quote an individual, as shown in the following example.

```
In reaction to the proposed budget cuts, Sam Dawson said
<q>This is crazy, they simply cannot turn off the Internet</q>.
Personally, I agree with Sam's comment.
```

 For a quick recap on how to mark up quotes in your HTML code, check out this video on Treehouse: `http://teamtreehouse.com/library/websites/html/text/quotes`.

Abbreviations

HTML has a number of elements for marking up key terms, abbreviations, and definitions in your text content. Using these elements also enables you to use CSS to apply a custom styling to these parts of your text that can be useful for indicating important terms or abbreviations. In this section, you are going to focus on the `<abbr>` element; however, check out Appendix A for information about how to mark up terms and definitions.

The `<abbr>` element can be used to identify abbreviations within your text content. You can also optionally use the `title` attribute to define the full text version of an abbreviation. Most browsers will display this full text version to a user if she hovers her mouse cursor over the abbreviation for a few seconds.

```
<p>The <abbr title="World Wide Web Consortium">W3C</abbr> is
  responsible for developing web standards.</p>
```

Using the `<abbr>` element allows computer programs to easily identify abbreviations in your text and understand what they mean. This contributes to building a smarter web.

Adding the About Page Text

The text on the About page will include both a quotation and an abbreviation, perfect candidates for the new HTML elements you have just learned about.

For this page, you are going to build on the content page template that you have already created in the `about.html` file.

The code for this exercise can be found in folder 4.

Follow these instructions to add the text content to your About page:

1. Open the `about.html` file.

2. Locate the `<section>` element with the ID `page-text`.

3. Create a new `<h1>` element within this `<section>` element. Add the following text to this new `<h1>` element: `About Joe's Pizza Co.` (including the period).

4. Create a new `<p>` element underneath the `<h1>` you just created and add the following text to your new `<p>` element:

   ```
   Established in 1984, Joe's Pizza Co. prides itself on serving
     up authentic Italian pizzas with a New York twist. Since
     opening their first restaurant at 310 West 38th Street, Joe's
     has expanded into two more restaurants distributed throughout
     New York.
   ```

5. Now create another `<p>` element underneath the previous one and add the following text to it. Note the use of the `<q>` element to mark up the quote within the text.

```
Our founder Joe Balochio has always said <q>"A great pizza
   starts with selecting quality, fresh ingredients from local
   suppliers."</q> This belief is embodied in the company and
   the pizzas that you will eat in our restaurants will never
   contain any poor quality or cheap ingredients. We take great
   pride in the quality of our pizzas.
```

6. Finally, add a third <p> element with the following text. This time, you are going to mark up the abbreviation using the <abbr> element.

```
Joe's Pizza Co. is a member of the National Restaurant
   Association (<abbr title="National Restaurant
   Association">NRA</abbr>).
```

7. Save the about.html file.

The code for your page-text section should now look like the following:

```
<!-- Page Text -->
<section id="page-text">
  <h1>About Joe's Pizza Co.</h1>
  <p>
    Established in 1984, Joe's Pizza Co. prides itself on serving
  up authentic Italian pizzas with a New York twist. Since opening
  their first restaurant at 310 West 38th Street, Joe's has
  expanded into two more restaurants distributed throughout New
  York.
  </p>
  <p>
    Our founder Joe Balochio has always said <q>"A great pizza
  starts with selecting quality, fresh ingredients from local
  suppliers."</q> This belief is embodied in the company and the
  pizzas that you will eat in our restaurants will never contain
  any poor quality or cheap ingredients. We take great pride in the
  quality of our pizzas.
  </p>
  <p>
    Joe's Pizza Co. is a member of the National Restaurant
  Association (<abbr title="National Restaurant Association">NRA</
  abbr>).
  </p>
</section>
```

Figure 4-4 shows how the About page should look in your web browser.

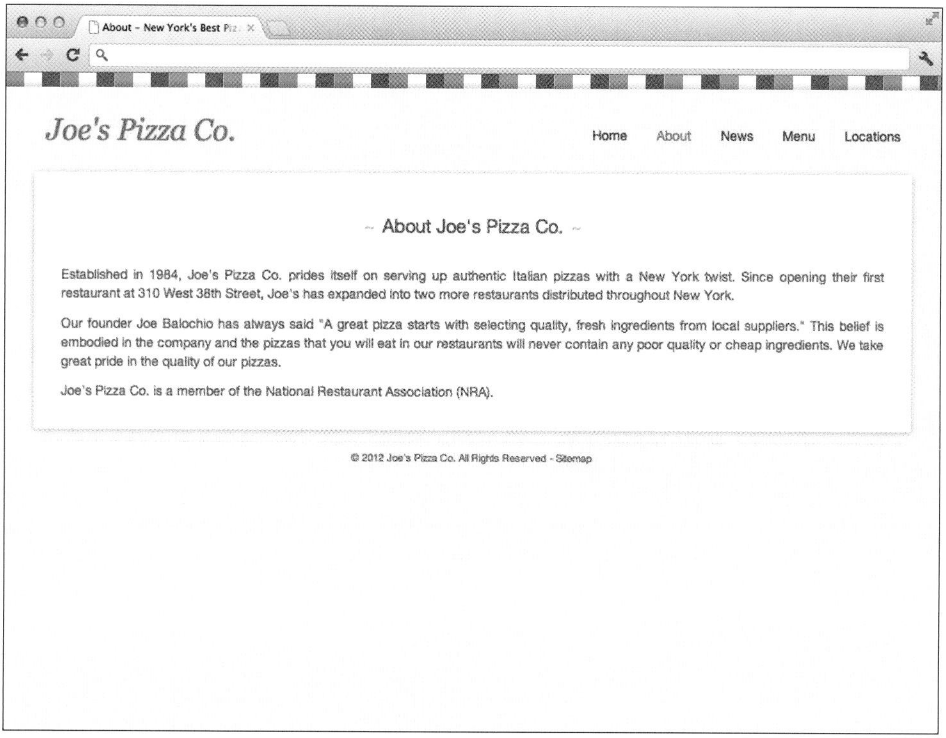

FIGURE 4-4 The About page.

Creating the Locations Page

Joe's Pizza Co. has three restaurant locations throughout New York. The Locations page will include the address, phone number, opening hours, and a map for each restaurant. All this information will be contained within individual <section> elements, one for each location.

You already know most of what is needed to create the Locations page. All that's left to learn is how to add images to your web pages so that you can add the maps.

Adding Images to Your Web Pages

So far you have only looked at how to use text within your web pages. The <img> element livens things up a little because it enables you to embed images.

The <img> element must have both a src attribute and an alt attribute. The src attribute should contain a path to the image file that you want to embed in your page. The alt attribute is used to provide some fallback text in case the image cannot be loaded. This text should describe the contents of the image. Here's an example.

```
<img src="pepperoni-pizza.jpeg"
     alt="A pepperoni pizza presented on a wooden chopping board">
```

Here we have defined an `<img>` element with a path to an image file and a text description of the image. Figure 4-5 shows how this image would be displayed in a web browser.

FIGURE 4-5 A simple image displayed in Google Chrome.
Pizza image reproduced by permission of iStockphoto.com/Lauri Patterson

 Notice that there is no end tag for `<img>` elements. This is because `<img>` is a *void* element.

You can also define the width and height that an image should be displayed at using the `width` and `height` attributes. These attributes should contain an integer that represents the dimension in pixels. The browser will automatically resize images to the specified dimensions if needed; however, it is better to supply an image that has already been sized to the proper dimensions. This will help to reduce the amount of time it takes the page to load.

The following example uses an `<img>` element that explicitly defines the `width` and `height` attributes. The image file here is already 240 pixels wide and 280 pixels high so the browser will not resize it. You should still explicitly define the image dimensions as this can help to speed up the page load time slightly.

```
<img src="pepperoni-pizza.jpeg"
     alt=" A pepperoni pizza presented on a wooden chopping board "
     width="240" height="280">
```

Adding Content to the Locations Page

Okay, so now you can add images using HTML. Next, let's start adding content for the Locations page.

The code for this exercise can be found in folder 5.

Follow these instructions:

1. First, download the following map images that you will be using in this section: `map1.png`, `map2.png`, and `map3.png`. These can be found in the `img` folder in folder 5. Place these in the `img` folder in your project directory.

2. Create a new `locations.html` file in your project folder.

3. Open the `about.html` file and copy its contents into your new `locations.html` file.

4. Update the `<title>` and `<meta>` elements to reflect the content of the new Locations page. I have provided some examples:

```
<title>Locations - Joe's Pizza Co.</title>
<meta name="description" content="Locations of Joe's Pizza Co.
restaurants in New York City.">
<meta name="keywords" content="new york pizza,pizza
restaurants,joe's pizza,joe's new york">
```

5. Remove the `class` attribute from the About link in the navigation and move this to the Locations link.

6. Locate the `<section>` element with the ID `page-text` and delete any content that is in this element.

7. Create a new `<h1>` element in this section and give it the text `Locations`.

8. Add the following code underneath this `<h1>` element. This provides the information about the first restaurant location. The `id` and `class` attributes here are used for styling purposes. The `<br>` element used here creates a line break in the text. You can find more information about the `<br>` element in Appendix A.

```
<section id="location1">
  <h1>310 West 38th Street, NY</h1>
  <img src="img/map1.png"
       alt="Joe's Pizza at 310 West 38th Street, NY ">
  <p class="location-phone">212 012 3456</p>
  <h2>Opening Hours:</h2>
  <p>
    Mon-Fri: 12:00 - 22:00<br>
    Sat-Sun: 11:00 - 23:00
  </p>
</section>
```

9. Underneath this, add the following code for restaurant location number 2.

```
<section id="location2">
  <h1>2450 Broadway, NY</h1>
  <img src="img/map2.png"
      alt="Joe's Pizza at 2450 Broadway, NY">
  <p class="location-phone">212 012 3457</p>
  <h2>Opening Hours:</h2>
  <p>
    Mon-Fri: 12:00 - 22:00<br>
    Sat-Sun: 11:00 - 23:00
  </p>
</section>
```

10. Finally, add the code for restaurant location number 3.

```
<section id="location3">
  <h1>200 West 44th Street, NY</h1>
  <img src="img/map3.png"
      alt="Joe's Pizza at 200 West 44th Street, NY">
  <p class="location-phone">212 012 3458</p>
  <h2>Opening Hours:</h2>
  <p>
    Mon-Fri: 12:00 - 22:00<br>
    Sat-Sun: 11:00 - 23:00
  </p>
</section>
```

11. Save your `locations.html` file.

Figure 4-6 shows how the new Locations page should look in your browser.

Creating the Sitemap Page

The Sitemap page should contain only a heading and a list of all the other pages on your website.

The code for this exercise can be found in folder 6.

FIGURE 4-6 The Locations page.
Map data 2012 © Google

Follow these instructions to create the Sitemap page:

1. First, create a new `sitemap.html` file in your project folder.

2. Open the `about.html` file and copy its contents into your new `sitemap.html` file.

3. Update the `<title>` and `<meta>` elements within the `<head>` element to reflect the content of the new Sitemap page.

4. Remove the `class` attribute from the About link in the navigation.

5. Locate the `<section>` element with the ID `page-text` and delete any content that is in this element.

6. Create a new `<h1>` element in this section and give it the text `Sitemap`.

7. Create a new `<ul>` element underneath this `<h1>` and give it the ID `sitemap`.

8. Create new `<li>` elements for each page in your website (you should have six).

9. Create a new `<a>` element in each of these `<li>` elements that links to each page in your website.

10. Set the anchor text of these links to the page names: Home, About, News, Menu, Locations, and Sitemap.

11. Set the `href` attributes on these links to point to the relevant HTML file: `index.html`, `about.html`, `news.html`, `menu.html`, `locations.html`, and `sitemap.html`.

12. Set the `title` attribute on these links to contain a description of the page you are linking to. You can use the same description that you used when building the navigation in Chapter 3.

13. Save the `sitemap.html` file.

Here is how your code should now look. You can also find this code in the `locations.html` file in folder 6.

```html
<section id="page-text">
  <h1>Sitemap</h1>
  <ul id="sitemap">
    <li>
      <a href="index.html" title="Joe's Pizza Co.">
        Home
      </a>
    </li>
    <li>
      <a href="about.html"
         title="Find out more about Joe's Pizza Co.">
        About
      </a>
    </li>
    <li>
      <a href="news.html"
         title="Latest News about Joe's Pizza Co.">
        News
      </a>
    </li>
    <li>
      <a href="menu.html"
         title="The restaurant menu for Joe's Pizza Co.">
        Menu
      </a>
    </li>
    <li>
      <a href="locations.html"
         title="Joe's Pizza Co. restaurant locations.">
        Locations
      </a>
    </li>
    <li>
      <a href="sitemap.html"
```

```
         title="Links to all the pages on this website ">
         Sitemap
      </a>
    </li>
  </ul>
</section>
```

Figure 4-7 shows how the Sitemap page should look in your web browser.

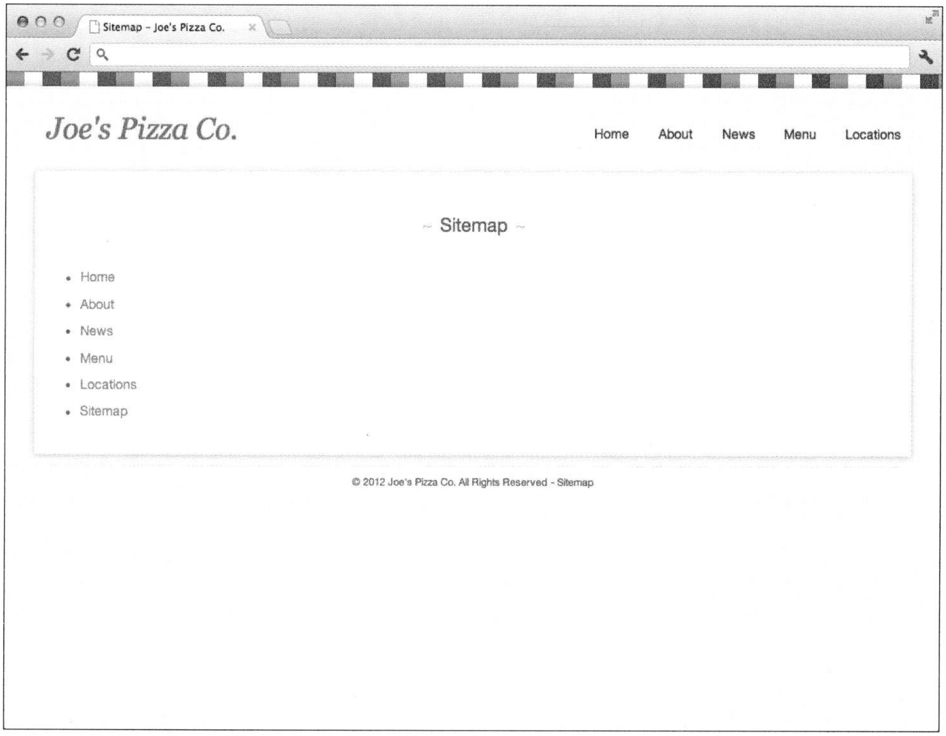

FIGURE 4-7 The Sitemap page.

Creating the Menu Page

The Menu page is going to display, well, the menu. You're also going to add some images of the menu items to jazz things up a little. (You don't want boring pages, do you?) The twist is that this time you are going to make these images into figures and give them captions using two new HTML5 elements, `<figure>` and `<figcaption>`.

This will be your first encounter with HTML tables. Tables are a fairly large topic so hang in there for the next few pages. You really do need to know this stuff!

Introducing Tables

If you have a lot of tabular data to present to your users, you can use the HTML <table> element. Table rows can be defined using the <tr> element and cells using the <td> element. Column headings are defined using the <th> element rather than a <td> element.

The following example creates a simple table that shows the results achieved by three students on their math exam.

```
<table border="1">
    <tr>
      <th>Pupil</th>
      <th>Result</th>
    </tr>
    <tr>
      <td>James</td>
      <td>85</td>
    </tr>
    <tr>
      <td>Alicia</td>
      <td>97</td>
    </tr>
    <tr>
      <td>Tom</td>
      <td>76</td>
    </tr>
</table>
```

The border attribute on the <table> tag adds a 1-pixel border to the table so that we can see the rows and columns clearly. The first row contains two <th> elements that make up the column headings; browsers will usually display these in bold text by default. We then define the records by creating three separate rows, each containing two <td> elements (table cells), one for the pupil's name and the one for his or her exam result. Figure 4-8 shows this table displayed in a browser.

FIGURE 4-8 A table of exam results.

Table Cell Attributes

Both `<td>` and `<th>` elements have a number of attributes that can be used to help format them. One example is the `colspan` (column span) attribute. Use the `colspan` attribute in instances where you need a particular table cell to span multiple columns. The following example uses the `colspan` attribute to create a cell that spans the whole table.

```
<table border="1">
    <tr>
      <th colspan="2">Class 2B</th>
    </tr>
    <tr>
      <th>Pupil</th>
      <th>Result</th>
    </tr>
    <tr>
      <td>James</td>
      <td>85</td>
    </tr>
    <tr>
      <td>Alicia</td>
      <td>97</td>
    </tr>
    <tr>
      <td>Tom</td>
      <td>76</td>
    </tr>
    <tr>
      <th colspan="2">Class 3A</th>
    </tr>
    <tr>
      <th>Pupil</th>
      <th>Result</th>
    </tr>
    <tr>
      <td>Ben</td>
      <td>82</td>
    </tr>
    <tr>
      <td>Louise</td>
      <td>92</td>
    </tr>
</table>
```

When this example is displayed in the browser, the `<th>` elements will span the full width of the table, as shown in Figure 4-9.

FIGURE 4-9 A table with <th> elements that use the colspan attribute.

As well as the `colspan` attribute, you can also specify a `rowspan` attribute. This effectively does the same thing as `colspan` but merges cells across rows instead of across columns.

Table Header, Body, and Footers

When working with tables, you can use the `<thead>`, `<tbody>`, and `<tfoot>` elements in order to give greater semantic meaning to your tables.

The <thead> Element

The `<thead>` element can be used to wrap the row of your table that contains the table headings. This enables computer programs and search engines to easily find the column headings. Using the `<thead>` element can also come in handy when writing CSS, because you may want to target just the elements within the `<thead>` with your CSS rules.

The <tfoot> Element

The `<tfoot>` element should contain a set of summaries for each of the columns in a table. Although it is a footer element, it is best to place the `<tfoot>` element under the `<thead>` in your table. The web browser will automatically move this content to bottom of the table, but by putting it under the `<thead>` you make it easier to find if you have a table with a lot of rows. See the next code extract for an example on how to use the `<tfoot>` element.

The <tbody> Element

The `<tbody>` element is used to define the rows of data that are being presented in the table. It should contain one or more `<tr>` elements.

Here's an example of a table that uses the `<thead>`, `<tbody>`, and `<tfoot>` elements.

```
<table border="1">
  <thead>
    <tr>
      <th>Pupil</th>
      <th>Result</th>
    </tr>
  </thead>
```

```
  <tfoot>
    <tr>
      <td>Average</td>
      <td>86</td>
    </tr>
  </tfoot>
  <tbody>
    <tr>
      <td>James</td>
      <td>85</td>
    </tr>
    <tr>
      <td>Alicia</td>
      <td>97</td>
    </tr>
    <tr>
      <td>Tom</td>
      <td>76</td>
    </tr>
  </tbody>
</table>
```

Viewing this in your browser, you should see the table shown in Figure 4-10.

FIGURE 4-10 A table that uses the <thead>, <tbody>, and <tfoot> elements.

For a quick recap on HTML tables, check out these videos on the Treehouse website.

- **Table Rows and Cells:** http://teamtreehouse.com/library/websites/html/tables/rows-and-cells

- **Table Headers and Footers:** http://teamtreehouse.com/library/websites/html/tables/headers-and-footers

Adding the Menu Tables

Every good restaurant website should contain a menu complete with prices. Joe's menu is split into three main sections: pizzas, garlic breads, and sides. You will be using <section> elements to explicitly define each of these sections, and then use <table> elements to display the menu data.

The code for this exercise can be found in folder 7.

Follow these instructions to create the Menu page:

1. First, create a new menu.html file in your project folder.

2. Open the about.html file and copy its contents into your new menu.html file.

3. Update the <title> and <meta> elements within the <head> element to reflect the content of the new Menu page.

4. Update the navigation so that the Menu link has the active class.

5. Locate the <section> element with the ID page-text and delete any content that is in this element.

6. Create a new <h1> element in this section and give it the text Menu.

7. Underneath this <h1> element, create a new <div> element with the ID menu-tables. This will be used to group all the menu tables together for styling purposes.

8. Within this new <div>, create three empty <section> elements. These will hold the three parts of the menu.

9. In the first <section> element, create a new <h1> with the text Pizzas.

10. Copy the following <table> underneath this heading. This table uses three columns. One for the name of the dish, one for a description of the dish, and one for the price. Each dish is presented on its own row.

```
<table id="pizzas">
  <thead>
    <tr>
      <th>Menu Item</th>
      <th>Description</th>
      <th>Price</th>
    </tr>
  </thead>
  <tbody>
    <tr>
```

```
        <td>Joe's Pepperoni Special</td>
        <td>
          Select pepperoni with our signature spicy tomato sauce
        </td>
        <td>13.00</td>
      </tr>
      <tr>
        <td>Margherita</td>
        <td>Oregano, mozzarella and tomato</td>
        <td>10.50</td>
      </tr>
      <tr>
        <td>Hawaiian</td>
        <td>Ham and Pineapple</td>
        <td>12.00</td>
      </tr>
      <tr>
        <td>Pollo</td>
        <td>Chicken and Roast Peppers</td>
        <td>12.00</td>
      </tr>
      <tr>
        <td>Mexican Chicken</td>
        <td>Spicy Chicken with jalapenos</td>
        <td>12.50</td>
      </tr>
    </tbody>
  </table>
```

11. In the second `<section>` element, create a new `<h1>` with the text `Garlic Breads`.

12. Copy the following table underneath this new heading. This table only has two columns because these two menu items do not need descriptions.

```
<table id="garlic-bread">
  <thead>
    <tr>
      <th>Menu Item</th>
      <th>Price</th>
    </tr>
  </thead>
  <tbody>
    <tr>
      <td>Garlic Bread</td>
      <td>4.00</td>
    </tr>
    <tr>
```

```
        <td>Garlic Bread with Double Cheese</td>
        <td>4.50</td>
      </tr>
      <tr>
        <td>Garlic Bread with Sun-Ripened Tomato</td>
        <td>4.80</td>
      </tr>
    </tbody>
  </table>
```

13. In the final `<section>` element, create a new `<h1>` with the text `Side Dishes`.

14. Copy the last table underneath this new heading. Again, this table only has two columns.

```
<table id="sides">
  <thead>
    <tr>
      <th>Menu Item</th>
      <th>Price</th>
    </tr>
  </thead>
  <tbody>
    <tr>
      <td>Potato Wedges</td>
      <td>3.00</td>
    </tr>
    <tr>
      <td>French Fries</td>
      <td>2.50</td>
    </tr>
    <tr>
      <td>6 Onion Rings</td>
      <td>3.50</td>
    </tr>
  </tbody>
</table>
```

15. Save the menu.html file.

Notice the `id` attributes applied to each of the menu tables. This is so that they can be easily targeted using CSS. The Menu page should look like Figure 4-11 when displayed in your web browser.

In Chapter 9, you will revisit the Menu page to make the menu table more accessible to users who rely on screen readers to browse your web pages.

Joe's Pizza Co.

Home   About   News   Menu   Locations

~ Menu ~

Pizzas

Menu Item	Description	Price
Joe's Pepperoni Special	Select pepperoni with our signature spicy tomato sauce	13.00
Margherita	Oregano, mozzarella and tomato	10.50
Hawaiian	Ham and Pineapple	12.00
Pollo	Chicken and Roast Peppers	12.00
Mexican Chicken	Spicy Chicken with jalapenos	12.50

Garlic Breads

Menu Item	Price
Garlic Bread	4.00
Garlic Bread with Double Cheese	4.50
Garlic Bread with Sun-Ripened Tomato	4.80

Side Dishes

Menu Item	Price
Potato Wedges	3.00
French Fries	2.50
6 Onion Rings	3.50

© 2012 Joe's Pizza Co. All Rights Reserved - Sitemap

FIGURE 4-11 The Menu page with the new table.

Figures and Captions

In the world of print, most images, charts, and diagrams include a caption to explain what it is they represent. HTML5 introduces two new elements, <figure> and <figcaption>, that allow you to add captions to the figures used in your web pages. This can help to give computer programs more information about what a figure contains.

The <figure> and <figcaption> elements are not supported by older versions of Internet Explorer and Mozilla Firefox.

The <figure> Element

This element should contain your content element and can optionally contain a <fig caption> element. Here is the earlier image example, this time contained within a <figure> element.

```
<figure>
  <img src="pepperoni-pizza.jpeg"
     alt="A pepperoni pizza presented on a wooden chopping board.">
</figure>
```

Most browsers will add a margin around your figure element; you can override this using CSS.

The <figcaption> Element

Often when you are using the <figure> element, you will want to add a short caption to describe the content of the figure. HTML5 brings the new <figcaption> element that allows you to do just that.

The <figcaption> element should only be used within a <figure> element and can be placed either above or below the contents of the figure.

Here is the image figure again, this time with a caption.

```
<figure>
  <img src="pepperoni-pizza.jpeg"
     alt="A pepperoni pizza presented on a wooden chopping board.">
  <figcaption>Joe's Special Pepperoni Pizza</figcaption>
</figure>
```

In your browser, this example should look like Figure 4-12.

FIGURE 4-12 A <figure> element with a <figcaption>.
Pizza image reproduced by permission of iStockphoto.com/Lauri Patterson

Because the caption is presented to the user, you will generally want the content of your <figcaption> element to be different from your alt text when you are using an image.

Adding Product Images

To make the Menu page look a bit more appetizing, you are now going to add three product images to the right side of the page. The CSS style sheet I provide will take care of positioning the images to the side.

You will be using multiple `<figure>`, `<img>`, and `<figcaption>` elements for these product images.

> The code for this exercise can be found in folder 8.

Let's get going!

1. First you need to download the new image files from the book's website. These can be found in the img folder in folder 8. Once you have these images, place them in the img folder in your project directory. The files you need are: `margherita-pizza.jpeg`, `pepperoni-pizza.jpeg`, and `pollo-pizza.jpeg`.

2. Open the `menu.html` file in your text editor.

3. Locate the `<div>` element that you created in the previous exercise. This holds all the menu tables and has the fitting ID `menu-tables`.

4. Underneath this `<div>`, create a new `<div>` element with the ID `menu-images`.

5. Next, you'll create three new `<figure>` elements, one for each of the product images. Here is the code for the first figure. Add this within your new `<div>` element.

```
<figure>
  <img src="img/pepperoni-pizza.jpeg"
     alt="A pepperoni pizza presented on a wooden chopping
        board."
     width="240" height="180">
  <figcaption>
    Joe's Pepperoni Special
  </figcaption>
</figure>
```

6. Now add the second figure underneath the first.

```
<figure>
  <img src="img/margherita-pizza.jpeg"
     alt="A margherita pizza with mozzarella, baby tomatoes and
        oregano."
     width="240" height="180">
```

```
      <figcaption>
        Margherita - Mozzarella and Oregano
      </figcaption>
    </figure>
```

7. Finally, add the last figure.

```
    <figure>
      <img src="img/pollo-pizza.jpeg"
         alt="A pollo pizza with roasted yellow peppers."
         width="240" height="180">
      <figcaption>
        Pollo - Chicken with Roast Peppers
      </figcaption>
    </figure>
```

8. Now save the menu.html file.

Note how the alt text for each of the images describes what is shown in the image, whereas the figure caption relates the image to the appropriate item on the menu. You have also explicitly defined the image dimensions using the width and height attributes.

Take a look at the updated menu.html file in your web browser. It looks much better with the pictures added! Figure 4-13 shows how your Menu page should look.

Creating the News Page

The News page a way for Joe's Pizza Co. to keep its customers up to date with what the company is up to as well as notify them of any current special offers.

To create the News page, you are going to use the same content page template that you have been using up to now. Each of the individual articles will then have its own <article> element (you were introduced to this element in Chapter 2).

In this section, you are also going to learn about a new HTML5 element that is a little bit specialist. This is the <time> element. It comes in handy for marking up things like the date a news article was published.

Menu

Joe's Pizza Co.   Home   About   News   Menu   Locations

~ Menu ~

Pizzas

Menu Item	Description	Price
Joe's Pepperoni Special	Select pepperoni with our signature spicy tomato sauce	13.00
Margherita	Oregano, mozzarella and tomato	10.50
Hawaiian	Ham and Pineapple	12.00
Pollo	Chicken and Roast Peppers	12.00
Mexican Chicken	Spicy Chicken with jalapenos	12.50

Joe's Pepperoni Special

Garlic Breads

Menu Item	Price
Garlic Bread	4.00
Garlic Bread with Double Cheese	4.50
Garlic Bread with Sun-Ripened Tomato	4.80

Margherita - Mozzarella and Oregano

Side Dishes

Menu Item	Price
Potato Wedges	3.00
French Fries	2.50
6 Onion Rings	3.50

Pollo - Chicken with Roast Peppers

© 2012 Joe's Pizza Co. All Rights Reserved - Sitemap

FIGURE 4-13 The updated Menu page with product images.
Pizza images reproduced by permission of iStockphoto.com/Lauri Patterson

Dates and Times

It can be notoriously hard for computer programs to find and make sense of dates in web pages. HTML5 aims to solve this problem by introducing the new `<time>` element. This element allows you to specify your dates in two ways, one for humans and one for computers. You do this by placing the human-readable date in the content of your `<time>` element and the machine-readable version in a special attribute, `datetime`.

Machine-Readable Date Formats

To help computer programs understand dates better, the HTML5 specification outlines a number of valid date and time formats that you should use. Dates and times are generally defined in the format YYYY-MM-DD HH:MM:SS.

Table 4-1 shows the valid formats you should use when specifying your dates and times in the datetime attribute.

Table 4-1   Date/Time Formats

Date/Time String	Human-Readable Version
2013	2013
2013-11	November 2013
2013-11-01	1st November 2013
16:20	20 minutes past 4
16:20:32	20 minutes and 32 seconds past 4
2013-11-01 16:20	20 minutes past 4 on 1st November 2013
2013-11-01 16:20+0100	20 minutes past 4 on 1st November 2013 (Showing the time difference from UTC)

The <time> Element

Using the <time> element allows you to write user-friendly dates and not worry about whether computers can understand them. Here is an example.

```
<time datetime="2013-11-06">Next Tuesday</time>
```

Here we give the user a nice readable date but also specify a valid machine-readable date that can be used by computer programs.

Adding Articles to the News Page

The News page will contain a number of articles. This is a perfect opportunity to make use of the <article> and <time> elements that you have learned about.

The code for this exercise can be found in folder 9.

To create the News page, follow these instructions:

1. First, create a news.html file in your project folder.

2. Open the about.html file and copy its contents into your new news.html file.

Using the <header> Element to Group Content

You have already learned about the <header> element in Chapter 2, but you can also use it to group together heading elements (such as h1, h2, h3) and metadata about the content of a section. This is especially useful if you are presenting blog posts on a web page.

Say each blog post includes a title and a date on which it was posted. The title is treated as a heading element and the posted date would be the metadata, as shown in the following example.

```
<article>
 <header>
  <h1>A Sample Blog Post</h1>
  <p>
   Posted on <time datetime="2013-11-01">1st November 2013</time>
  </p>
 </header>
 <p>
  Here is my blog posts text content.
 </p>
</article>
```

3. Update the <title> and <meta> elements within the <head> element to reflect the content of the News page.

4. Remove the class attribute from the About link in the navigation and place it on the News link.

5. Locate the <section> element with the ID page-text and delete any content that is in this element.

6. Create a new <h1> element in this section and give it the text Latest News.

7. Create an <article> element underneath this heading. This element will hold the first of your news articles.

8. Within this <article> element, create a new <header> element to hold the article title and metadata.

9. Use a <h1> element for the article title. The first article is New Restaurant Opening! (including the exclamation mark).

10. Now create a <p> element underneath this <h1> that will contain the date the article was posted.

11. You can use the <time> element to mark up the *posted on* date. Add the following code to your new <p> element. Note the use of the datetime attribute.

```
Posted on
<time datetime="2013-11-01">1st November 2013</time>.
```

12. Create a new `<div>` element underneath the `<header>` element to hold the main article content.

13. Add the following content to this `<div>`. Here you use `<p>` elements to mark up each paragraph of text.

```
<p>
  We've just opened a brand new restaurant at 200 West 44th
Street.
</p>
<p>
  To celebrate this new opening we're giving all of our
customers the chance to get 10% off their next order. Just
mention this post when placing your order.
</p>
```

14. Now create two more articles to go underneath the one you just added. I have provided two examples here that you might want to use, or you could come up with your own.

```
<article>
  <header>
    <h1>Joe's Pepperoni Special Named New York's Best Pizza
  </h1>
    <p>
      Posted on
      <time datetime="2013-10-18">18th October 2013</time>.
    </p>
  </header>
  <div>
    <p>
      We are very happy to announce that one of our pizzas has
been voted the best pizza in New York. Our Joe's Pepperoni
Special is a favorite amongst our customers and we would like
to thank everybody that voted for us.
    </p>
    <p>
      As an extra thank-you we are giving everybody 20% off a
Joe's Pepperoni Special pizza for the next 2 weeks. Just
quote the promo code NYBESTPIZZA when placing your order.
    </p>
  </div>
</article>

<article>
  <header>
    <h1>Joe's Wins Annual Basketball Game</h1>
```

```
    <p>
        Posted on
        <time datetime="2013-10-12">12th October 2013</time>.
    </p>
</header>
<div>
    <p>
        On Saturday we geared up for our annual basketball game
    with local rivals, Antonio's Pasta. It was a close game but
    we just managed to clinch it at the end with a basket from
    none other than Joe Balochio himself. The game ended 94-89.
    </p>
</div>
</article>
```

15. Save the news.html file.

You can add more news articles if you would like. Just follow the same template that you have used in this section.

Figure 4-14 shows how the News page should be displayed in your browser.

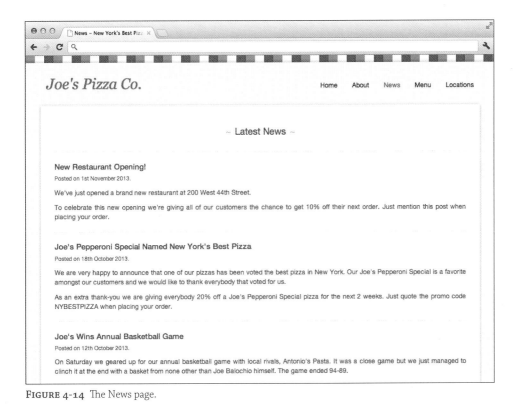

FIGURE 4-14 The News page.

Summary

In this chapter, you accomplished a lot. You put to use the templates that you created in the previous chapters in order to create all the pages for your website. You then added content to each page using your growing knowledge of HTML elements.

As you progressed through this chapter, you learned about some pretty important HTML elements, including tables and a whole bunch of elements used for marking up text. Appendix A also contains information on a few more elements that can be used for giving your text greater semantic meaning. I couldn't quite fit them into this chapter, but this would be a great time to read through that appendix. Although you won't be using these elements in the example website you are building, they are good to know and may come in useful in future, real projects.

In Chapter 5, you start learning how to collect data from users using HTML forms. As I mentioned earlier in this book, HTML5 actually evolved out of an effort to make web forms better. The next chapter introduces loads of new HTML5 goodies.

part 2

Dealing with Data

chapter five
Working with Forms

THE WORLD WIDE WEB is the single greatest tool ever invented for collecting information. Web forms are responsible for this. We use them every day, whether we are purchasing something online, doing research using our favorite search engine, or logging into our e-mail. Web forms have become an essential part of our everyday browsing experience; in fact, without them, the Internet would be a rather dull place (yes, really).

Joe's website needs a web form so that customers can book a table directly through the website. This chapter teaches you how to create a simple web form and embed it within your web pages. First, you will create the new Bookings page with a barebones form. Once you have your page set up, you will start adding a number of different form fields to it using a range of HTML elements, such as `<input>`, `<label>`, `<select>`, and `<textarea>`. You will finish by updating the site navigation and sitemap to include the new Bookings page.

In this chapter you are just going to focus on creating a basic form using elements that were present in HTML4. Once you have this form set up, Chapters 6 and 7 will teach you how to use new HTML5 features to enhance your web forms. These new features include specialized input types that make it easier for users to input data and tools for validating the data inputted by users. Figure 5-1 shows the completed Bookings page that you will be building in these three chapters.

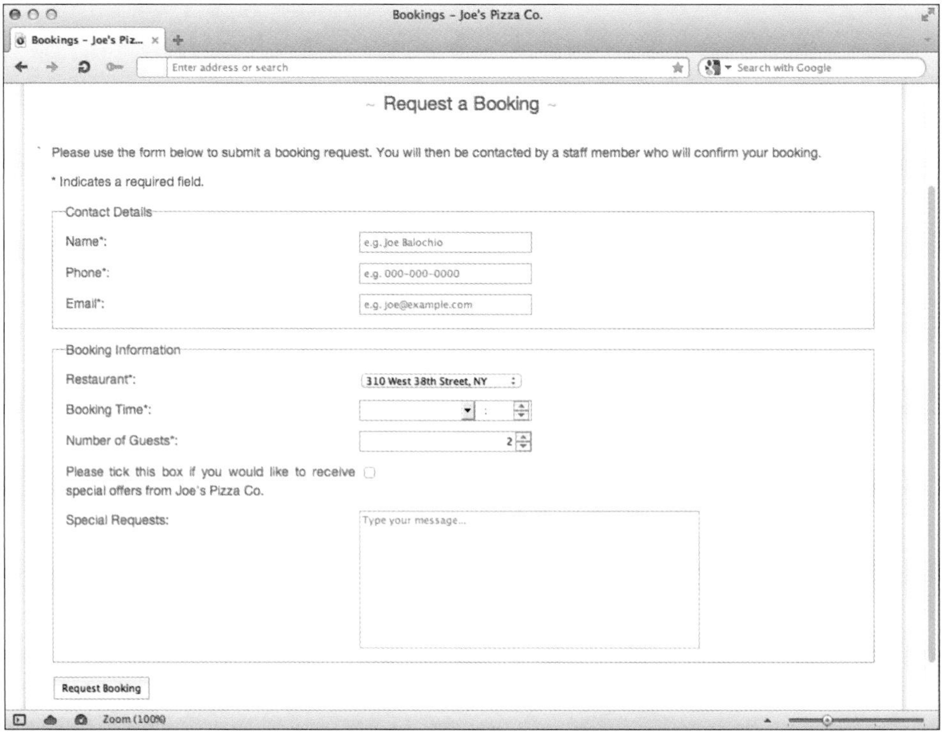

FIGURE 5-1 The completed Bookings page, displayed in Opera.

Setting Up the Bookings Page with the <form> Element

Throughout this chapter, you are going to work on building a bookings form for the Joe's Pizza Co. website that will enable users to request reservations through the website. In this section, you learn about the <form> element and also create the new Bookings page.

To create a web form, you use the <form> element. This element will contain all your form fields, labels, and buttons.

The <form> element requires two attributes, action and method, as in the following example:

```
<form action="search.php" method="GET">
  <div class="field">
    <label for="query">Query:</label>
    <input type="text" name="query" id="query">
  </div>
  <div class="field">
```

```
      <input type="submit" value="Search">
  </div>
</form>
```

For now, this is all you need to know about the `<form>` element to begin building your book-ings form. You will be diving deeper into forms and inputs later in this chapter, but first let's set up the Bookings page.

As usual, this code can be downloaded from the book's website at `http://www.wiley.com/go/treehouse/html5foundations`. The code for this exercise can be found in the code for Chapter 5, folder 1.

Follow these instructions to create the new Bookings page.

1. Create a new file called `bookings.html` in your favorite text editor and save it in the root of your project folder.

2. Open the `about.html` file and copy its contents into your new `bookings.html` file. Don't forget to update the `<title>` and `<meta>` elements and remove the `active` class from the Home link in this new file.

3. Clear out the contents of the `<section>` element that has the ID `page-text`.

4. Within this `<section>` element, create a new `<h1>` element with the text `Request a Booking`.

5. Underneath this heading, add the following paragraph of text using a `<p>` element.

```
<p>
  Please use the form below to submit a booking request. You
  will then be contacted by a staff member who will confirm
  your booking.
</p>
```

6. Below this paragraph, create a new `<form>` element.

```
<form></form>
```

7. Set the `action` attribute on this `<form>` element to `bookings.php`.

```
<form action="bookings.php"></form>
```

8. Set the `method` attribute on this `<form>` element to `POST`.

```
<form action="bookings.php" method="POST"></form>
```

9. Save your `bookings.html` file.

Figure 5-2 shows how your Bookings page should look at this stage.

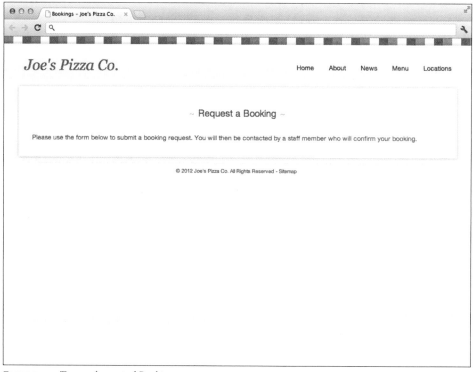

FIGURE 5-2 The newly created Bookings page.

The action Attribute

The `action` attribute is used to specify the location of the file that the form data should be sent to. This should be an absolute or relative path. The file referenced in the `action` attribute would then perform an *action*, such as saving the data to the database or checking a user's log-in details.

For more information on absolute and relative paths, check out the "Relative and Absolute Paths" section in Chapter 2.

If you look at the form that you just added to the Bookings page, you can see that the `action` attribute references a `bookings.php` file.

```
<form action="bookings.php" method="POST">
```

The fact that you have used a relative path here means that the `bookings.php` file must be in the same folder as the `bookings.html` file.

Don't worry that you don't actually have a `bookings.php` in your project folder. We are just going to pretend that it's there and that it will create a new booking when the form is submitted.

To be able to process the data, you would need to write a program using a programming language such as PHP, Ruby or Python, which is beyond the scope of this book. If you are interested in learning more about server-side programming, check out this Treehouse course by Jim Hoskins and Jason Seifer `http://teamtreehouse.com/library/programming-2/build-a-simple-version-of-facebook`.

The method Attribute

The `method` attribute is used to specify how you want the form data to be sent to the server. There are two ways of sending form data, GET requests and POST requests. If you forget to specify a method attribute on your form, the GET method is used by default.

The GET Method

The GET method sends your form data within a URL. This method is commonly used when performing tasks that just need to fetch existing data from a web server, such as searches or product filters on e-commerce websites. When a user submits the form, the browser will start to create a new URL to send the user to. This will look something like the URL below.

```
http://www.html5foundations.com/bookings.php?name=Joe%20Balochio
&restaurant=310%20West%2038th%20Street,%20NY
```

This URL has a number of different parts. Let's look at them in more detail.

The Domain Name

The first part of the generated URL is made up of the protocol (http://) and the fully qualified domain name (`www.html5foundations.com`).

If you are using an absolute URL, you would have explicitly defined this domain name in your `action` attribute.

Should you be using a relative URL in your `action` attribute, the browser will automatically take the domain name from the page the form is submitted from. For example, if your form is on the `www.html5foundations.com/bookings.html` page, the browser will use `www.html5foundations.com` as the domain name.

The Path

The path segment of the URL represents the path to the file that will process the form data. I have highlighted the path segment of our example URL in bold.

```
http://www.html5foundations.com/bookings.php?name=Joe%20Balochio
&restaurant=310%20West%2038th%20Street,%20NY
```

The URL Parameters

The final segment of our URL is the parameters. This is where the data from your form is transmitted.

The browser will first add a question mark character (?) after the path to signify that everything after this point in the URL is data.

```
http://www.html5foundations.com/bookings.php?name=Joe%20Balochio
&restaurant=310%20West%2038th%20Street,%20NY
```

Each of the form fields is then added to the URL as a key-value pair. The key is taken from the name attribute on the form control (more on this later), and the value is just the value of the form control at the time the form was submitted. In the example below, the key for the first piece of data is name and the value is Joe%20Balochio. Each key-value pair is separated using an ampersand (&); this is highlighted in bold in the following example.

```
http://www.html5foundations.com/bookings.php?name=Joe%20Balochio
&restaurant=310%20West%2038th%20Street,%20NY
```

Once the browser finishes constructing the URL, it loads the new URL in the current browser window.

Browsers do put a limit on the length of URLs, and therefore, the amount of data that you can submit using the GET method. This limit varies depending on the browser, but a limit of 2,000 characters is typical. If you have a fairly large form or are using <textarea> elements, you should use the POST method instead.

An advantage of using the GET method is that the URL that is generated when the form is submitted can be bookmarked. For example, if you use the GET method on a search form the user can bookmark the results page as the form data that contains the search term is present in the page URL. If you use the POST method they could not do this because the data is passed 'behind the scenes.'

Form Data Encoding

You may have noticed some strange characters that appear within the example URL (these are in bold below):

name=Joe**%20**Balochio&restaurant=310**%20**West**%20**38th**%20**Street,**%20**NY

Surely humans didn't write these?

Correct. URLs cannot contain spaces or special characters, and so the browser automatically encodes any spaces or special characters in your data by changing them to a hexadecimal ASCII code. You don't need to worry too much about this; just note that the browser encodes data for you.

The POST Method

The POST method should be used when performing any action that will involve data being saved to a database. While it is also technically possible to save data using the GET method, it is considered a security best practice to use POST for these actions.

The URL for forms that use the POST method is constructed in largely the same way. The difference is that the form data is not added to the URL as parameters (but it is still encoded). Instead, the data is effectively sent in the background and completely hidden from the URL. The data can still be picked up and processed by the server.

The POST method has some security benefits. For example, you would not want to use the GET method for a log-in form, as a user's log-in details would be visible in the URL (including his or her password!). Also, as the data is passed in the URL there is nothing to stop a user from easily modifying this data by editing the URL in the address bar. This can sometimes break your applications if they do not have the appropriate measures in place for dealing with incorrect data. It is important to note, though, that using the POST method will not solve all of these problems and is not enough to make your forms completely secure (but it helps).

Adding the Form Fields to the Bookings Page with <input> and <label> Elements

The main form control element that you will use in your web forms is the <input> element. This element is a jack of all trades kind of guy because it can be used for collecting all sorts of data from your users. You can specify what sort of data you want to collect using the type attribute; in most browsers, this will also alter the way the element is displayed. By default, all <input> elements have the type text. You will learn about the different input types that you can use later in this chapter and in Chapter 6.

Form fields are useless unless the user knows what he should be inputting into each box. The <label> element enables you to associate a text label with a form field. The following example shows an <input> element with an associated <label> element.

```
<label for="firstName">First Name:</label>
<input name="firstName" type="text" id="firstName">
```

Figure 5-3 shows how this example would be displayed in a browser.

FIGURE 5-3 A simple text input and label.

When you create an <input> element you should also create a <label> element and associate it with the input. To do this you need to give the <input> element an ID and then specify a for attribute on the <label> element with the value set to the ID of the input, as in the preceding example.

Creating labels for <input> elements is important for a number of reasons. Assistive technologies such as screen readers will rely on these labels in order to understand your forms and help users to fill them out. Properly associating labels with inputs will also cause the label itself to become an extended click target for the input field. This means that when the user clicks on the label, the associated <input> element will gain focus in the browser. This is especially useful for items like checkboxes or radio buttons (more on these coming up) that are themselves, fairly small targets for a user to click on.

To start, the bookings form will include seven fields: Name, Phone, Email, Restaurant, Booking Time, Guests, and Marketing. Here you will be creating <input> and <label> elements for each of these.

The code for this exercise can be found in folder 2.

Follow these steps to add each of the input fields to your form:

1. Open your bookings.html file in your favorite text editor.

2. Create a new <div> element within the <form> element and set its class to field. This class will be used purely for styling purposes. (You will need to create a new <div> element like this one for each <input> element that you add.)

   ```
   <div class="field"></div>
   ```

3. Within this first <div> element, create a new <input> element with the type text.

   ```
   <div class="field">
     <input type="text">
   </div>
   ```

4. Set both the name and id attributes of this input to name. The reason for setting both attributes is because it is possible for multiple elements to have the same name value. This occurs when dealing with groups of inputs such as radio buttons. The id value, however, should always be unique. This means if you wanted to target this individual <input> element with CSS or JavaScript, you would need to use the ID.

   ```
   <div class="field>
     <input type="text" name="name" id="name">
   </div>
   ```

5. Create a `<label>` element and assign it to this `<input>` element using the `for` attribute.

```
<div class="field">
  <label for="name">Name:</label>
  <input type="text" name="name" id="name">
</div>
```

6. Below this `<div>` element create a new `<div>` (again with the class `field`) with an `<input>` element that has the type `text` and the name and ID `phone`. Then create a label for this input.

```
<div class="field">
  <label for="phone">Phone:</label>
  <input type="text" name="phone" id="phone">
</div>
```

7. Now create a new `<div>` element with an `<input>` element that has the type `text` and the name and ID `email`. Create a label for this input.

```
<div class="field">
  <label for="email">Email:</label>
  <input type="text" name="email" id="email">
</div>
```

8. Create a new `<div>` element that has an `<input>` element with the type `text` and the name and ID `restaurant`. You should also create a label for this input.

```
<div class="field">
  <label for="restaurant">Restaurant:</label>
  <input type="text" name="restaurant" id="restaurant">
</div>
```

9. Create another new `<div>` element with an `<input>` that has the type `text` and the name and ID `bookingTime`. Don't forget the label!

```
<div class="field">
  <label for="bookingTime">Booking Time:</label>
  <input type="text" name="bookingTime" id="bookingTime">
</div>
```

10. Create a `<div>` element with an `<input>` that has the type `text` and the name and ID `guests`. Add a label for this input.

```
<div class="field">
  <label for="guests">Number of Guests:</label>
  <input type="text" name="guests" id=" guests">
</div>
```

11. Create a final `<div>` element with an `<input>` element. This time set the type to `checkbox` and the name and ID to `marketing`. Set the `value` attribute to 1. Then create a label for this element with the text shown in the following code.

```html
<div class="field">
  <label for="marketing">Please tick this box if you would like
  to receive special offers from Joe's Pizza Co.</label>
  <input type="checkbox" name="marketing" id="marketing"
  value="1">
</div>
```

12. Save the `bookings.html` file.

Here is how your `<form>` element should now look:

```html
<form action="bookings.php" method="POST">
  <div class="field">
    <label for="name">Name:</label>
    <input type="text" name="name" id="name">
  </div>
  <div class="field">
    <label for="phone">Phone:</label>
    <input type="text" name="phone" id="phone">
  </div>
  <div class="field">
    <label for="email">Email:</label>
    <input type="text" name="email" id="email">
  </div>
  <div class="field">
    <label for="restaurant">Restaurant:</label>
    <input type="text" name="restaurant" id="restaurant">
  </div>
  <div class="field">
    <label for="bookingTime">Booking Time:</label>
    <input type="text" name="bookingTime" id="bookingTime">
  </div>
  <div class="field">
    <label for="guests">Number of Guests:</label>
    <input type="text" name="guests" id="guests">
  </div>
  <div class="field">
    <label for="marketing">Please tick this box if you would like
    to receive special offers from Joe's Pizza Co.</label>
    <input type="checkbox" name="marketing" id="marketing"
    value="1">
  </div>
</form>
```

Figure 5-4 shows how the Bookings page should look with these new input fields.

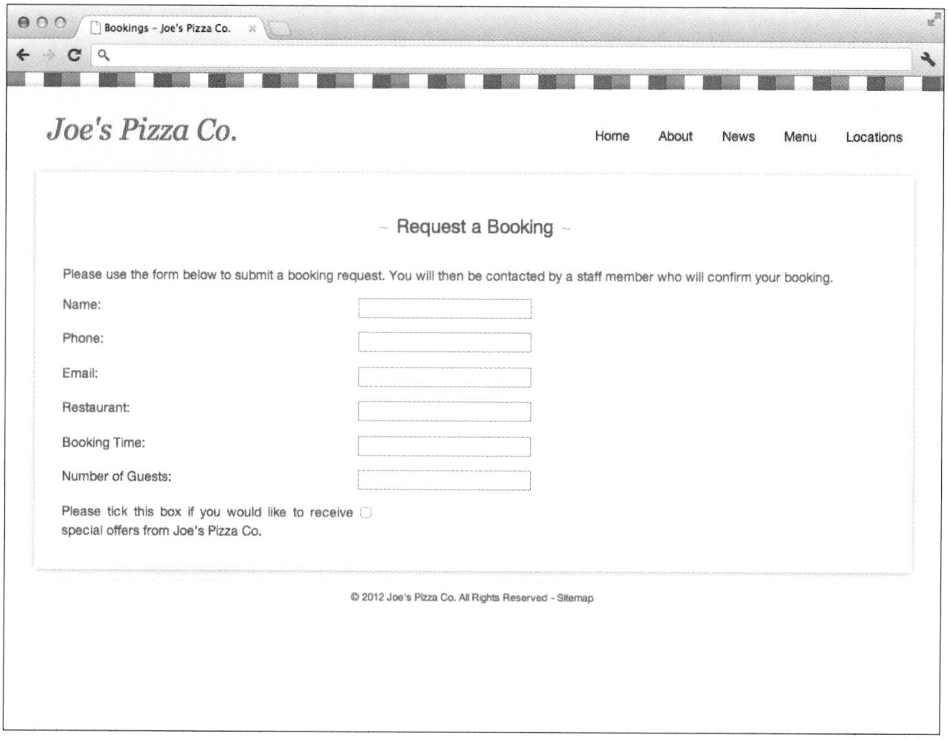

FIGURE 5-4 The updated Bookings page.

In the following sections, you will learn about the different types of inputs that you can use as well as each of the different attributes that you can apply to the <input> element. Here you are just going to cover the widely supported types and attributes from HTML4. In Chapter 6 you will learn about the new input types and attributes introduced in HTML5.

Input Attributes

As well as the standard global attributes that you looked at in Chapter 3, the <input> element has a number of specialized attributes, some of which you have already used in the Bookings page.

Naming Inputs

Although it is not strictly required, all your input elements *should* have a name attribute. If you intend on sending the data to a server, you will need to specify a name attribute. Otherwise, the browser will not send your data.

```
<label for="name">Name:</label>
<input type="text" name="name" id="name">
```

As I mention earlier in this chapter, the value of the name attribute will form the key that the input data will be associated with when it is sent to the server.

Setting Default Values

You can set a default value for an input element using the value attribute. When the browser loads the page, it will automatically place the value of the value attribute into the input box, or set a specialized control to this value.

Here is an example of how you could set the default value of the guests input to be 2.

```
<input type="text" name="guests" id="guests" value="2">
```

Disabling Fields

You have two ways to disable a form field so that a user cannot alter its value. The first is to use the disabled attribute; alternatively, you can use the readonly attribute.

```
<input type="text" name="name" disabled>
```

```
<input type="text" name="name" readonly>
```

The difference between these two attributes is that the value of <input> elements with the readonly attribute will still be sent to the server, whereas <input> elements that have the disabled attribute will not send any data. The disabled attribute is ignored if the input type is hidden.

Size

The size attribute is used to specify the number of characters that should be visible to a user at any one time, therefore altering the physical size of the <input> element. The default size is 20.

The size attribute does not limit the number of characters that a user can input into a field; for that, you use the maxlength attribute that you will look at in Chapter 7.

```
<label for="name">Name:</label>
<input type="text" name="name" id="name" size="65">
```

Input Types

There are a number of different input types that you can use to make it easier for users to fill out your web forms. In this section you are going to learn about the input types that are widely supported by web browsers. In Chapter 6 you will learn about the new input types that have been introduced in HTML5.

Text

The text input type has traditionally been the most commonly used type on `<input>` elements. As the name suggests, the text input type is used for instances where you need to collect some text from the user. This is also the default type for the `<input>` element, so if you forget to specify a type attribute or are using a type that a user's browser does not support, the browser will simply display a text field.

The name input in your form uses the text type.

```
<label for="name">Name:</label>
<input type="text" name="name" id="name" autofocus>
```

Passwords

The password type can be used to indicate that an input is expecting a password. The browser won't display the input that is typed into a password field in plain text; this stops those sneaky devils from catching a glance of your password over your shoulder. Instead, password inputs display characters as black dots or asterisks, as shown in Figure 5-5.

FIGURE 5-5 A password input field.

Here is an example of an `<input>` element of type password.

```
<label for="pass">Password:</label>
<input type="password" name="pass" id="pass">
```

Checkboxes

The checkbox type is useful when you need to collect a true or false answer from the user. By default the checkbox will be displayed as unticked; however, you can change this by adding the checked attribute to the `<input>` element.

Inputs with the checkbox type should also specify a value attribute; this is the data that will be sent to the server if the checkbox is selected when the form is submitted.

Here is an example of an `<input>` element with the type checkbox set to display as ticked by default. The value has been set to 1 because this is the common convention for true answers. Use 0 for false.

```
<label for="contact">Receive updates from Joe's Pizza Co?</label>
<input type="checkbox" name="contact" id="contact" value="1"
checked>
```

A checkbox element is shown in Figure 5-6.

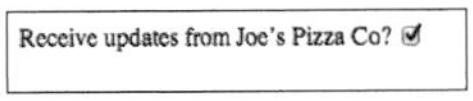

Receive updates from Joe's Pizza Co? ☑

FIGURE 5-6 A simple checkbox.

Radio Buttons

The `radio` type is used to display a radio button. This is useful if you have a number of different options to present to users but only want them to choose one of these options.

When using multiple radio buttons as options, each `<input>` element should have the same name attribute. The data that is associated with an option should be stored in the `value` attribute.

As with checkboxes, you can also set a default for radio inputs using the `checked` attribute.

Here is an example of how you might use multiple `<input>` elements with the type `radio` in order to collect a user's favorite color.

```
<p>
  What is your favorite color?
</p>
<div>
  <label for="green">Green</label>
  <input name="favColor" id="green" type="radio" value="green">
  <label for="red">Red</label>
  <input name="favColor" id="red" type="radio" value="red" checked>
  <label for="orange">Orange</label>
  <input name="favColor" id="orange" type="radio" value="orange">
  <label for="blue">Blue</label>
  <input name="favColor" id="blue" type="radio" value="blue">
</div>
```

Notice how, in this example, all the `<input>` elements have the same name attribute. We have also indicated that red should be the default option using the `checked` attribute.

Figure 5-7 shows how this example should look in your web browser.

What is your favorite color?
Green ○ Red ⊙ Orange ○ Blue ○

FIGURE 5-7 Multiple input elements with the type radio.

Submit Buttons

The submit type can be used to define a submit button for your form. The text for the button should be set in the value attribute.

Here is an example of a submit button.

```
<input type="submit" value="Send">
```

You can also create Submit buttons using the <button> element that you learn about later in this chapter.

Hidden Fields

There may be times that you want to send data up to the server but hide that data from your users. The hidden type is designed to enable you to do this.

When using the hidden type, you should specify a name for your <input> element and set the value of the value attribute to the data that you want to send with the form.

Here is an example of a hidden <input> element that sends a user ID to the server.

```
<input type="hidden" name="id" value="123">
```

You've covered a lot in this section so far. For a quick recap, check out Nick Pettit's video about inputs on Treehouse: http://teamtreehouse.com/library/websites/html/forms/inputs.

Adding a Message Box with the <textarea> Element

In addition to the fields that you have already added to your form, it would be nice to have a text box where users can leave comments about their bookings. Input elements are great, but they are not very user friendly when it comes to inputting large amounts of text, especially if that text needs to span multiple lines. Instead, you can add the <textarea> element to your form for text-heavy input fields.

The <textarea> element shares many of the same attributes as the <input> element, such as autofocus, name, and placeholder; however, it also has the attributes cols and rows. The cols attribute can be used to specify how many characters should fit on a single line in the text area, and the rows attribute specifies how many rows should be visible to the user. Using these two attributes, you can theoretically set the height and width of the <textarea> (although you may want to do this using CSS instead).

Here is an example of a `<textarea>` element that uses the `cols` and `rows` attributes to specify its size.

```
<textarea name="message" cols="50" rows="10"></textarea>
```

Notice how the `<textarea>` element has an end tag. Unlike the `<input>` element, `<textarea>` is not a void element. Any text content that you place between the start and end tags will be displayed in the text area.

 The code for this exercise can be found in folder 3.

Follow these steps:

1. Open the `bookings.html` file.

2. Below the existing form fields, create a new `<div>` element with the class `field`.

3. Within this `<div>` element, create a new `<textarea>` element.

4. Set both the `id` and `name` attributes on this `<textarea>` to be message.

5. Set the `cols` attribute on this `<textarea>` to be 50.

6. Set the `rows` attribute to be 10.

7. Above this `<textarea>` element, create a new `<label>` element.

8. Set the `for` attribute on this `<label>` to be message.

9. Add the following text within the `<label>` element: Special Requests:.

10. Save the `bookings.html` file.

You have now added a `<textarea>` to your form that visitors can use to provide some extra comments about their booking requests. Here's how your new code should look.

```
<div class="field">
  <label for="message">Special Requests:</label>
  <textarea name="message" id="message" cols="50" rows="10">
  </textarea>
</div>
```

Figure 5-8 shows how your bookings form should look in your browser.

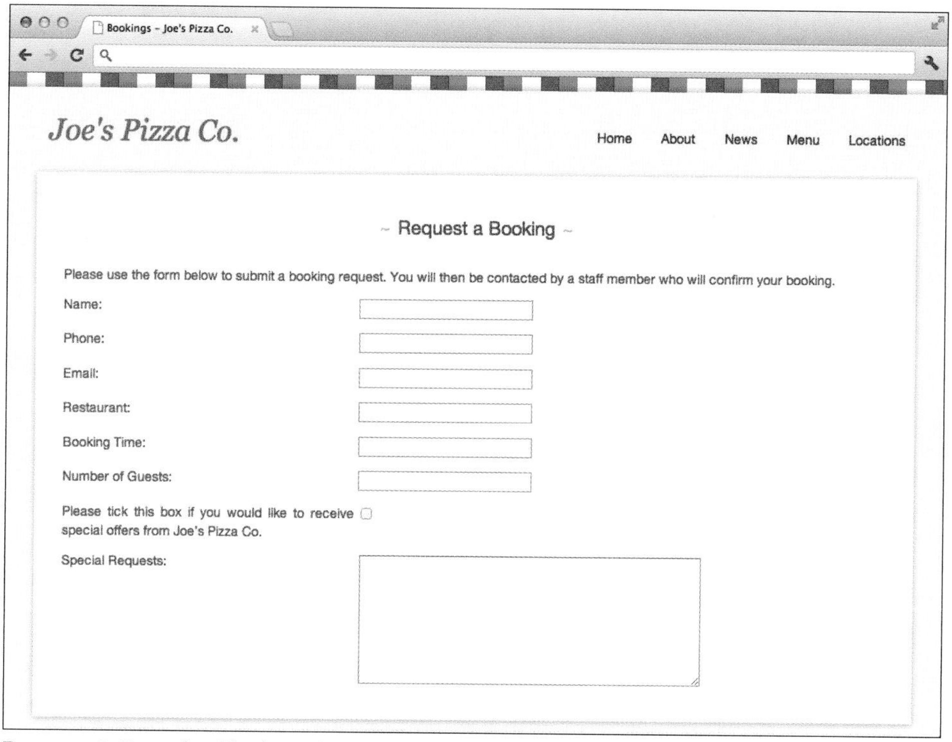

FIGURE 5-8 The updated bookings form with the message box added.

Adding a Submit Button to Your Bookings Page

Your booking form is nearly complete, but it is missing one important component—a Submit button that users can click to send off their requests for a reservation. The <button> element has a number of different functions that can be defined using its type attribute. For your Bookings page, you will use the submit type, but you can also use the reset or button types for other functions, as described shortly. If you forget to specify a type, submit will be used by default.

To create a button that will submit a form, you use the submit type, as in the following example:

```
<button type="submit">Submit Form</button>
```

The text within the button element will appear on the button.

The code for this exercise can be found in folder 4.

Follow these steps to add a Submit button to your form:

1. Open the bookings.html file.

2. Create a new <div> element just before the end tag of the <form> element and give it the class field.

3. Within this <div> element, create a new <button> element.

4. Set the type attribute on this <button> to submit.

5. Add the following text between the tags of the <button> element: Request Booking.

6. Save the bookings.html file.

Here's how this portion of your code should look:

```
<div class="field">
  <button type="submit">Request Booking</button>
</div>
```

You should now have a Submit button at the end of your form so visitors can request bookings. Figure 5-9 shows how your updated bookings form should look in your browser.

With the <button> element, you can create a button that is similar to one created using <input type="submit">. The difference is that you can place other HTML elements within a <button> element; for example, you could have an <img> element within a button.

Reset Buttons

By setting the type attribute of a <button> element to reset, you can create a button that will reset all the fields in a form. Here's an example of how you can create a Reset button for your forms.

```
<button type="reset">Reset Form</button>
```

Dumb Buttons

There is one other type that can be used on the <button> element—button. I like to refer to these buttons as *dumb buttons* because they do not actually perform any actions. In order to make these buttons "smart," you need to use JavaScript to tell the browser to execute some JavaScript code when the button is pressed. This JavaScript code could then perform an action, such as starting or stopping the playback of a video. You will learn how to do this in Chapter 11.

Here is an example of a dumb button.

```
<button type="button">Do Something</button>
```

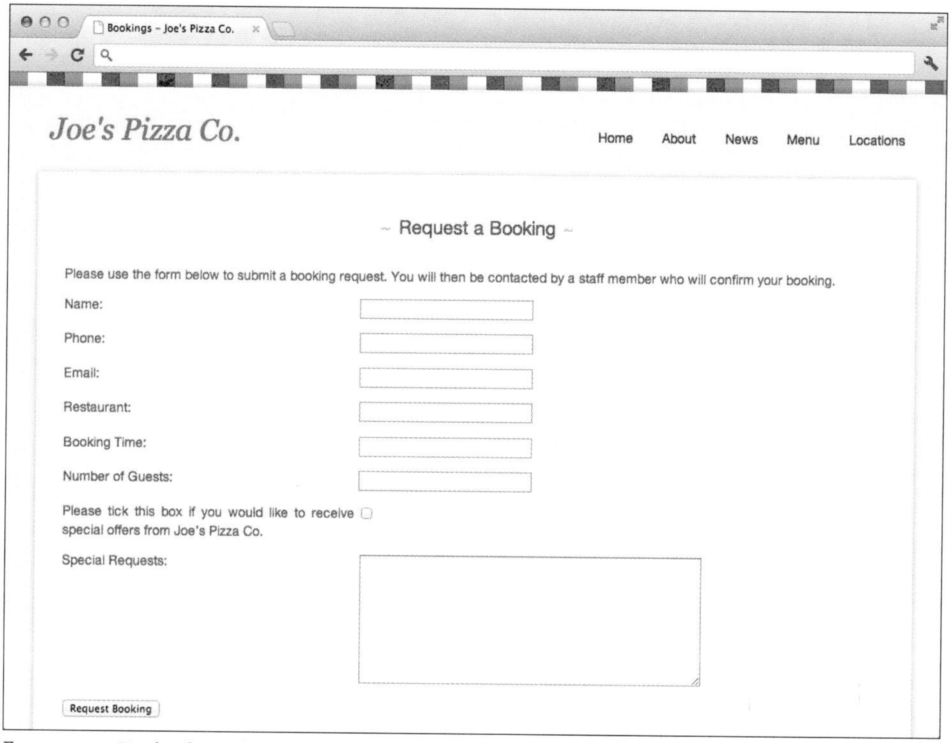

FIGURE 5-9 The bookings form with the new Submit button.

Adding a Drop-Down Menu to Your Bookings Page

You've already learned how you can use radio buttons to create multiple options for users to choose from. In this section, you learn how to use the `<select>` and `<option>` elements to create a drop-down menu. You will then use these elements to create a drop-down menu for the restaurant field on your Bookings page, eliminating the need for the user to type in the restaurant location.

The <select> and <option> Elements

To create a drop-down menu, you use a <select> element. This element serves a similar purpose to the <input> element in that it is used to set the name of the form control as well as other attributes, such as its class and id.

The <select> element is also responsible for grouping the options together and should contain one or more <option> elements, as shown in the following example.

```
<select name="color" id="color">
  <option>Green</option>
  <option>Red</option>
  <option>Blue</option>
</select>
```

Each of these <option> elements represents a potential value for the form control (the text contained within the element is used as the value here). The concept is similar to how multiple radio buttons work. Here is how the previous example would look if it were implemented using radio buttons.

```
<label for="green">Green</label>
<input type="radio" name="color" id="green" value="Green">
<label for="red">Red</label>
<input type="radio" name="color" id="red" value="Red">
<label for="blue">Blue</label>
<input type="radio" name="color" id="blue" value="Blue">
```

The main difference is that all the options are displayed at once when using radio buttons, whereas the <select> element will group the options and display them in a drop-down menu. This is particularly useful if you have a large number of options to choose from, because the screen space taken up by the drop-down menu does not increase when you add more options. Figure 5-10 shows how these two examples differ.

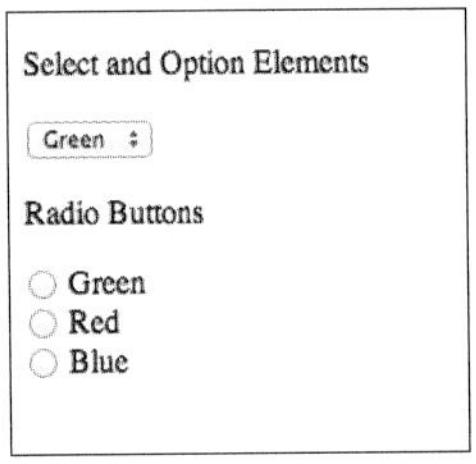

Select and Option Elements

Green ⇕

Radio Buttons

○ Green
○ Red
○ Blue

FIGURE 5-10 Using the <select> element with <option> elements versus using radio buttons.

Adding the Restaurant Drop-Down Menu to Your Page

The restaurant field in your bookings form is used to tell the bookings coordinator at which restaurant the customer would like to make a reservation. Currently, this field just uses a normal text input; however, this is a bad practice because it relies on the customer to type an accurate address into the location field. A better solution would be to create a drop-down menu that already contains the three restaurant locations so that customers can select the restaurant they want rather than having to type in the location.

> The code for this exercise can be found in folder 5.

Follow these steps to modify the restaurant field on the Bookings page.

1. Open the bookings.html file.

2. Locate the <input> element that is currently used for the restaurant field and remove it.

   ```
   <div class="field">
     <label for="restaurant">Restaurant:</label>
     <input type="text" id="restaurant" name="restaurant">
   </div>
   ```

3. Create a new <select> element in its place.

   ```
   <div class="field">
     <label for="restaurant">Restaurant:</label>
     <select></select>
   </div>
   ```

4. Set the name and id attributes on this <select> element to restaurant.

   ```
   <select name="restaurant" id="restaurant"></select>
   ```

5. Within this <select> element, create a new <option> element with the text 310 West 38th Street, NY.

   ```
   <option>310 West 38th Street, NY</option>
   ```

6. Create another <option> element underneath that one with the text 2450 Broadway, NY.

   ```
   <option>2450 Broadway, NY</option>
   ```

7. Finally, create one more `<option>` element with the text 200 West 44th Street, NY.

```
<option>200 West 44th Street, NY</option>
```

8. Save the `bookings.html` file.

Your restaurant field should now look like the following.

```
<div class="field">
  <label for="restaurant">Restaurant:</label>
  <select id="restaurant" name="restaurant">
    <option>310 West 38th Street, NY</option>
    <option>2450 Broadway, NY</option>
    <option>200 West 44th Street, NY</option>
  </select>
</div>
```

Figure 5-11 shows how this new drop-down menu should look in your web browser.

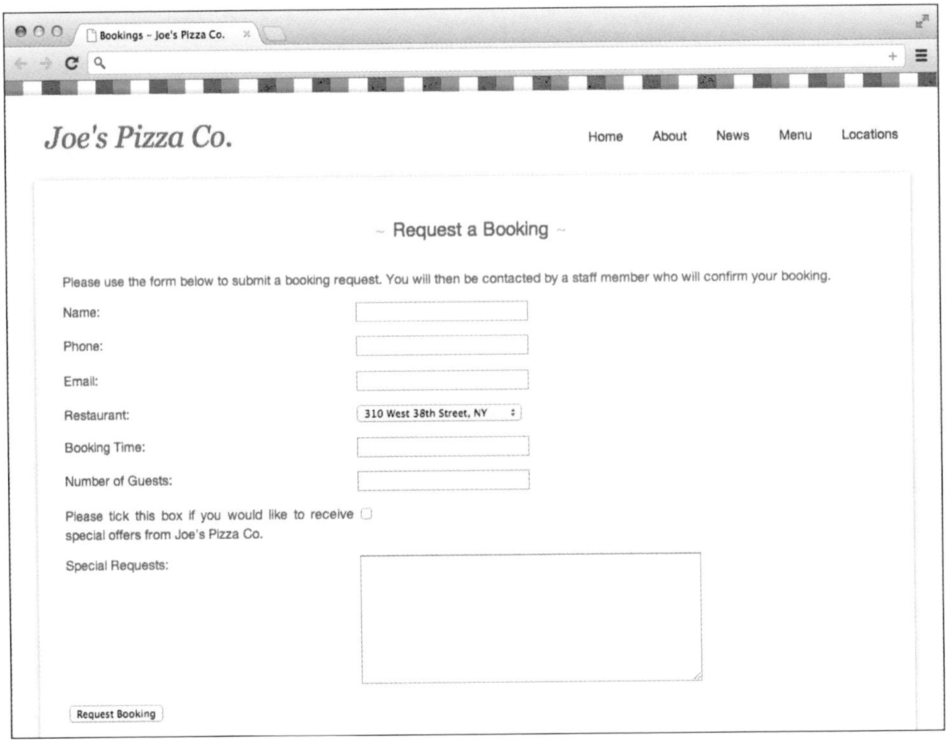

FIGURE 5-11 The updated restaurant field with a drop-down menu.

More about Using Options

So far in this section, you have learned how to create basic drop-down menus using the `<select>` and `<option>` elements. Now you are going to learn some slightly more advanced techniques that enable you to do things like setting the default option, adding a value that is different from the option text, and how to group options into sub-groups in the drop-down menu.

Setting a Default Option

To set the default option in a drop-down menu, you simply need to apply the `selected` attribute to the desired `<option>` element.

```
<select name="color" id="color">
  <option>Green</option>
  <option selected>Red</option>
  <option>Blue</option>
</select>
```

In this example, the Red option would be selected by default.

Using the value Attribute for the `<option>` Element

There will be times when the text inside an `<option>` element needs to be different from the value that is sent when the form is submitted.

An example would be if you needed to collect a user ID. It is unlikely that an admin user would be able to remember the numeric user ID of every user on the system, so you would want the users' names to be displayed in the drop-down menu but their IDs to be sent in the form. You can do this by adding a `value` attribute to the `<option>` element.

```
<option value="23">Joe Balochio</option>
```

When the form is submitted, the value will be used rather than the text contained between the `<option>` tags.

Allowing Multiple Selections

You can allow your users to select more than one option. Specifying the `multiple` attribute on the `<select>` element will allow you to do this. Users will then have to press and hold the CTRL key (or the CMD key on a Mac) to select multiple options from the list.

Grouping Options

When you have a `<select>` element with several options, you may want to use the `<opt group>` element to make it easier for your users to find the one they want. The `<optgroup>` element should be placed inside the `<select>` element and should contain all the `<option>` elements that are related to the group. You can specify a name for an options group using its `title` attribute.

This example code shows how you could create a drop-down menu that has multiple option groups.

```
<select name="food" id="food">
  <optgroup title="Dairy">
    <option>Milk</option>
    <option>Egg</option>
    <option>Cheese</option>
  </optgroup>
  <optgroup title="Bakery">
    <option>Bread</option>
    <option>Rolls</option>
    <option>Baguette</option>
  </optgroup>
</select>
```

Figure 5-12 shows this example displayed in a web browser.

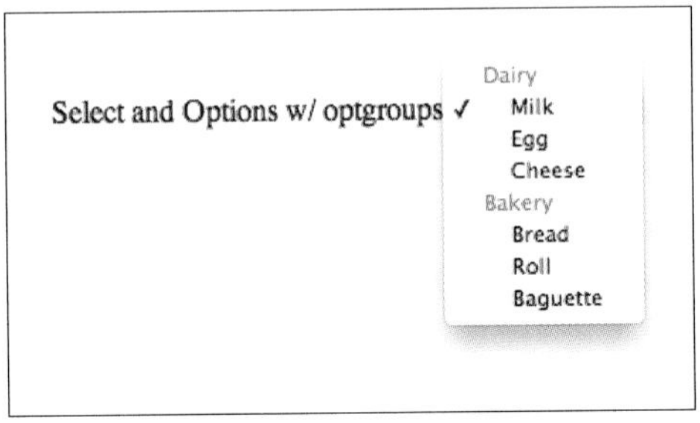

FIGURE 5-12 A `<select>` element with multiple `<option>` and `<optgroup>` elements, as displayed in Google Chrome.

Handling Files

So far, you have learned how you can gather text from a user and how you can create drop-down menus and radio buttons to restrict input values. Now it's time to look at how you can enable users to upload files. For this task, you use yet another type for the `<input>` element: `file`.

The file Input Type

The `file` input type displays a button that launches a file browser so that users can select a file from their hard drive to upload to your website. An example of a `file` input in its simplest form is shown in the following code example.

```
<input name="avatar" type="file">
```

Figure 5-13 shows the file browser displayed in Mac OS X.

FIGURE 5-13 The file browser displayed when a user clicks the file input in Mac OS X.

Selecting Multiple Files

Before HTML5 came along, the only way that you could confidently handle multiple file uploads was to use Adobe's Flash technology. This caused a few headaches for developers who just wanted a simple solution for multiple file uploads. Yet again, HTML5 has come to the rescue by allowing multiple file uploads with the simple use of the `multiple` attribute.

The following example shows how you can allow a user to select multiple files using a single `<input>` element.

```
<label id="pictures">Upload Pictures:</label>
<input name="pictures" id="pictures" type="file" multiple>
```

This is a new addition in HTML5. Older web browsers do not support the `multiple` attribute.

Specifying Accepted File Types

If you are expecting a user to upload a picture of himself to use as an avatar on your social networking site, you want to be sure that he doesn't try to upload a spreadsheet instead. The accept attribute enables you to specify what type of file you are expecting so that the browser can launch a file browser that will only allow the user to select those types of files.

Some possible values for the accept attribute are: image/*, audio/*, and video/*. You can find a full list of these values (also known as MIME types) here: http://www.webmaster-toolkit.com/mime-types.shtml.

Here is an example of a file <input> that only accepts image files.

```
<label id="photos">Upload Photos:</label>
<input name="photos" id="photos" type="file" accept="image/*"
        multiple>
```

The accept attribute is a new addition in HTML5, so it won't work in older web browsers.

Grouping the Input Fields in Your Bookings Page Using <fieldset> and <legend>

When creating larger web forms, you will often find it useful to group relevant form fields together. You can do that using the <fieldset> and <legend> elements.

The <fieldset> element is used to define a group of inputs and should contain all the form elements related to that group. The <legend> element is used to specify a name for a field-set group and should be placed after the start tag of the <fieldset> element, as shown in the following example.

```
<fieldset>
  <legend>Contact Details</legend>
  <div class="field">
    <label for="name">Name:</label>
    <input type="text" name="name" id="name">
  </div>
  <div class="field">
    <label for="email">Email:</label>
    <input type="text" name="email" id="email">
  </div>
</fieldset>
```

You can also set the `disabled` attribute on a `<fieldset>` element. This will disable all the fields within the fieldset so that the user cannot edit them.

Check out this Treehouse video where Nick Pettit covers fieldsets, legends, and labels: `http://teamtreehouse.com/library/websites/html/forms/fieldsets-and-labels`.

You are now going to add the final touches to your bookings form, creating two groups of input fields: one for the customer's contact details and one for the booking details.

The code for this exercise can be found in folder 6.

Follow these steps to create your two `<fieldset>` elements.

1. Open your `bookings.html` file.
2. Create a new `<fieldset>` element at the top of your form, just below the start tag for the `<form>` element.
3. Within this `<fieldset>`, create a `<legend>` element with the text `Contact Details`.
4. Now move the name, phone, and e-mail inputs into this `<fieldset>` element, directly below the `<legend>` element.
5. Below this `<fieldset>`, create another `<fieldset>` element.
6. Create a new `<legend>` in this `<fieldset>` with the text `Booking Information`.
7. Move the restaurant, booking time, guests, marketing, and message form fields into this `<fieldset>` element, leaving the button outside of it.
8. Save the `bookings.html` file.

You should now have two groups of form fields, as shown in the following code.

```
<form action="bookings.php" method="POST">
  <fieldset>
    <legend>Contact Details</legend>
    <div class="field">
      <label for="name">Name:</label>
      <input type="text" name="name" id="name">
    </div>
```

```
    <div class="field">
      <label for="phone">Phone:</label>
      <input type="text" name="phone" id="phone">
    </div>
    <div class="field">
      <label for="email">Email:</label>
      <input type="text" name="email" id="email">
    </div>
  </fieldset>
  <fieldset>
    <legend>Booking Information</legend>
    <div class="field">
      <label for="restaurant">Restaurant:</label>
      <select name="restaurant" id="restaurant">
        <option>310 West 38th Street, NY</option>
        <option>2450 Broadway, NY</option>
        <option>200 West 44th Street, NY</option>
      </select>
    </div>
    <div class="field">
      <label for="bookingTime">Booking Time:</label>
      <input type="text" name="bookingTime" id="bookingTime">
    </div>
    <div class="field">
      <label for="guests">Number of Guests:</label>
      <input type="number" name="guests" id="guests">
    </div>
    <div class="field">
      <label for="marketing">Please tick this box if you would like
      to receive special offers from Joe's Pizza Co.</label>
      <input type="checkbox" name="marketing" id="marketing"
      value="1">
    </div>
    <div class="field">
      <label for="message">Special Requests:</label>
      <textarea id="message" name="message" cols="50" rows="10">
      </textarea>
    </div>
  </fieldset>
  <div class="field">
    <button type="submit">Request Booking</button>
  </div>
</form>
```

Most browsers will usually put a border around `<fieldset>` elements to make the groups of form controls more visible.

Congratulations! You have now finished the bookings form (for now). Submitting this form won't actually do anything because you do not have a `bookings.php` file to process the data. Figure 5-14 shows how your Bookings page should look. In the next two chapters you will be learning how to use HTML5 to make this web form a bit more exciting.

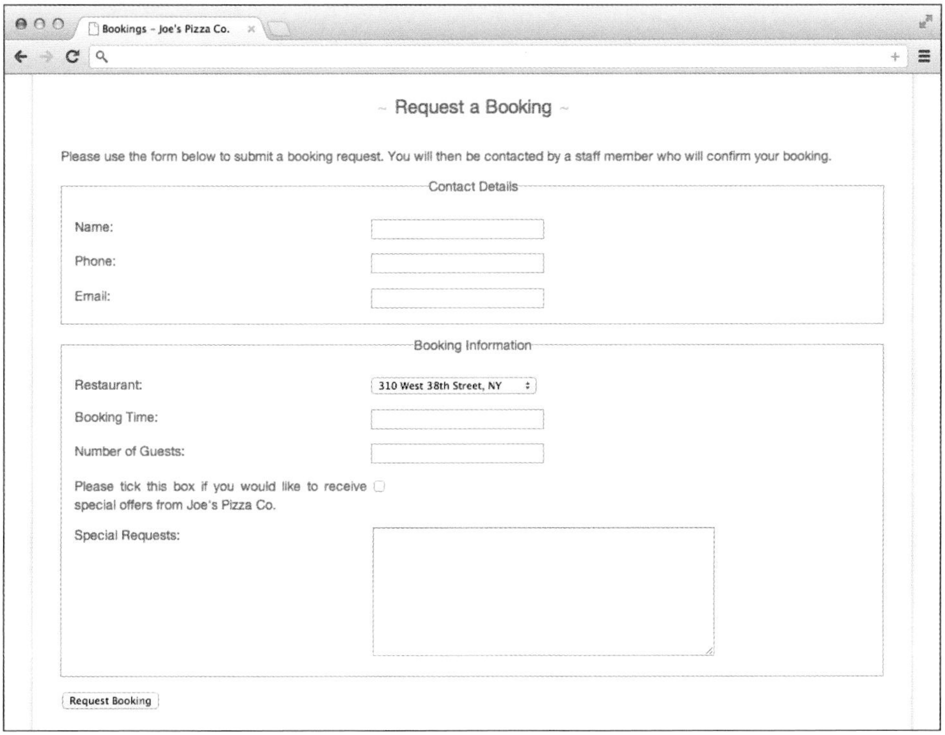

![Browser window showing the finished Bookings page with the title "Request a Booking" and a form containing Contact Details and Booking Information fieldsets.]

FIGURE 5-14 The finished Bookings page.

Updating the Site Navigation and Sitemap

As your websites mature, you will find yourself adding new pages. Each time you do this, you will need to update the site navigation on each of your pages as well as update the list of pages on the Sitemap page.

Now that you have created your Bookings page, you need to update the site navigation and sitemap to include links to this new page.

 The code for this exercise can be found in folder 7.

Follow these steps:

1. Open the sitemap.html file.

2. Locate the <nav> element in the page header.

3. At the end of the navigation list, create a new <li> element.

4. Within this <li> element, create a new link using the <a> element:

```
<li>
  <a href="bookings.html" title="Make a booking">Bookings</a>
</li>
```

5. Save this file and repeat Steps 1 to 4 for each page in your website. You might find it easier to just copy and paste the new <li> element into the navigation section in each of the files. Don't forget to add the active class to the link when adding it to the Bookings page.

6. Go back to the sitemap.html and locate the list of links that make up the sitemap. This <ul> element has the ID sitemap.

7. Using the code from Step 4, add a new link to the sitemap.

8. Save the sitemap.html file.

Figure 5-15 shows how the updated Sitemap page should look in your web browser.

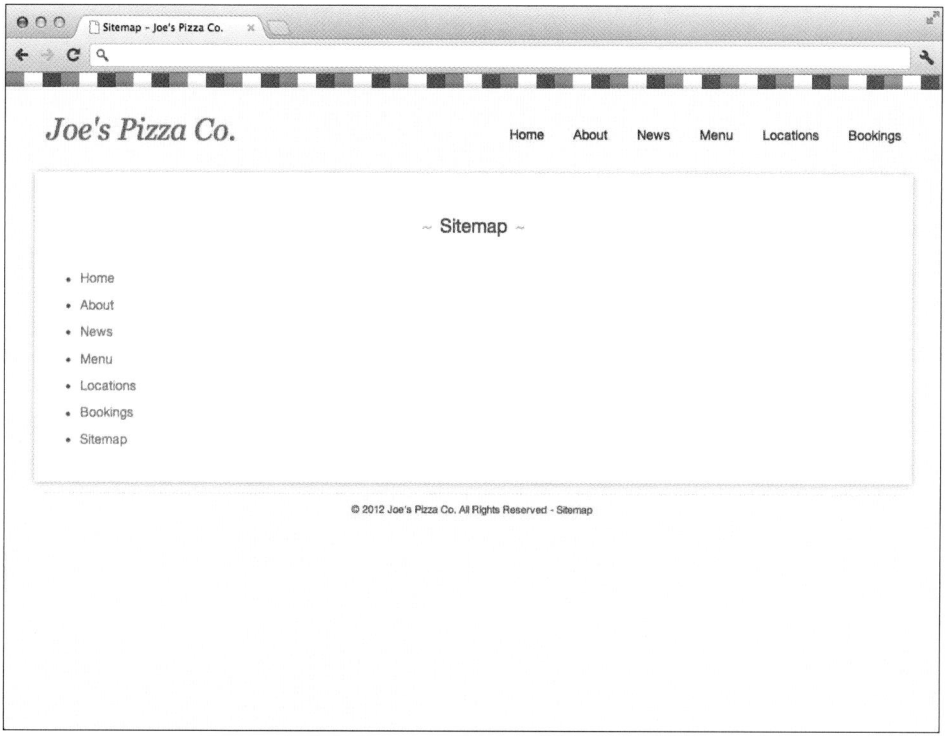

FIGURE 5-15 The updated Sitemap page.

Summary

It's been another long chapter and you've covered a lot of content, so let's have a quick recap. The chapters get shorter from now on. Honest.

In this chapter, you learned about the `<form>` element and the different elements that you can use to define form fields, including `<input>`, `<select>`, and `<textarea>`. You have also learned about a number of widely supported input types that make it easier to collect data from your users.

In Chapter 6 you'll learn how to use HTML5 to enhance your web forms. You will be introduced to client-side validations (*client-side* means that they happen on the user's computer, not on a web server), datalists, and loads of new HTML5 input types. See you there!

chapter six

Enhancing Your Web Forms with HTML5

IN CHAPTER 5 you learned how to create web forms using elements such as `<form>`, `<input>`, `<select>`, and `<option>`. In this chapter you are going to learn how you can make your forms more delightful for users by taking advantage of the new range of input types and attributes that have been introduced in HTML5.

For example, the new `datetime` input types enable you to display a small calendar to the user when you need to collect a date. This makes it much easier for the user, as she can simply click on a date in the calendar instead of needing to manually type the date into a text field. The new `<datalist>` element enables you to easily create autocomplete lists similar to those that you see when you type a query into the search box on Google. This makes things much easier for users as it reduces the amount that they need to type. In this chapter you will learn how to use both of these new features as well as a lot of other fantastic HTML5 additions.

It is important to note that the input types and attributes that you will be learning about in this chapter are not yet widely supported. If a browser does not support an input type, then the `text` type will be used. If an attribute is not supported it will simply be ignored.

Web Forms and HTML5

HTML5 really started with web forms. When the World Wide Web Consortium (W3C) decided not to pursue the development of HTML, it was a small group from Opera that picked up on their work and developed the Web Forms 2.0 specification, rekindling excitement for HTML. The Web Forms 2.0 specification has since become part of the official HTML5 spec.

Adding HTML5 to Your Bookings Form

Let's dive straight in to using some HTML5 in your bookings form. You are going to use a number of input types and attributes that you have not encountered before. Don't worry. I will explain each of these in detail later in this chapter.

You will add placeholder text to your input fields to give your users hints about what data they should enter into your form fields, and specialized input types such as email and tel to give the web browser more information about the data you are trying to collect.

Follow these steps to supercharge your bookings form with HTML5.

 The code for this exercise can be found in the download code for Chapter 6, folder 1.

1. Open the bookings.html file in your text editor of choice.

2. Add an autofocus attribute to the name input. This will tell the browser that this input element should be automatically focused when the page loads. This is a Boolean attribute so you do not need to set a value.

   ```
   <input type="text" name="name" id="name" autofocus>
   ```

3. Now add a placeholder attribute to this same <input> element and set its value to e.g. Joe Balochio. This placeholder text will provide a hint to the user, telling them what they should type into the input field.

   ```
   <input type="text" name="name" id="name" placeholder="e.g Joe Balochio" autofocus>
   ```

4. Set the type of the phone <input> element to be tel and add a placeholder attribute to this element with the value 000-000-0000.

   ```
   <input type="tel" name="phone" id="phone" placeholder="e.g. 000-000-0000">
   ```

5. Change the type of the email `<input>` element to be `email` and add a `placeholder` element with the following value: `e.g. joe@example.com`.

    ```
    <input type="email" name="email" id="email" placeholder="e.g.
    joe@example.com">
    ```

6. For the Booking Time `<input>` element, change the input type to `datetime-local`. This will prompt browsers that support this input type to display a date/time picker to help the user fill out this form field.

    ```
    <input type="datetime-local" name="bookingTime"
    id="bookingTime">
    ```

7. Also add a `placeholder` attribute to the Booking Time field that has the value `e.g. 2012-09-06 12:14`. This placeholder text will only be displayed if the browser does not support the `datetime-local` input type and will help the user to provide a date/time combo in the right format. This is not ideal, but it is better than having no hint at all.

    ```
    <input type="datetime-local" name="bookingTime"
      id="bookingTime"placeholder="e.g. 2012-09-06 12:14">
    ```

8. Change the type of the Number of Guests `<input>` element to be `number` and set a default value of 2 using the `value` attribute.

    ```
    <input type="number" name="guests" id="guests" value="2">
    ```

9. Finally, add a `placeholder` attribute to the `<textarea>` element and set its value to `Type your message....`

    ```
    <textarea id="message" name="message" cols="50" rows="10"
    placeholder="Type your message...">
    </textarea>
    ```

10. Save the `bookings.html` file.

Congratulations! You've now upgraded your bookings form to use HTML5! In Chapter 7 you will take this even further by adding validations. Figure 6-1 shows how your form should look at this stage.

In the remainder of this chapter you are going to take a deeper look at the input types and attributes that you have just added to your bookings form, as well as some that you have not yet encountered.

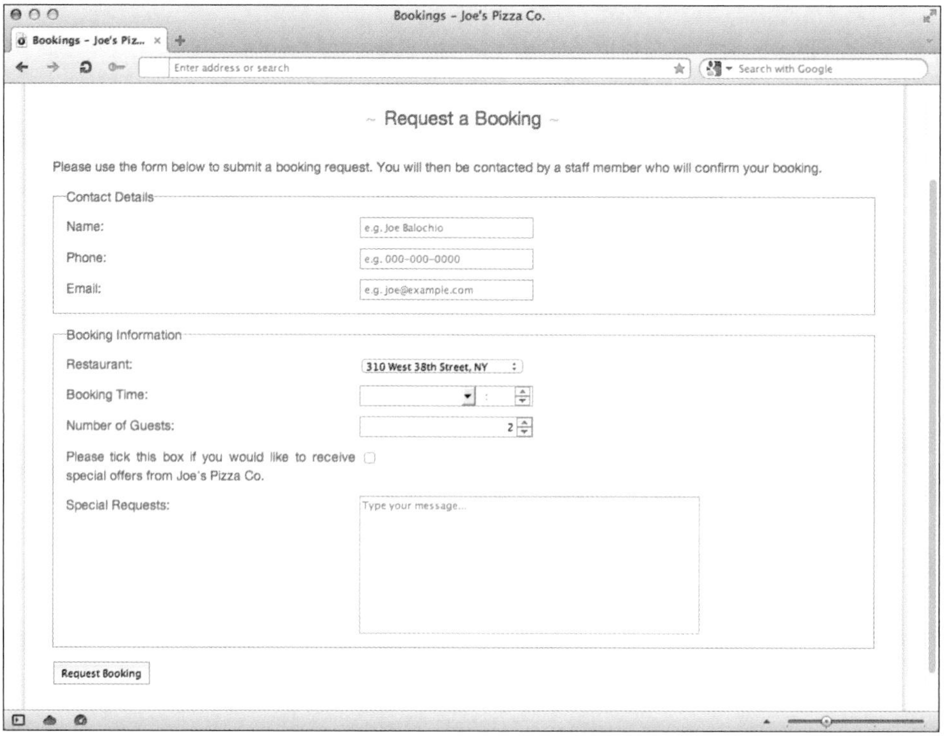

FIGURE 6-1 The bookings form with HTML5 input types and attributes (shown in Opera).

HTML5 Input Types

HTML4 included a number of input types for creating basic form controls. However, as the demands of the modern web user have increased, the need arose to extend these types to give developers a wider range of form controls to play around with. HTML5 introduces a range of new input types that make it easier for users to fill in forms by providing easy-to-use form controls.

Many of the latest mobile devices, such as smartphones and tablets, use software keyboards that have the capability to alter their layout depending on the type of data that is being collected. The new input types introduced in HTML5 provide signals to mobile browsers so that they can display customized keyboards that make it easier for users to enter data.

Telephone Numbers

HTML5 introduces the new tel input type for collecting telephone numbers. By specifying this special input type, devices that use software keyboards (such as touch devices) can display a slightly different keyboard that makes it easier for the users to input their data. For example, iOS will display a keyboard with numbers rather than letters, as shown in Figure 6-2.

FIGURE 6-2 The iOS keyboard displayed for input elements with the type tel.

> The device shown in Figure 6-2 uses a UK keyboard layout and therefore displays a pound sign (£) instead of a dollar ($).

You used the `tel` input type for the phone field in your bookings form:

```
<input type="tel" name="phone" id="phone"
  placeholder="000-000-0000">
```

E-mail Addresses

The `email` type is another newbie introduced in HTML5 and brings with it the double-barreled goodness that is customized keyboards and browser validations (more on validations in Chapter 7). Figure 6-3 shows the keyboard displayed in iOS for `email` input elements.

FIGURE 6-3 The iOS keyboard displayed for input elements with type email.

At first glance, not much has changed here but you might notice that @, underscore (_), and minus (-) symbols have replaced the regular keys in the bottom-right corner of the keyboard.

Browsers with built-in support for validation will check that the e-mail address is supplied in a valid format and prompt the user if there is a problem.

You have already used the `email` type for the e-mail field in your bookings form.

```
<input type="email" name="email" id="email" placeholder="e.g.
joe@example.com">
```

Numbers

If you are collecting a numeric value, such as a quantity or age, you can use the `number` input type. By default, the `number` type will expect an integer value and browsers that support validation will reject any non-integer values that a user might attempt to provide. You can change this behavior by setting the `step` attribute to be a decimal number.

Browsers with support for the `number` type may display up and down arrows in the input field. Figure 6-4 shows how a number field is displayed in Google Chrome.

FIGURE 6-4 An input element with the type number, displayed in Google Chrome.

The `number` type will also trigger the numbers keyboard to be displayed on devices that use software keyboards. Refer to Figure 6-2 for how this keyboard looks in iOS.

In your bookings form, you used the `number` type for the Number of Guests field.

```
<input type="number" name="guests" id="guests" value="2">
```

URLs

The input type `url` is also new in HTML5 and enables you to specify that you are expecting a web address as the input. Again, devices with software keyboards may present a customized keyboard to users. Figure 6-5 shows the keyboard presented in iOS. This time, the space bar has been replaced with the special characters commonly used in URLs.

FIGURE 6-5 The iOS keyboard displayed for input elements with the type url.

Browsers that support form validation will also validate the contents of url inputs when the form is submitted. This is to check that the format of the URL supplied by the user is valid.

Here is a short snippet that shows how to create an <input> element with the type url.

```
<input type="url" name="website" id="website">
```

Search

The search type is much the same as the text input type, with the only real difference being how the field is displayed in the browser. Input elements with the search type will inherit the operating system's natural styling for search fields. This helps users to quickly recognize search forms on your web pages because the search forms are styled in a way that users recognize. Figure 6-6 shows how the following search input would be displayed in Google Chrome on Mac OS X.

```
<input type="search" name="term" id="term">
```

FIGURE 6-6 An input element with the type search, as displayed in Google Chrome on Mac OS X.

Ranges

The range type is used to collect a numeric value from a user that must be between a minimum and maximum value; browsers will display a slider to help users input this value. Before HTML5 introduced the range type, creating a slider to collect a value from a user involved writing some fairly fancy JavaScript that tended to be a bit of a pain.

Pro Tip: Displaying Recent Searches

If you add a results attribute to a search input element, WebKit-based browsers (Google Chrome and Safari) will display a small magnifying glass in the input box. If the user clicks on this it will display her recent searches. The value that you set in the results attribute tells the browser how many recent searches to display.

```
<input type="search" results="5">
```

The results attribute is not officially part of the HTML5 specification, but it is an example of an instance when a browser vendor will implement a new feature that will likely be added to the specification in the future.

The default range scale is between 0 and 100; however, you can change this using the `max`, `min`, and `step` attributes.

Figure 6-7 shows the interactive slider displayed to users.

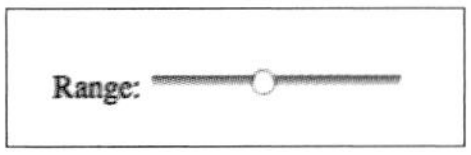

FIGURE 6-7 An input element with the type range, as displayed in Google Chrome.

Here is an example of a basic `<input>` element with the type `range` that specifies a default scale of 0 to 1 with a step of 0.01 (the minimum increment between values).

```
<input type="range" min="0" max="1" step="0.01">
```

The problem with range sliders in their default state is that users cannot actually see the value that they are selecting. However, range sliders can be very useful for creating features like seek bars and volume controls. In Chapter 11 you will use range sliders when creating custom controls for a video.

Colors

The colors used by computers are represented by hexadecimal color codes that define the amounts of red, green, and blue needed to create the desired color. This is great for computers, but the likelihood of humans remembering these color codes is very slim. Giving users the capability to visually select a color previously required an elaborate JavaScript solution that wasn't very developer friendly.

Luckily, HTML5 has come to the rescue with the `color` type for `<input>` elements. Using this type will trigger the browser to display a button that can be used to launch a visual color picker. The user can then use this to pick the color she wants, without having to deal with color codes. It's awesome!

Figure 6-8 shows the button and color picker that are displayed in Google Chrome on Mac OS X.

Here is an example of a basic `<input>` element with the type `color`.

```
<input type="color" name="favColor" id="favColor">
```

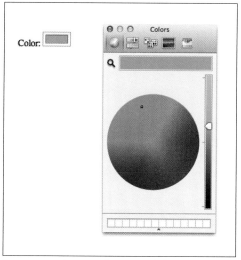

FIGURE 6-8 An input element with the type color, as displayed in Google Chrome on Mac OS X.

Date and Time

The `datetime` type can be used to collect a date and time from a user. This date/time combo should be a valid Coordinated Universal Time (UTC) string. UTC time is the standardized time used by computers.

Fortunately, specifying the `datetime` type will instruct the browser to display a date picker to help the users input their date in the correct format. This usually takes the form of a small calendar. The time segment is inputted using a text field with helper controls similar to those displayed with a number field. Figure 6-9 shows an example of a `datetime` field with the date picker displayed.

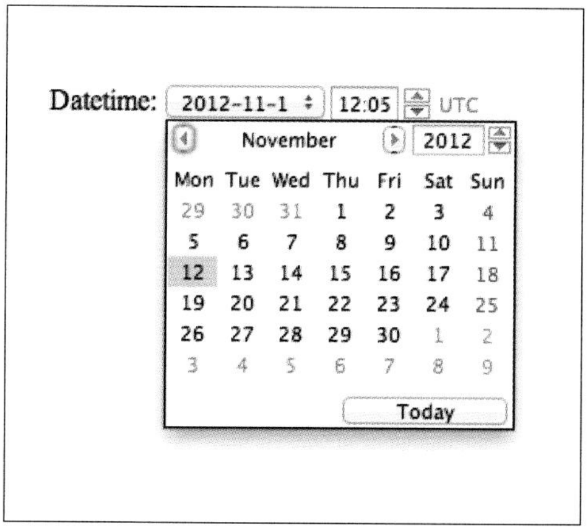

FIGURE 6-9 An input element with the type datetime, as displayed in Opera.

Here is an example of an `<input>` element with the type `datetime`.

```
<input type="datetime" name="eventStart" id="eventStart">
```

Date

There will be times when you just want to collect a date from your users; for example, you might want to collect their date of birth. The `date` type is very useful for such occasions.

As you've probably already guessed, the `date` type is exactly the same as `datetime`, just without the time part. Browsers that support the `date` type will still display a date picker to help the user easily select a date.

Here is an example of an `<input>` element with the type `date`.

```
<input type="date" name="dob" id="dob">
```

Time

There's a date type so there must to be a `time` type too. Again, this will still prompt the browser to display some helper controls. Figure 6-10 shows the controls displayed in Opera.

FIGURE 6-10 An input element with the type time, as displayed in Opera.

Here is an example of a time input.

```
<input type="time" name="startTime" id="startTime">
```

 At the time of writing this book, only Opera and mobile Safari have full support for the new `date` and `time` types. Google Chrome has partial support (only the `date` type), but other browsers will just display a standard text input.

Week and Month

As well as collecting a complete date, you can also specify that you would like just a week or month using the `week` and `month` types.

Using the week type will prompt the browser to display a picker that will help the user select a week in the year. This value is then converted to a formatted string. For example: 2012-W29.

The month type will also prompt the browser to display a date picker, this time just for selecting a month.

Figures 6-11 and 6-12 show <input> elements with the week and month types. Note how the browser highlights only weeks/months for selection.

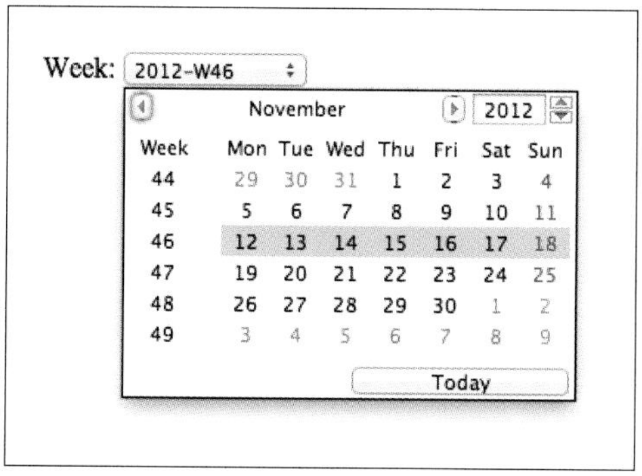

FIGURE 6-11 An input element with the type week, as displayed in Opera.

FIGURE 6-12 An input element with the type month, as displayed in Opera.

Here are two simple <input> elements with the types week and month.

```
<input type="week" name="week" id="week">
<input type="month" name="month" id="month">
```

Local Date and Time

The datetime-local type is used to collect a date and time from users in a format that is consistent with their local time zone. It is usually best to collect date and time combinations from the users using this type; otherwise, the users would have to do the time conversion themselves (which is a pain and could lead to incorrect data).

Here is an example of a <input> element with the type datetime-local.

```
<input type="datetime-local" name="localDT" id="localDT">
```

HTML5 Input Attributes

As well as new input types, HTML5 also introduces a number of new attributes that can be used to make it easier for users to fill in your web forms. In this section you learn how you can use these attributes to improve your forms.

AutoComplete

Many web browsers have a feature called auto-complete that will fill in common form fields for you based on values that you have used in the past, such as username, password, name, and telephone. The autocomplete attribute enables you to control whether the browser should use its auto-complete feature for a certain field. The attribute has three possible values: on, off, and default.

Setting the autocomplete value to default will inherit the browser's auto-completion setting. This is important because some users like to turn this feature off. Often, this can be done in the web browser's settings menu.

It sometimes can be useful to explicitly turn off auto-completion. For example, you might want to force users to input their password into a log-in form rather than let the browser fill this field in for them.

Here is an example of how you could turn off auto-completion for the phone input in your form using the autocomplete attribute.

```
<input type="tel" name="phone" id="phone" placeholder="e.g. 000-
000-0000" autocomplete="off">
```

AutoFocus

The autofocus attribute can make it easier for users to start filling in a form because it will put the cursor into the <input> element when the page loads. This prevents the need for the users to select the element with their mouse. This might seem like a small optimization, but it can have a big impact on making your web pages easier to use.

You should apply the `autofocus` attribute only to one element on your page. If you apply it to more than one, the browser will autofocus the last element that has the attribute in your HTML.

You used the `autofocus` attribute on the name input in your form.

```
<input type="text" name="name" id="name" placeholder="e.g. Joe
Balochio" autofocus>
```

Min and Max

The `min` and `max` attributes can be used to limit the range of valid entries for an `<input>` element. You don't have to use both of these attributes together; you can specify a `min` but no `max` and vice versa.

```
<input type="number" name="guests" id="guests" value="2"
min="1" max="12">
```

These attributes should only be used on `<input>` elements with the `number` or `datetime` types.

Step

The `step` attribute is used to specify the accuracy of the data you are collecting. It is usually used on inputs that collect numeric data or times.

For example, if you wanted to get the price of an object, you would want the value submitted to have no more than two decimal places. This could be achieved by setting the `step` attribute to 0.01. You are basically setting the step to a cent (or penny, for our British friends).

```
<input type="number" name="price" id="price" step="0.01">
```

Setting the `step` attribute will also affect the helper controls displayed for `number` and `range` `<input>` elements.

Placeholder

The `placeholder` attribute can be used to temporarily display a hint within an `<input>` element. When the `<input>` element gains focus, this text will disappear. Before HTML5 introduced the `placeholder` element, this sort of functionality could only be achieved using JavaScript, which was a bit of a pain to set up if you had a lot of inputs that needed placeholders.

You used the `placeholder` attribute to display a hint to the user in your bookings form.

```
<input type="email" name="email" id="email" placeholder="e.g.
joe@example.com">
```

Datalists

You may have noticed that sometimes when you start typing into a form field, the browser will offer suggestions to help you complete your input quicker. Until recently, this functionality was created using JavaScript and clever CSS positioning. However, HTML5 makes it a lot easier for developers to add these suggestions using the <datalist> element.

The <datalist> element enables developers to specify a number of different options that a user could type into an input field. Each of these options is defined using an <option> element. To link this list of possible options up to your <input> element, you will first need to give the <datalist> element a unique ID using its id attribute. You can then link this <datalist> to your <input> element by setting the list attribute to the ID of the <datalist>, as shown in the following example code.

```
<input type="text" name="coffee" list="coffees">

<datalist id="coffees">
  <option value="Americano">
  <option value="Cappuccino">
  <option value="Flat White">
  <option value="Latte">
</datalist>
```

As the user starts to type, the browser will display a list of options that match the user's input, as shown in Figure 6-13.

FIGURE 6-13 An <option> element that is linked to a <datalist>, as displayed in Opera.

Browser support for the <datalist> element is increasing, but at the time of writing this book, the majority of mobile web browsers and the Safari desktop browser do not have support.

If in doubt, check out the compatibility table here: http://caniuse.com/#searmenuch=datalist.

Summary

HTML5 has introduced a lot of changes to how web forms can be created. In this chapter you learned how to use new input types such as `number`, `search`, and `datetime-local` to create form controls that make it even easier for users to fill in your web forms.

This chapter has also introduced you to a number of new input attributes that can be used to make the overall user experience of filling in your web forms better. You have learned how you can use attributes such as `autocomplete` and `autofocus` to control a web browser's behavior, as well as learning how to provide hints to users using the `placeholder` attribute.

In Chapter 7 you start exploring the world of browser validations, another new feature in HTML5. You will learn how to require an input from a user as well as more complex validations such as creating patterns to validate the format of data.

chapter seven

Validating Form Data Using HTML5

COLLECTING DATA FROM a user is one thing; making sure that data is what you wanted is another. If you're asking for someone's date of birth, you don't want the name of his cat. This may sound silly, but you would be surprised what some people will decide to enter into your web forms.

HTML5 introduces a number of new features that you can use to validate data. You can now *require* an input to make sure that the user gives you something to work with. You can perform *pattern* (or *format*) validations to check that the data supplied by the user has been provided in a valid format (think e-mail addresses and URLs). You can also restrict the *length* of an input (this was feasible in HTML4) or restrict the *possible values* that can be submitted. All of these validation methods can help to make your life easier when it comes to processing the data.

Adding Validations to Your Bookings Form

Your bookings form currently makes use of built-in pattern validations introduced in HTML5 by using the email input type; however, you can do much more. In this section, you are going to apply a number of validations to your bookings form using the following attributes: required, maxlength, min, and max. You will learn about each of these attributes in more detail later in this section.

157

Before you start writing code, take a look at Table 7-1, which shows the validations that each of the fields will have. Planning out your validations in this way is useful to ensure that you don't miss anything.

Table 7-1 Input Validations

Input Field	Validation Rules
Name	Required Maxlength is 65 characters.
Phone	Required This must be in the following format: 000-000-0000
Email	Required This must be a valid e-mail address.
Restaurant	Required
Booking Time	Required
Guests	Required The maximum number of guests is 12. The minimum number of guests is 1.
Message	Maxlength is 250 characters.

Table 7-1 shows that all the form fields are required, with the exception of the message. Some of these form fields also have validations for their length.

 The code for this exercise can be found in the download files for Chapter 7, folder 1.

Here are the steps to add validations to your form fields.

1. Open the `bookings.html` file.

2. Locate the name `<input>` element and add a `required` attribute. Add a `maxlength` attribute and set its value to 65.

   ```
   <input type="text" name="name" id="name" placeholder="e.g. Joe
   Balochio" autofocus required maxlength="65">
   ```

3. Locate the phone `<input>` element and add a `required` attribute. Also add a `pattern` attribute with the following value: `[0-9]{3}[-][0-9]{3}[-][0-9]{4}` (this will be explained in detail later). As you are using pattern validation here you should also provide a tip to users telling them how to format their data. You do this using the `title` attribute.

   ```
   <input type="tel" name="phone" id="phone" placeholder="e.g.
   000-000-0000"
   ```

```
pattern="[0-9]{3}[-][0-9]{3}[-][0-9]{4}" required
title="Please provide your phone number in the following
format: 000-000-0000">
```

4. Locate the email `<input>` element and add a `required` attribute. The browser will take care of checking that the e-mail address is valid because you have used the input type `email`.

```
<input type="email" name="email" id="email" placeholder="e.g.
joe@example.com" required>
```

5. Locate the restaurant `<select>` element and add a `required` attribute.

```
<select name="restaurant" id="restaurant" required>
```

6. Locate the booking time `<input>` element and add a `required` attribute.

```
<input type="datetime-local" name="bookingTime"
id="bookingTime" placeholder="e.g. 2012-09-06 12:14" required>
```

7. Locate the guests `<input>` element and add the `required` attribute. Add a `max` attribute to this element and set its value to 12. Add a `min` attribute and set the value to 1.

```
<input type="number" name="guests" id="guests" value="2"
required min="1" max="12">
```

8. Locate the message `<textarea>` element. Add a `maxlength` attribute to this element and set its value to 250.

```
<textarea id="message" name="message" cols="50" rows="10"
placeholder="Type your message..." maxlength="250">
```

9. Now add an asterisk next to the text label for each of the form fields that is required, following this example:

```
<label for="email">Email*:</label>
<input type="email" name="email" id="email" required>
```

10. Create a new `<p>` element at the top of the form.

11. Add a `class` attribute to this `<p>` element and set its value to `validation-tip`. This will be used for styling purposes.

12. Now add the following text to this `<p>` element.

```
<p class="validation-tip">
  * Indicates a required field.
</p>
```

13. Save the `bookings.html` file.

You have now applied validations to all of the form fields!

If you view the updated bookings form in your web browser, you should see that only the text labels and validation tip have changed, as shown in Figure 7-1.

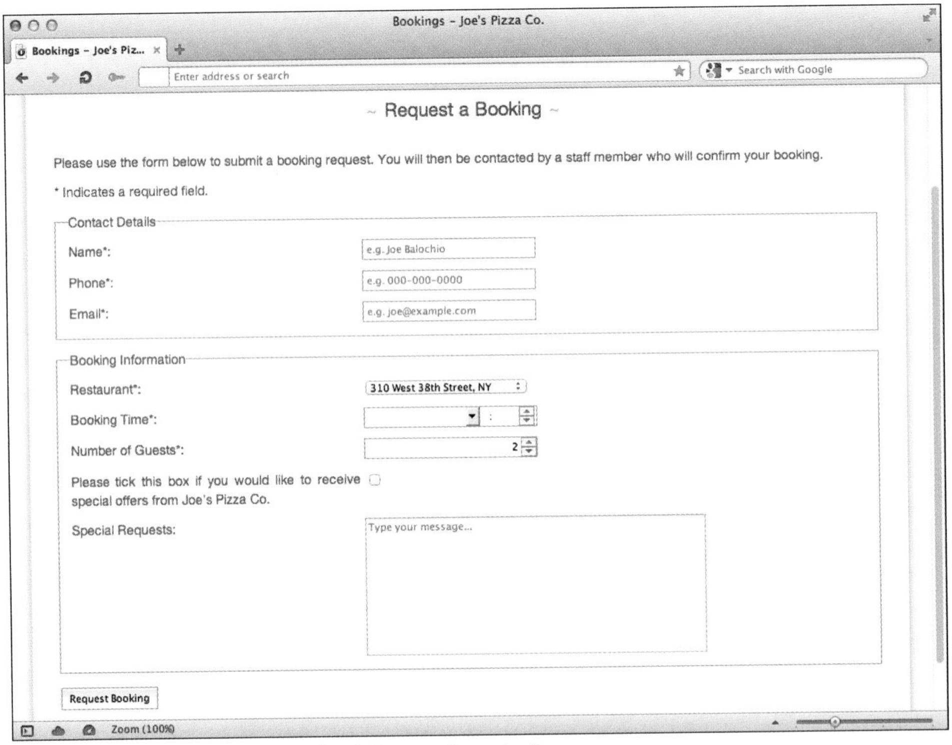

FIGURE 7-1 The bookings form with validations, shown in Opera.

Requiring Data from the User

Requiring data from a user is relatively easy. It's just a matter of including the new `required` attribute on the form field that you want the user to fill in, as you did on a number of the fields in your bookings form.

```
<input type="email" id="email" name="email" placeholder="e.g.
joe@example.com" required>
```

If the user fails to fill in a required form field, the browser will prevent the form from being submitted and will display a tip to the user as shown in Figure 7-2.

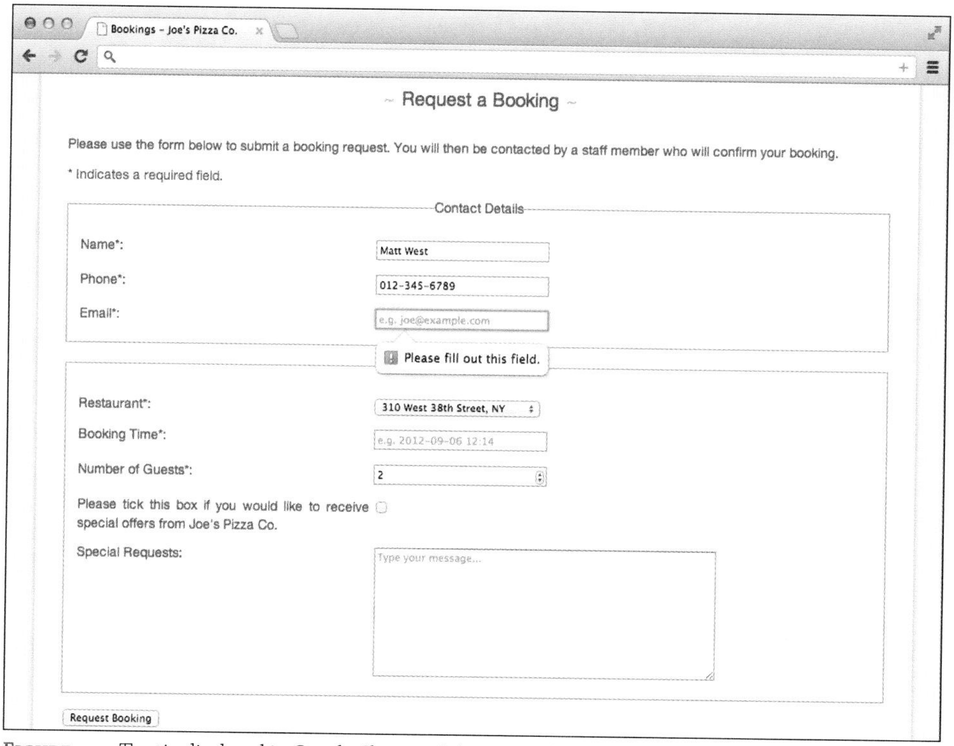

FIGURE 7-2 The tip displayed in Google Chrome if the user fails to fill in a required form field.

If you are going to require that users fill in certain fields in your form please, please, please let them know! There is nothing worse for them than hitting the Submit button and then finding out that they have to go back and fill in those fields that they didn't complete. It's annoying and makes for a terrible user experience.

Some browsers will highlight required fields in a dull red, but never rely on this. If you decide to apply some styling to your forms fields, you could override this behavior. Simply place an asterisk (*) next to the required fields with a little note at the top explaining to the users that they must fill in these fields (you did this for the bookings form). That's all you need and most users will see the asterisk and know straight away that this field is required.

Restricting Length

It can sometimes be useful to restrict the length of the data provided by a user. For these occasions, you can use the `maxlength` attribute on an `<input>` or `<textarea>` element and pass in the maximum number of characters that the user can supply. When the user reaches the character limit, the browser will no longer allow anything the user types to be added to the field.

In your bookings form, you used the `maxlength` attribute to restrict the length of the message to 250 characters.

```
<textarea id="message" name="message" cols="50" rows="10"
placeholder="Type your message..." maxlength="250">
```

The `maxlength` attribute was present in HTML4 so you can rely on it being supported by web browsers.

Restricting Range

In your bookings form, you used the `min` and `max` attributes on the Guests input in order to restrict the range of the input to between 1 and 12. These two attributes can also be used to restrict date inputs.

For example, suppose you are building a form for a brewery website that collects data about potential customers. Let's say that the brewery has no interest in collecting the data of people under the age of 21 as they are not yet old enough to buy their products. Here you could use the max attribute to specify a date that is 21 years in the past, therefore preventing anybody under the age of 21 from completing the form (without being dishonest).

Here is an example of how that `<input>` element would look.

```
<input type="date" max="1991-04-24">
```

This would restrict the input to dates on or before April 24, 1991.

Computer Time

I know what you're thinking. Why `max`? Surely that would be `min`, as in *minimum* age?

When computers encounter dates they convert them into an integer number known as a *Unix timestamp*. This is generated by calculating the number of seconds between the date and January 1, 1970 (the *Unix epoch*). Therefore, dates in the future will have a larger timestamp because the gap between the date and the Unix epoch is larger.

If you want to set a minimum age you use the `max` attribute because the Unix timestamp will get larger the younger the person is. This is because their date of birth is further from the Unix epoch.

Matching Patterns

HTML5 introduces another new attribute for `<input>` elements, the `pattern` attribute. This attribute can be used to check whether the data the user has input conforms to a certain format or pattern. The pattern attribute can only be used on `<input>` elements with the types `text`, `search`, `tel`, `url`, or `email`.

The `pattern` attribute should contain a *regular expression* (sometimes written *RegExp*). This is sort of like a code that defines which characters and symbols can be used, in what quantities, and in what order. The user's input is then compared to this *code* to see whether it matches or not. You will learn the basics of regular expressions very soon, but here's a quick example of an `<input>` element that uses the `pattern` attribute.

```
<input name="initials" type="text" pattern="[A-Z]+" title="Your
   initials should be supplied in uppercase with no spaces.">
```

This example restricts the input to uppercase characters between A and Z only. For example, MW would be valid, but Mw would not. That's because Mw includes a lowercase character. This pattern also does not allow spaces, numbers, or special characters.

When using the `pattern` attribute, you should specify a `title` attribute that describes the rules that the user should stick to. The browser *may* present this to the user if the match fails. Figure 7-3 shows the validation tip that would be displayed if a user enters an incorrect phone number in your bookings form. Notice how the value of the `title` attribute is displayed in the tip.

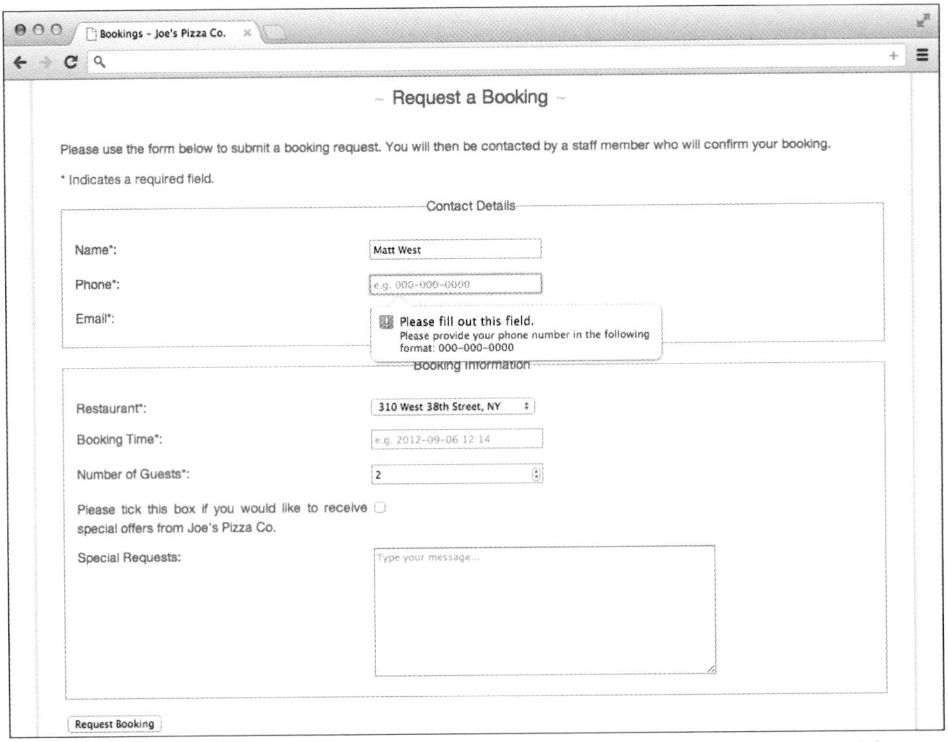

FIGURE 7-3 The validation tip displayed in Google Chrome when the input does not match the validation pattern.

Regular Expression Basics

Regular expressions can be a bit daunting at times; people have written whole books about them (they're truly terrifying—the books, not the people!). There are thousands of different patterns that you could create, but in this section, I want to walk you through the basics and show you some of the most common patterns you might need to use when building web forms.

Validating Characters

You can restrict the characters that can be used by specifying them in a pattern. To do this, you first create a set of square brackets [] that you will place your valid characters inside. If you wanted to limit the input to an alphanumeric string that does not allow spaces of special characters, for example, you could use the following code.

```
[A-Za-z0-9]+
```

This example accepts characters from 0 to 9 and A to Z, both upper and lowercase. Patterns are case sensitive so you need to include both the uppercase and lowercase characters in order to get things working correctly. The + sign here means that this rule can happen one or more times, therefore you cannot have zero characters.

Validating Length

Usually, you should use the `maxlength` attribute if you want to restrict the length of a whole input, but sometimes you may want to specify the length of one section of the input. You can specify an exact length for a section within curly braces `{}`.

```
[A-Za-z0-9]{3}
```

This pattern validates an alphanumeric string that is three characters long. You could also specify a range using two numbers.

```
[A-Za-z0-9]{3,5}
```

This pattern validates an alphanumeric string that is between three and five characters long.

Validating Format

Now that you have a grasp of the basics, let's look at an example of how you can use regular expressions to validate the format of some text.

The following pattern can be used to match a U.S. telephone number. It will validate that a telephone number begins with a three digit area code, followed by a dash, then the first three-digits of the phone number, followed by another dash, and finally the last four digits of the phone number; for example 000-000-0000.

```
[0-9]{3}[-][0-9]{3}[-][0-9]{4}
```

The HTML5 specification outlines that browser vendors should implement pattern validations for `<input>` elements that use specialized types such as `url` or `email`. This is great because it means that you don't need to worry about dealing with more complicated regular expressions. But if you are really serious about building websites, you'll benefit from getting a solid understanding of regular expressions. They are incredibly useful tools.

> You can find a really handy list of common regular expressions for your pattern attributes at `http://html5pattern.com/`.

Summary

Data validation is important, but it is also one of the first things to get dropped when a deadline is looming and the project is rapidly running out of time.

Validation should not be an optional extra. It should be a requirement. Validation is as beneficial to your users as it is to you as a developer because it helps them to fill in your forms correctly and avoid problems down the line. While HTML5 browser validation is a wonderful thing and I believe that everyone should be using it, not all web browsers currently support this new feature. This means that there is a large group of users out there for whom browser validations will not work. This is why it is important not to rely solely on HTML5 browser validation. If you are building a website that will be interacting with a database or performing some other action based on data provided by a user, you need to make sure that you validate this data in your *server-side* application code. Not doing so could leave your website vulnerable to attack by hackers.

Chapter 8 focuses on how you can make your web pages more useful to computer programs using *microdata*. This involves using special markup syntax and element attributes to give your content greater semantic meaning.

chapter eight
Using Microdata

THIS CHAPTER FOCUSES on how you can use advanced markup syntax to enable computer programs to understand the data presented in your web pages. The web is full of structured data—the details of a local business, the properties of an item for sale on an e-commerce website, or someone's profile information on a social networking site. All of these examples follow a structured data model. The problem is that when this data is displayed on a web page, it's difficult for computer programs to make sense of it. For a long time there was no set specification for how data should be presented or how markup could be used to help make your web pages more meaningful to computer programs. Microdata changed this.

Microdata aims to bring structured data models into our web pages by enabling developers to define, use, and share schemas that outline the structure of their data. Think of these schemas as templates of items. They define all the properties that an item could have. A simple schema for a human, for example, would have properties such as height, weight, eye color, hair color, and age.

Enabling computer programs to extract data from your web pages opens up a realm of new possibilities to developers. It allows developers to build web applications that can interact with each other without necessarily needing to know the specifics of how the other application is built. For example, Google has already started looking for microdata when it crawls web pages and will often display this data alongside a website in the search results if it thinks that the data might be relevant to the user's search. Google is currently doing this for local businesses, products, and reviews, and plans to expand on this in the future.

Microdata is still in its infancy and therefore a lot of possible applications for this technology have not even been thought about yet. In this chapter you are going to learn how you can use microdata to mark up local businesses, events, people, and products to make them more visible to search engines.

About Schema.org

Microdata will only truly succeed in enabling computer programs to make sense of the data in your web pages if the schemas that you use when defining your items are consistent. This problem has been recognized by some of the world's largest search engines, many of which are already using microdata in order to display better results to their users. Schema.org is a collaborative effort between Bing, Yahoo!, Google, and Yandex to come up with a set of consistent schemas that developers can use to mark up their structured data.

Many schemas have been developed by the contributors to the schema.org project. In this chapter, you learn about the schemas that you will be using most frequently: LocalBusiness, Event, Person, and Product.

You can find a full list of schemas on the schema.org website: `http://schema.org/docs/full.html`.

Using Microdata

You add microdata to your web pages using a series of new HTML attributes. These are `itemscope`, `itemprop`, `itemtype`, `itemid` and `itemref`. To teach you about these attributes you will learn how to mark up a LocalBusiness item about a Joe's Pizza Co. restaurant.

Here is the original HTML for one of the restaurant locations in your website. In the next few sections you will learn how to apply the new microdata attributes to this HTML code.

```
<section id="location1">
  <h1>310 West 38th Street, NY</h1>
  <img src="img/map1.png"
      alt="Joe's Pizza at 310 West 38th Street, NY">
  <p class="location-phone">212 012 3456</p>
  <h2>Opening Hours:</h2>
  <p>
    Mon-Fri: 12:00 - 22:00<br>
    Sat-Sun: 11:00 - 23:00
  </p>
</section>
```

The itemscope Attribute

The itemscope attribute is used to define the scope of an item. It tells the browser that all the properties defined within this element belong to a single item.

```
<section id="location1" itemscope>
  <h1>310 West 38th Street, NY</h1>
  <img src="img/map1.png"
       alt="Joe's Pizza at 310 West 38th Street, NY">
  <p class="location-phone">212 012 3456</p>
  <h2>Opening Hours:</h2>
  <p>
    Mon-Fri: 12:00 - 22:00<br>
    Sat-Sun: 11:00 - 23:00
  </p>
</section>
```

In the case of our restaurant location the itemscope attribute would go on the <section> element. This is because this element contains all of the data related to that specific location.

The itemtype Attribute

The itemtype attribute is used to indicate what an item *is*—it might be a person, a business, or an event, for example. The attribute should contain a URL to a web page that outlines the item schema (the template that defines all the properties that the item can have). A computer program can use this schema to identify which properties it should look for within an item.

```
<section id="location1" itemscope
         itemtype="http://schema.org/LocalBusiness">
  <h1>310 West 38th Street, NY</h1>
  <img src="img/map1.png"
       alt="Joe's Pizza at 310 West 38th Street, NY">
  <p class="location-phone">212 012 3456</p>
  <h2>Opening Hours:</h2>
  <p>
    Mon-Fri: 12:00 - 22:00<br>
    Sat-Sun: 11:00 - 23:00
  </p>
</section>
```

The itemprop Attribute

The itemprop attribute is used to define each of the properties of an item. The value of this attribute should be set to a property name from your chosen schema.

```
<section id="location1" itemscope
        itemtype="http://schema.org/LocalBusiness">
  ...
  <img src="img/map1.png"
      alt="Joe's Pizza at 310 West 38th Street, NY"
      itemprop="image">
  <p class="location-phone" itemprop="phone">
    212 012 3456
  </p>
  ...
</section>
```

If you take a look at the LocalBusiness schema (`http://schema.org/LocalBusiness`) you will notice that two of the properties the item has are `image` and `phone`. Here I have added the `itemprop` attribute to the `<img>` element and the `<p>` element that contains the phone number and have set the value of these attributes to `image` and `phone`.

Usually, the value of the item property will be the text content contained within the element; however, if you are using the `itemprop` attribute on an `<img>`, `<video>`, or `<audio>` element, it will use the value of the `src` attribute. When you use `itemprop` on an `<a>` element it will use the value of the `href` attribute.

LocalBusiness items also have a property called `openingHours`. The opening hours for a business may not be the same for every day of the week. You can accommodate this by having multiple instances of the same property.

```
<section id="location1" itemscope
        itemtype="http://schema.org/LocalBusiness">
  <h1>310 West 38th Street, NY</h1>
  <img src="img/map1.png"
      alt="Joe's Pizza at 310 West 38th Street, NY"
      itemprop="image">
  <p class="location-phone" itemprop="phone">
    212 012 3456
  </p>
  <h2>Opening Hours:</h2>
  <p>
    <time itemprop="openingHours" datetime="Mo-Fr 12:00-22:00">
      Mon-Fri: 12:00 - 22:00
    </time><br>
    <time itemprop="openingHours" datetime="Sa,Su 11:00-23:00">
      Sat-Sun: 11:00 - 23:00
    </time>
  </p>
</section>
```

Notice how the `openingHours` property is used twice in this example.

> Ignore that this example is now using multiple `<time>` elements with `datetime` attributes for now. You will learn why this is the case later in this chapter.

The itemid Attribute

The `itemid` attribute can be used to specify a unique ID for an item. This can then be used by computer programs to determine whether two microdata items actually refer to the same object. This attribute doesn't really apply to the restaurant location example we have been working with as the restaurant doesn't have a unique ID so I'm going to use a different example for the moment.

If I use microdata to mark up information about this book on my website, and Amazon uses microdata to mark up information about this book in its store, and we both used an `itemid` attribute with the same value, a computer program would be able to understand that we are both referring to the same object. The `itemid` should be a unique identifier such as a URL or the ISBN of a book.

```
<div itemscope itemtype="http://schema.org/Book"
     itemid="urn:isbn:978-1-907828-03-4">
  <span itemprop="name">HTML5 Foundations</span> by
  <span itemprop="author">Matt West</span>.
</div>
```

> The "urn" in the `itemid` attribute here is a Uniform Resource Name. This is similar to a URL but only specifies a name for identification purposes and not the location of a resource.

The itemref Attribute

There may be times when a property of the item you are defining lies outside the element with the `itemscope` defined on it. In these cases, the `itemref` attribute can be very useful. The `itemref` attribute can be used to link properties to your item by using a space-separated list of IDs from HTML elements.

Going back to our restaurant location example, each LocalBusiness item should have a name property that defines the company name. This poses a potential issue, as we are displaying three locations on the same page. Rather than adding the company name to each location separately we can add it to the page once and then reference that single HTML element using the `itemref` attribute on each LocalBusiness item. This is what it would look like:

```
<meta id="company-name" itemprop="name" content="Joe's Pizza Co.">

<section id="location1" itemscope
        itemtype="http://schema.org/LocalBusiness"
        itemref="company-name">...</section>

<section id="location2" itemscope
        itemtype="http://schema.org/LocalBusiness"
        itemref="company-name">...</section>

<section id="location3" itemscope
        itemtype="http://schema.org/LocalBusiness"
        itemref="company-name">...</section>
```

Here you have a single element that defines the item name property. This property is then linked to the three LocalBusiness items using the elements ID and `itemref` attributes.

Notice the use of a `<meta>` element here to define the `name` property. This element can be used for much more than just meta keywords, descriptions and charsets. As this element does not display any content to the user it can come in very handy when you want to add some data to your page that is purely for the benefit of computer programs. When using a `<meta>` element to define microdata the value of the item property will be taken from the `content` attribute.

Commonly Used Schemas

Many schemas have been developed by the contributors to the schema.org project. The following sections describe the schemas that you will be using most frequently: LocalBusiness, Event, Person, and Product.

LocalBusiness

Marking up data about a local business and where it is located can be very useful for search engines that display location-aware results to their users. By using microdata for this application, you give search engines more information and therefore increase the chances that they will display this extra information alongside your listing in search results.

For more information about how Google uses microdata in its search results, check out this page on the webmaster tools website: `http://support.google.com/webmasters/bin/answer.py?hl=en&answer=99170`.

You can define a LocalBusiness item using a URL to the schema on schema.org.

```
<div itemscope itemtype="http://schema.org/LocalBusiness"></div>
```

You have already taken a look at some of the properties that a LocalBusiness item can have; however, there are a lot more. I won't bore you with the obscure properties that you will probably never use, but the following list shows the more commonly used ones. You can find the full schema at `http://schema.org/LocalBusiness`.

- name—This is simply the name of the local business.

  ```
  <span itemprop="name">Joe's Pizza Co.</span>
  ```

- description—This property should contain a short description of the business.

  ```
  <p itemprop="description">
      Joe's Pizza Co. offers a fantastic selection of pizzas
      made using traditional techniques.
  </p>
  ```

- image—The image property could contain a photo of the business or the business's logo. In the LocalBusiness item example shown earlier we used the map image as the image property.

  ```
  <img itemprop="image" src="joes-pizza.png"
      alt="A photo of the Joe's Pizza restaurant on Broadway">
  ```

  As the itemprop attribute has been used on an <img> element, computer programs will use the content of the src attribute.

- url—If the business has a website, you can use the url property to specify the web address.

  ```
  <a itemprop="url" href="http://example.com">
      Joe's Pizza Co.</a>
  ```

  Here, computer programs will use the absolute URL found in the href attribute.

- address—To define the address for your LocalBusiness, use the address property. Schema.org provides a separate schema for marking up postal addresses, PostalAddress.

  ```
  <div itemprop="address" itemscope
      itemtype="http://schema.org/PostalAddress">
    <span itemprop="streetAddress">123 Fake Street</span>
    <span itemprop="addressLocality">Town</span>,
    <span itemprop="addressRegion">State</span>,
    <span itemprop="postalCode">P0ST C0D3</span>
  </div>
  ```

Here we have created a nested PostalAddress item that forms the `address` property for your master LocalBusiness item. Nesting microdata items within other items is perfectly fine.

- map—The `map` property should contain a URL to a map of the location. This could be a link to a Google map, for example.

```
<a itemprop="map" href="http://maps.google.com">See map</a>
```

- telephone—As the name suggests, this property is for a telephone number.

```
<span itemprop="telephone">01234 123123</span>
```

- faxNumber—It's a little old school, but I'm told some people still use fax machines.

```
<span itemprop="faxNumber">01234 123124</span>
```

- email—You could either use a <span> element for defining the e-mail, or alternatively, link it up using an <a> element. Both of the following examples would be fine.

```
<a itemprop="email" href="mailto:joe@example.com">
    Email Joe</a>

<span itemprop="email">joe@example.com</a>
```

- openingHours—Defining the opening hours can be a little trickier. Programs will take the data from the `datetime` attribute of a <time> element as the value for the openingHours property. When specifying this property you should first define the day(s) using two-letter representations (Mo, Tu, We, Th, Fr, Sa, Su) and then specify the times.

Here is an example of opening times between 9 a.m. and 5 p.m., Monday to Friday.

```
<time itemprop="openingHours" datetime="Mo-Fr 09:00-17:00">
  Monday to Friday 9am-5pm
</time>
```

Here is an example that uses the same opening hours but is closed on Wednesdays.

```
<time itemprop="openingHours" datetime="Mo,Tu,Th,Fr 09:00-
17:00">
  9am-5pm Weekdays (closed Wednesdays)
</time>
```

Schema.org specifies that you should use two-letter representations for days, but be aware that this will cause your markup validations to fail. This is an example of when achieving 100% validation is not possible.

Using Microdata in Your Restaurant Website

Now that you have an understanding of microdata and how it should be used, take another look at the website you are building for Joe's Pizza. Your Locations page currently contains the information of all three restaurants run by Joe's Pizza Co.

In this example, you are going to use the LocalBusiness item to mark up each restaurant location. To do this, follow these instructions.

The code for this exercise can be found in the download code for Chapter 8, folder 1.

1. Open the `locations.html` file in your text editor.

2. Create a new `<meta>` element below the `<h1>` element in the page text. This will be used to specify the company name.

3. Add an `id` attribute to this `<meta>` element and set its value to be `company-name`.

    `<meta id="company-name">`

4. Now add an `itemprop` attribute and set its value to `name`.

    `<meta id="company-name" itemprop="name">`

5. Finally add a `content` attribute, and set its value to `Joe's Pizza Co.` (including the period). The new line should like this:

    `<meta id="company-name" itemprop="name" content="Joe's Pizza Co.">`

6. Locate the `<section>` elements with the following IDs: `location1`, `location2`, and `location3`.

7. Add the `itemscope` attribute to each of these elements. Remember that you do not need to give this attribute a value.

    `<section id="location1" itemscope>...</section>`

8. Now add an `itemtype` attribute to each of these `<section>` elements and set the values to `http://schema.org/LocalBusiness`.

    `<section id="location1" itemscope itemtype="http://schema.org/LocalBusiness">...</section>`

9. Finally, you need to add an `itemref` attribute to each of the `<section>` elements and set its value to `"company-name"`. This will link the `<meta>` element you created

earlier to each of these LocalBusiness items, therefore setting the company name without the need for three separate elements. Here's the new code for location1:

```
<section id="location1" itemscope
        itemtype="http://schema.org/LocalBusiness"
        itemref="company-name">
```

10. Locate the <h1> element within the first <section> element you found in Step 6.

11. Add the itemprop attribute to this element and set its value to address.

```
<h1 itemprop="address">310 West 38th Street, NY</h1>
```

12. Add the itemscope attribute to this element.

```
<h1 itemprop="address" itemscope>310 West 38th Street, NY</h1>
```

13. Add the itemtype attribute to this element and set its value to http://schema. org/PostalAddress. This creates a new PostalAddress item within your original LocalBusiness item.

```
<h1 itemprop="address" itemscope
    itemtype="http://schema.org/PostalAddress">
  310 West 38th Street, NY
</h1>
```

14. You now need to mark up the address within this <h1> element. Create a new <span> element around the text that comes before the comma (310 West 38th Street).

```
<h1 itemprop="address" itemscope
    itemtype="http://schema.org/PostalAddress">
  <span>310 West 38th Street</span>, NY
</h1>
```

15. Add an itemprop attribute to this <span> element and set its value to streetAddress.

```
<h1 itemprop="address" itemscope
    itemtype="http://schema.org/PostalAddress">
  <span itemprop="streetAddress">310 West 38th Street</span>,
  NY
</h1>
```

16. Create a new <span> element around the state text (NY).

```
<h1 itemprop="address" itemscope
    itemtype="http://schema.org/PostalAddress">
  <span itemprop="streetAddress">310 West 38th Street</span>,
  <span>NY</span>
</h1>
```

17. Add an `itemprop` attribute to this `<span>` element and set its value to `addressRegion`.

```
<h1 itemprop="address" itemscope
    itemtype="http://schema.org/PostalAddress">
  <span itemprop="streetAddress">310 West 38th Street</span>,
  <span itemprop="addressRegion">NY</span>
</h1>
```

18. Now locate the `<img>` element and add an `itemprop` attribute to it. Set the value of this attribute to be `image`.

```
<img src="img/map1.png"
    alt="Joe's Pizza at 310 West 38th Street, NY"
    itemprop="image">
```

19. Locate the `<p>` element that contains the location phone number and add an `itemprop` attribute to it. Set the value of the attribute to be `telephone`.

```
<p class="location-phone" itemprop="telephone">212 012 3456</p>
```

20. You now need to mark up the opening hours. To do this, you need to create a new `<time>` element for each line that specifies opening hours. Create a new `<time>` element and place the human-readable text for the Monday to Friday opening hours between the element tags.

```
<time>Mon-Fri: 12:00 - 22:00</time>
```

21. Add an `itemprop` attribute to this `<time>` element and set its value to `openingHours`.

```
<time itemprop="openingHours">Mon-Fri: 12:00 - 22:00</time>
```

22. Add a `datetime` attribute to the element and set its value to reflect the opening hours; in this case it would be: `Mo-Fr 12:00-22:00`. (See the `opening Hours` bullet earlier in this chapter for help with calculating the value for the `datetime` attribute.)

```
<time itemprop="openingHours" datetime="Mo-Fr 12:00-22:00">
Mon-Fri: 12:00 - 22:00</time>
```

23. Repeat Steps 20 through 22 for each line in the `openingHours` section. Here is how this section should look when you're done.

```
<h2>Opening Hours:</h2>
<p>
  <time itemprop="openingHours" datetime="Mo-Fr 12:00-22:00">
  Mon-Fri: 12:00 - 22:00</time><br>
  <time itemprop="openingHours" datetime="Sa,Su 11:00-23:00">
  Sat-Sun: 11:00 - 23:00</time>
</p>
```

24. Your first item should now be complete. Repeat Steps 10 through 23 for each of the locations in your code.

25. Save the `locations.html` file.

If all went well, you should not see any visual difference when viewing the Locations page in your browser, but a computer program examining your website would now be able to easily extract data about the three restaurant locations from the page. To test this go to `https://www.google.com/webmasters/tools/richsnippets` and copy the code for your Locations page into the textarea. If you click the Preview button you should see that the tool extracts three LocalBusiness items and three PostalAddress items from your HTML, as shown in Figure 8-1.

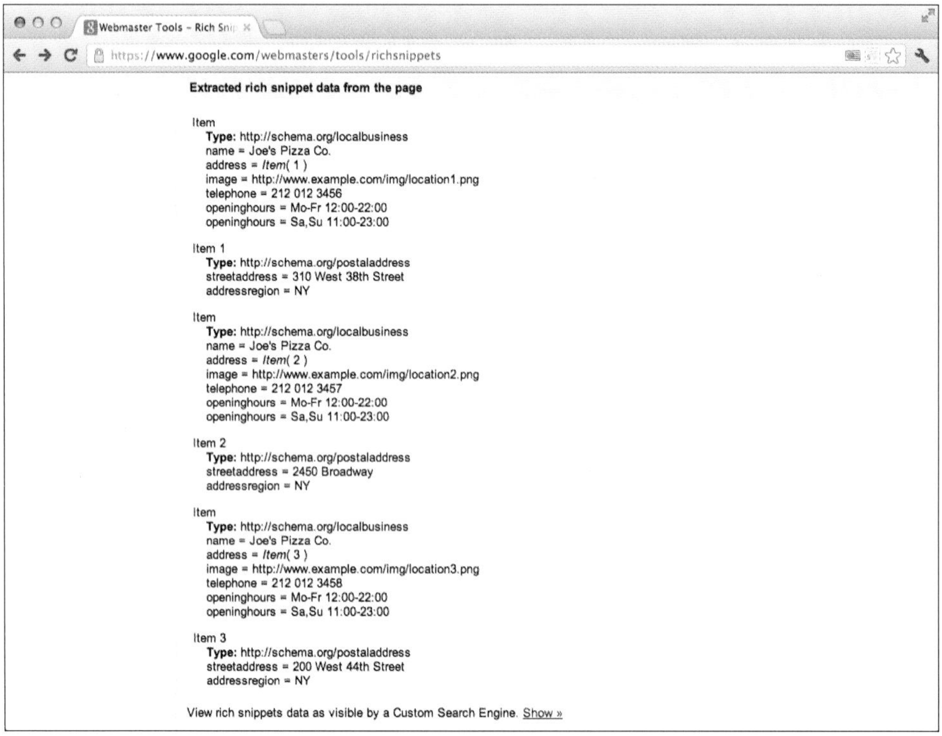

FIGURE 8-1 Extracting microdata from the Locations page using the Google Rich Snippets Tool.

Here is how your updated HTML code should look.

```
<section id="page-text">
  <h1>Locations</h1>
  <meta id="company-name" itemprop="name" content="Joe's Pizza
  Co.">
```

```
<section id="location1" itemscope
         itemtype="http://schema.org/LocalBusiness"
         itemref="company-name">
  <h1 itemprop="address" itemscope
      itemtype="http://schema.org/PostalAddress">
    <span itemprop="streetAddress">310 West 38th Street</span>,
    <span itemprop="addressRegion">NY</span>
  </h1>
  <img src="img/map1.png"
       alt="Joe's Pizza at 310 West 38th Street, NY"
       itemprop="image">
  <p class="location-phone" itemprop="telephone">212 012 3456</p>
  <h2>Opening Hours:</h2>
  <p>
    <time itemprop="openingHours" datetime="Mo-Fr 12:00-22:00">
    Mon-Fri: 12:00 - 22:00</time><br>
    <time itemprop="openingHours" datetime="Sa,Su 11:00-23:00">
    Sat-Sun: 11:00 - 23:00</time>
  </p>
</section>

<section id="location2" itemscope
         itemtype="http://schema.org/LocalBusiness"
         itemref="company-name">
  <h1 itemprop="address" itemscope
      itemtype="http://schema.org/PostalAddress">
    <span itemprop="streetAddress">2450 Broadway</span>,
    <span itemprop="addressRegion">NY</span>
  </h1>
  <img src="img/map2.png"
       alt="Joe's Pizza at 2450 Broadway, NY"
       itemprop="image">
  <p class="location-phone" itemprop="telephone">212 012 3457</p>
  <h2>Opening Hours:</h2>
  <p>
    <time itemprop="openingHours" datetime="Mo-Fr 12:00-22:00">
    Mon-Fri: 12:00 - 22:00</time><br>
    <time itemprop="openingHours" datetime="Sa,Su 11:00-23:00">
    Sat-Sun: 11:00 - 23:00</time>
  </p>
</section>

<section id="location3" itemscope
         itemtype="http://schema.org/LocalBusiness"
         itemref="company-name">
  <h1 itemprop="address" itemscope
```

```
        itemtype="http://schema.org/PostalAddress">
      <span itemprop="streetAddress">200 West 44th Street</span>,
      <span itemprop="addressRegion">NY</span>
    </h1>
    <img src="img/map3.png"
         alt="Joe's Pizza at 200 West 44th Street, NY"
         itemprop="image">
    <p class="location-phone" itemprop="telephone">212 012 3458</p>
    <h2>Opening Hours:</h2>
    <p>
      <time itemprop="openingHours" datetime="Mo-Fr 12:00-22:00">
      Mon-Fri: 12:00 - 22:00</time><br>
      <time itemprop="openingHours" datetime="Sa,Su 11:00-23:00">
      Sat-Sun: 11:00 - 23:00</time>
    </p>
  </section>
</section>
```

Now that you are finished with the Locations page, take a look at the rest of the pages on the website. Are there any other areas of content that you think would benefit from the use of microdata? Try adding microdata to those areas (you might need to read the rest of this chapter first).

Events

Marking up your events data enables computer programs to use this data for a number of possible applications. For example, imagine if when you did a web search for an event, the important details about the event appeared right there in the search results, saving you the job of having to find the correct link in the results and then scan the web page for details about the event. That could be really useful.

Google already does something similar to this. If you search for your favorite sports team Google will show you a summary of recent results and upcoming games above the normal search results.

Every October Joe's Pizza Co. runs a number of special events in celebration of national Italian-American heritage month. In this section you learn how to use microdata to mark up one of these events.

You can define an event by using the Event schema.

```
<div itemscope itemtype="http://schema.org/Event"></div>
```

Events have the same four basic properties that all schema.org items have: name, description, image, and url, plus the properties outlined in the following list.

- startDate—Your `startDate` should be supplied in a machine-readable format. It's usually best to use a `<time>` element when specifying dates and times with microdata. Computer programs will use the contents of the `datetime` attribute. The Joe's Pizza Co. event will start at 9am on Saturday 5th October.

```html
<time itemprop="startDate" datetime="2013-10-05T09:00">
  Saturday 5th October at 9am
</time>
```

> Refer to the "Dates and Times" section in Chapter 4 for more information about machine-readable datetime formats.

- endDate—The `endDate` should follow the same rules as the `startDate`. The Joe's Pizza Co. event is a one-day event that finishes at 5:30pm.

```html
<time itemprop="endDate" datetime="2013-10-05T17:30">
  Saturday 5th October at 5:30pm
</time>
```

- duration—The `duration` should also be specified using a machine-readable time.

```html
<time itemprop="duration" datetime="T8H30M">
  8 Hours and 30 Minutes
</time>
```

The `datetime` attribute here uses a T to specify that this is a time, followed by the number of hours and an H character (signifying hours), and finishes with the number of minutes followed by an M character (signifying minutes).

- location—The `location` property should be either a PostalAddress or Place item. The Joe's Pizza Co. event will be held at the restaurant on Broadway.

```html
<div itemprop="location" itemscope
     itemtype="http://schema.org/PostalAddress">
  <span itemprop="streetAddress">2450 Broadway</span>,
  <span itemprop="addressRegion">NY<span>
</div>
```

- performer—You can also include a list of performers who are going to be at the event. These could be musicians, speakers, or actors, for example. These should be marked up using either the Person or Organization item. For our event some of the chefs will be participating in an extreme pizza tossing demonstration, so we can add them to the event as performers.

```html
<ul>
  <li itemprop="performer" itemscope
      itemtype="http://schema.org/Person">
    <span itemprop="name">Giorgio Giove</span>
  </li>
```

```
      <li itemprop="performer" itemscope
          itemtype="http://schema.org/Person">
        <span itemprop="name">Joe Balochio</span>
      </li>
    </ul>
```

Here, we have defined two performers for the Joe's Pizza Co. event, using the `per-former` property and Person items.

- attendee—Websites such as lanyrd.com hold lists of all the people who have booked onto events so that you can see if anybody you know is going. This has become quite a popular feature, especially within the web industry.

  Using the `attendee` property, you can mark up all this data so that it is useful for computer programs, too. Here's how we would add attendees to our event:

```
    <ul>
      <li itemprop="attendee" itemscope
          itemtype="http://schema.org/Person">
        <span itemprop="name">Matt West</span><br>
        <a itemprop="url" href="http://twitter.com/MattAntWest">
          @MattAntWest
        </a>
      </li>
      <li itemprop="attendee" itemscope
          itemtype="http://schema.org/Person">
        <span itemprop="name">Tom Meier</span><br>
        <a itemprop="url" href="http://twitter.com/pommytom">
          @pommytom
        </a>
      </li>
    </ul>
```

  Here we have defined two attendees, with a link to their Twitter profiles. This link also acts as the `url` property for the Person item.

- subEvent—If you were planning a big event, such as a music festival, you might have a number of smaller events take place during the main event. You can use microdata to define these by nesting Event objects using the `subEvent` property.

  We could also use subevents to mark up the different activities that will be taking place during the Joe's Pizza Co. event.

```
    <div itemprop="subEvent" itemscope
         itemtype="http://schema.org/Event">
      <span itemprop="name">Extreme Pizza Tossing</span><br>
      Starts <time itemprop="startDate" datetime="2013-10-
      05T12:00"> 12 noon on Saturday</time>
    </div>
```

Here, we have defined a subevent for the extreme pizza tossing demonstration.

- superEvent—A super event is the opposite of a subevent (but you already figured that out). If we had a web page that was solely dedicated to the extreme pizza tossing demonstration we could link this subevent to the main event by defining a superevent using the superEvent property.

```
<div itemprop="superEvent" itemscope
    itemtype="http://schema.org/Event">
  <span itemprop="name">Joe's Pizza Co. Family Fun Day</span>
</div>
```

An Example Event

It's time to put all of this together into a full example. Here is the Joe's Pizza Co. event in all its glory.

```
<div itemscope itemtype="http://schema.org/Event">
  <h1 itemprop="name">Joe's Pizza Co. Family Fun Day</h1>
  <img src="family-fun-day.png" alt="A family at Joe's Pizza"
  itemptop="image">
  <p itemprop="description">
    In celebration of national American-Italian heritage month,
    Joe's Pizza Co. will be hosting a family fun day at its
    restaurant on Broadway. Come along for the day and take part in
    exciting activities like extreme pizza tossing!
  </p>
  <p>
    Starts: <time itemprop="startDate" datetime="2013-10-05T09:00">
    Saturday 5th October at 9am</time><br>
    Ends: <time itemprop="endDate" datetime="2013-10-05T17:30">
    Saturday 5th October at 5:30pm</time><br>
    Duration: <time itemprop="duration" datetime="T8H30M">
    8 Hours and 30 Minutes</time>
  </p>

  <h2>Activities</h2>
  <div itemprop="subEvent" itemscope
      itemtype="http://schema.org/Event">
    <span itemprop="name">Welcome from Joe</span><br>
    Starts <time itemprop="startDate" datetime="2013-10-05T09:00">
    9am on Saturday</time>
  </div>
  <div itemprop="subEvent" itemscope
      itemtype="http://schema.org/Event">
    <span itemprop="name">Italian Food Tasting</span><br>
    Starts <time itemprop="startDate" datetime="2013-10-05T09:30">
    9:30am on Saturday</time>
```

```
    </div>
    <div itemprop="subEvent" itemscope
        itemtype="http://schema.org/Event">
      <span itemprop="name">Extreme Pizza Tossing</span><br>
      Starts <time itemprop="startDate" datetime="2013-10-05T12:00">
      12 noon on Saturday</time>
    </div>

    <h2>Performers</h2>
    <ul>
      <li itemprop="performer" itemscope
          itemtype="http://schema.org/Person">
        <span itemprop="name">Giorgio Giove</span>
      </li>
      <li itemprop="performer" itemscope
          itemtype="http://schema.org/Person">
        <span itemprop="name">Joe Balochio</span>
      </li>
    </ul>

    <h2>Attendees</h2>
    <ul>
      <li itemprop="attendee" itemscope
          itemtype="http://schema.org/Person">
        <span itemprop="name">Matt West</span><br>
        <a itemprop="url" href="http://twitter.com/MattAntWest">
          @MattAntWest
        </a>
      </li>
      <li itemprop="attendee" itemscope
          itemtype="http://schema.org/Person">
        <span itemprop="name">Tom Meier</span><br>
        <a itemprop="url" href="http://twitter.com/pommytom">
          @pommytom
        </a>
      </li>
    </ul>
</div>
```

Here we have defined an event complete with subevents, performers, and attendees.

Person

Schema.org has a specific schema for the Person item. Again, I have omitted some of the more obscure properties, but you can see them all at `http://schema.org/Person`.

- givenName—When defining a person's name, you can use more specific properties than the general name property. The givenName (or first name) is one of these.

  ```
  <span itemprop="givenName">Joe</span>
  ```

- additionalName—The additionalName property can be used for a person's middle name.

  ```
  <span itemprop="additionalName">Antonio</span>
  ```

- familyName—Finally, there is a property for the family name.

  ```
  <span itemprop="familyName">Balochio</span>
  ```

- gender—You can also specify a person's gender.

  ```
  <span itemprop="gender">Male</span>
  ```

- birthDate—A birthDate can be a very useful piece of data. From a birth date, you can calculate someone's age and birthday.

  ```
  <time itemprop="birthDate" datetime="1966-10-06">
    6th October 1966
  </time>
  ```

- deathDate—If you are creating a history website, you might find the deathDate property useful.

  ```
  <time itemprop="deathDate" datetime="1920-01-23">
    23rd January 1920
  </time>
  ```

The Person item also has properties for defining contact details: telephone, faxNumber, and email. You can see how to use these properties in the example of a LocalBusiness item.

Example Person

Here is an example of a Person item that uses the details of our friend Joe Balochio.

```
<div itemscope itemtype="http://schema.org/Person">
  <h1 itemprop="name">
    <span itemprop="givenName">Joe</span>
    <span itemprop="additionalName">Antonio</span>
    <span itemprop="familyName">Balochio</span>
  </h1>
  <p>
    Born: <time itemprop="birthDate" datetime="1966-10-06">
    6th October 1966</time><br>
    Gender: <span itemprop="gender">Male</span>
  </p>
  <h2>Contact Details</h2>
```

```
    <p>
      Telephone: <span itemprop="telephone">01234 123123</span><br>
      Fax Number: <span itemprop="faxNumber">01234 123124</span><br>
      Email: <a itemprop="email" href="mailto:joe@example.com">
      joe@example.com</a>
    </p>
</div>
```

In this example, I have placed the `givenName`, `additionalName`, and `familyName` properties within an `<h1>` element that defines the more general name property.

Here is how this example would look to a computer program.

```
name: Joe Antonio Balochio
givenName: Joe
additionalName: Antonio
familyName: Balochio
birthDate: 1966-10-06
gender: Male
telephone: 01234 123123
faxNumber: 01234 123124
email: joe@example.com
```

Product

The last item type that you are going to look at is Product. As with all other items, the Product schema has the same basic name, `description`, `image`, and `url` properties as well as some more specific properties.

You are going to be using the Product schema available from schema.org:

```
<div itemscope itemtype="http://schema.org/Product"></div>
```

- `productID`—The `productID` property can be used to define the unique ID of a product, such as an ISBN.

  ```
  <meta itemprop="productID" content="isbn:978-1118356555">
  ```

  In this example, I have used the `<meta>` element to define the ID of the product. As I mentioned earlier, this will not display anything to the user but will be useful for computer programs.

- brand—The brand property should contain an Organization item (`http://schema.org/Organization`).

```
<div itemprop="brand" itemscope
    itemtype="http://schema.org/Organization">
    <span itemprop="name">Joe's Pizza Co.</span>
</div>
```

- model—The `model` property should just be some text. This could be the model number of the product or the name of a particular model in a range of products.

```
Model Number: <span itemprop="model">147JFK932</span>
```

- manufacturer—The manufacturer property should contain an Organization item (`http://schema.org/Organization`).

```
<div itemprop="manufacturer" itemscope
     itemtype="http://schema.org/Organization">
  <span itemprop="name">ACME Co.</span>
</div>
```

Example Product

Here is an example of a Product item (to be more accurate, it's the lamp sitting on my desk).

```
<div itemscope itemtype="http://schema.org/Product">
    <h1 itemprop="name">Anglepoise Desk Lamp</h1>
  <figure>
    <img itemprop="image" src="desk-lamp.png"
         alt="A silver Anglepoise desk lamp">
  </figure>
  <p itemprop="description">
    A desk lamp designed by Kenneth Grange, a leading British
    industrial designer.
  </p>
  <h2>Product Specifications</h2>
  <p>
    Brand: <span itemprop="brand manufacturer" itemscope
                 itemtype="http://schema.org/Organization">
            <span itemprop="name">Anglepoise</span>
          </span><br>
    Model: <span itemprop="model">Type 75</span>
  </p>
</div>
```

Here the brand and manufacturer properties are the same, so we can define them both using a single itemprop attribute.

Summary

Microdata promises to reduce the headache for developers who are trying to create programs that can mine data from web pages. Moving toward a more semantic web can only be a good thing, but using microdata does not really eradicate this headache: It merely redistributes it.

Instead of the problem being in the realm of a relatively small number of developers building highly complex algorithms for understanding the data hidden away within web pages, it is being distributed among all the developers who are creating websites. Using microdata increases development overhead in both time and complexity. I am a big supporter of microdata, but I fear it may meet its demise because of the overhead issues.

The truth is, we have to find a healthy balance between creating pages that are easy for computers to understand and creating pages that are maintainable. The more you use microdata, the more complex your code becomes, and this can make it harder to maintain. For this reason, I recommend that you only use microdata for marking up structured data that is important, such as contact information or product specifications. Don't bloat your pages with microdata code unless you feel that it's going to have a positive, productive impact.

In Chapter 9, you look at how to make your web pages more accessible for users who have disabilities. You learn about the tools that these individuals use in order to browse websites—and how you can make your websites work well with these tools.

chapter nine

Ensuring Accessibility

JOE WANTS TO make sure that all the visitors to his new website can check out the menu, find special offers, and place a booking online. Sometimes, it is easy to forget that not all users can enjoy the same rich experience as we do when browsing a website. For users with visual or motor impairments, browsing the web can actually be quite a difficult task. We need to make sure that we build accessibility features into the Joe's Pizza Co. website so that these users can easily read the content and navigate the pages.

Accessibility is affected by both your markup and your visual design. In this chapter, you focus on the markup side of this problem. You learn how to write markup that makes your websites more accessible to assistive technologies such as screen readers. It's no good learning about the principles of accessibility if you have no way to test them, so this chapter also covers a variety of tools that you can use to test both your website markup and visual design.

Why Is Accessibility Important?

Building websites that are accessible is crucial to maintaining a web that anyone can use, regardless of whether he or she has a disability. This section addresses three major reasons why you should ensure that your websites are accessible.

Reason #1: It's the Right Thing to Do

Making your websites accessible is simply the right thing to do. As a web developer, you should carefully consider your entire audience, not only the typical user, but the entire spectrum. What if your user is blind? How will she be able to access your content?

Think about the other extreme "power users" who might use your web applications multiple times a day and will want features like keyboard shortcuts so that they can accomplish tasks quickly. This functionality is also useful for people with motor impairments who may not be able to use a mouse.

Reason #2: It Leads to Best Practices and Better Code

Creating accessible websites means you will follow recognized web standards. This means picking up coding best practices that will make your web pages more accessible and improve your overall coding abilities. Everybody wins!

A big part of a web developer's job is considering all possible situations and creating applications that can handle all these edge cases. Incorporating accessibility features to serve your entire audience is a valuable skill that can serve you well as you learn more about web technologies.

Reason #3: It Fulfills Legal Requirements

Disclaimer: I'm not a lawyer, so none of this should be taken as legal advice.

Many countries have laws requiring that certain organizations make their web applications and websites accessible to users with disabilities. In 1998, the U.S. Congress amended the Rehabilitation Act of 1973 with section 508, requiring Federal agencies to make their electronic information accessible to all. The U.K. has a British Standard (BS8878) that makes non-technical recommendations about how web applications should be made accessible. However, unlike in the United States, this is just a standard and not the law.

Many of these laws and standards are based around the Web Content Accessibility Guidelines (WCAG) published by the World Wide Web Consortium (W3C). This specification outlines the principles that web developers should follow in order to create accessible websites.

You can view the full WCAG (version 2.0) specification on the W3C website at
http://www.w3.org/WAI/intro/wcag.php.

Screen Readers

Browsing the web can be a challenging experience for users with visual impairments. Depending on the level of the impairment, these users may use a computer program called a *screen reader* to navigate between pages and consume content. Screen readers read aloud the page content and enable users to browse using only their keyboard. This means that developers have a responsibility to create websites that can easily be understood by screen readers.

Take a look at some of the most popular screen readers in the following list. I recommend you download or activate a tool appropriate for your operating system so you can test your code as you add accessibility features to your website.

- **Apple Voice Over**—Apple's Mac OS X operating system comes with a built-in screen reader called VoiceOver (`http://www.apple.com/accessibility/voiceover/`). This program enables users to navigate their laptop or desktop computer using a number of keyboard shortcuts. You can activate VoiceOver using a keyboard shortcut: Cmd + F5.

- **Orca for Linux**—The most popular screen reader amongst Linux users is Orca (`http://projects.gnome.org/orca/`). Orca is a free and open-source piece of screen reading software that was originally developed by Sun Microsystems to enable users with disabilities to access the various programs on their computer (not just websites).

  Linux distributions that use the GNOME desktop environment, such as Ubuntu, often come with Orca preinstalled. The program can be accessed from the main menu or the new unity launcher in the latest versions of Ubuntu.

- **NVDA for Windows**—For Windows users, there is a free and open-source screen reader called NVDA, for Non-Visual Desktop Access. You can download NVDA from the project's website at `http://www.nvda-project.org`.

Figure 9-1 shows VoiceOver in action. Notice how the program highlights the text that is currently being spoken by placing a thick black box around it. The semi-transparent black box at the bottom of this screenshot shows the text the screen reader spoke.

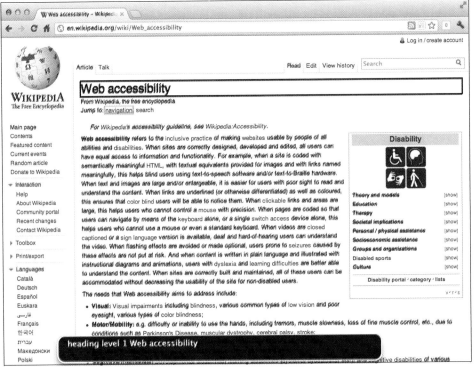

The content inside the browser screenshot reads:

en.wikipedia.org/wiki/Web_accessibility

Log in / create account

Article Talk   Read Edit View history   Search

Web accessibility
From Wikipedia, the free encyclopedia
Jump to: navigation, search

For Wikipedia's accessibility guideline, see Wikipedia:Accessibility.

Web accessibility refers to the inclusive practice of making websites usable by people of all abilities and disabilities. When sites are correctly designed, developed and edited, all users can have equal access to information and functionality. For example, when a site is coded with semantically meaningful HTML, with textual equivalents provided for images and with links named meaningfully, this helps blind users using text-to-speech software and/or text-to-Braille hardware. When text and images are large and/or enlargeable, it is easier for users with poor sight to read and understand the content. When links are underlined (or otherwise differentiated) as well as coloured, this ensures that color blind users will be able to notice them. When clickable links and areas are large, this helps users who cannot control a mouse with precision. When pages are coded so that users can navigate by means of the keyboard alone, or a single switch access device alone, this helps users who cannot use a mouse or even a standard keyboard. When videos are closed captioned or a sign language version is available, deaf and hard-of-hearing users can understand the video. When flashing effects are avoided or made optional, users prone to seizures caused by these effects are not put at risk. And when content is written in plain language and illustrated with instructional diagrams and animations, users with dyslexia and learning difficulties are better able to understand the content. When sites are correctly built and maintained, all of these users can be accommodated without decreasing the usability of the site for non-disabled users.

The needs that Web accessibility aims to address include:

- **Visual:** Visual impairments including blindness, various common types of low vision and poor eyesight, various types of color blindness;
- **Motor/Mobility:** e.g. difficulty or inability to use the hands, including tremors, muscle slowness, loss of fine muscle control, etc., due to conditions such as Parkinson's Disease, muscular dystrophy, cerebral palsy, stroke;

heading level 1 Web accessibility

Sidebar panel:

Disability

Theory and models   [show]
Education   [show]
Therapy   [show]
Societal implications   [show]
Personal / physical assistance [show]
Socioeconomic assistance   [show]
Groups and organizations   [show]
Disabled sports   [show]
Culture   [show]

Disability portal · category · lists

Left navigation:
Main page
Contents
Featured content
Current events
Random article
Donate to Wikipedia

▼ Interaction
  Help
  About Wikipedia
  Community portal
  Recent changes
  Contact Wikipedia

▶ Toolbox
▶ Print/export
▼ Languages
  Català
  Deutsch
  Español
  Euskara
  فارسی
  Français
  한국어
  עברית
  Македонски
  Polski

FIGURE 9-1 The VoiceOver screen reader in action.

Screen readers can be tricky to use at first, and the keyboard shortcuts for using them vary depending on which screen reader you use. As you progress through this chapter, you need to use a screen reader to test out the accessibility modifications that you make to the Joe's Pizza Co. website. So select one and activate or install it now. The following list provides links to the user guides for the three screen readers mentioned in this book:

- **Apple Voice Over**—http://help.apple.com/voiceover/info/guide/10.8/English.lproj/index.html

- **Orca**—http://library.gnome.org/users/gnome-access-guide/2.32/gnome-access-guide.html#enable-orca

- **NVDA**—http://www.nvda-project.org/documentation/userGuide.html

The Treehouse website has a great video that covers all these screen readers in a bit more detail: http://teamtreehouse.com/library/websites/accessibility/websites/screen-readers.

HTML5 Semantic Markup

In order for screen readers to operate effectively, they need to be able to identify key areas on the page, such as the navigation or main content section. HTML5 aims to make this task easier with the introduction of new semantic markup.

The new HTML5 elements such as `<header>`, `<nav>`, and `<article>` can help computer programs identify the location of key content on a web page. As the HTML5 specification explicitly defines what sort of content should be contained within these elements, computer programs can make an educated guess that a `<nav>` element on a page contains the navigation links, for example.

In theory, this concept works great, but in reality many screen readers are not yet harnessing the full potential of these new semantic elements. Instead, many screen readers rely on something called *WAI-ARIA landmark roles*. WAI-ARIA is an accessibility standard that was developed before HTML5 existed. The landmark roles defined in this specification do essentially the same job as the new HTML5 semantic elements; however, instead of using special element tags, they use `role` attributes on standard HTML elements. For this book, you focus on using pure HTML5 to define the key areas on your pages. (You already did this when you created the page templates using HTML5 elements.) Some screen readers don't have fantastic support for the pure HTML5 approach yet, but it is getting better.

If you are interested in learning more about WAI-ARIA landmark roles, check out Opera's guide at `http://dev.opera.com/articles/view/introduction-to-wai-aria/#landmarks`.

Making Web Forms Accessible

Web forms can pose a problem for users who rely on screen readers. If your forms are not accessible, it can be hard for users to navigate through your form fields or actually input data. This section shows you two ways to make your web forms more accessible to users with disabilities.

Using Labels

One of the best ways to make your web forms more accessible is to make sure that you use labels with all your form controls. Chapter 5 looks at labels more in-depth, but here's a quick refresher.

You use the `<label>` elements for attribute to assign an `<input>` element using the ID of that `<input>` element, like this:

```
<label for="name">Name:</label>
<input type="text" name="name" id="name">
```

Using labels offers two accessibility benefits. First, although users with visual impairments may not be able to read the screen, if you include a label, a screen reader can tell the user what to input into a form field by reading the label aloud. The other main benefit is for users who have motor impairments and may not be able to control their mouse precisely. When you assign a label to an input, that label becomes a click target for the form field. So if a user clicks the label, the browser focuses or checks the linked <input> element. This is especially useful for checkbox and radio inputs because these form controls are small targets for a user to click on.

Here is an extract of the form from your Bookings page. Notice how you already assigned a <label> to each <input> element:

```
<form action="bookings.php" method="POST">
  <fieldset>
    <legend>Contact Details</legend>
    <div class="field">
      <label for="name">Name*:</label>
      <input type="text" name="name" id="name"
             placeholder="e.g. Joe Balochio" autofocus required
             maxlength="65">
    </div>
    <div class="field">
      <label for="phone">Phone*:</label>
      <input type="tel" name="phone" id="phone"
             placeholder="e.g. 000-000-0000"
             pattern="[0-9]{3}[-][0-9]{3}[-][0-9]{4}" required
             title="Please provide your phone number in the
             following format: 000-000-0000">
    </div>
    <div class="field">
      <label for="email">Email*:</label>
      <input type="email" name="email" id="email"
             placeholder="e.g. joe@example.com" required>
    </div>
  </fieldset>
  ...
</form>
```

View the Bookings page in your web browser and try clicking on one of the text labels. You should see that the input field gains focus.

The tabindex Attribute

Users can navigate your web forms by using the Tab key to move between form fields. This feature is popular with power users, but it is also very useful for users with disabilities.

The order in which these form fields are focused is determined by the order of the HTML elements in the code. The default order is usually fine; but there may be times when you need to change this tab order without rearranging the elements in your code. You can do this using the `tabindex` attribute.

The `tabindex` attribute for each element should contain a number that represents that particular element's position in the tab order, starting at 1 for the first element.

To illustrate this, you are going to add the `tabindex` attribute to the form fields in your bookings form.

You can download the code used in this book from the book's website at `http://wiley.com/go/treehouse/html5foundations`. The code for this exercise can be found in the download code for Chapter 9, folder 1.

Here are the steps to follow:

1. Open the `bookings.html` file in your text editor.

2. Add `tabindex` attributes to each of the form fields as I have done in the following code extract. Notice that the `tabindex` values do not follow a sequential order.

```
<form action="bookings.php" method="POST">
  <p class="validation-tip">
    * indicates a required field.
  </p>
  <fieldset>
    <legend>Contact Details</legend>
    <div class="field">
      <label for="name">Name*:</label>
      <input type="text" name="name" id="name"
             placeholder="e.g. Joe Balochio" autofocus required
             maxlength="65" tabindex="1">
    </div>
    <div class="field">
      <label for="phone">Phone*:</label>
      <input type="tel" name="phone" id="phone"
             placeholder="e.g. 000-000-0000"
             pattern="[0-9]{3}[-][0-9]{3}[-][0-9]{4}" required
             title="Please provide your phone number in the
             following format: 000-000-0000" tabindex="2">
    </div>
    <div class="field">
      <label for="email">Email*:</label>
```

```html
        <input type="email" name="email" id="email"
                placeholder="e.g. joe@example.com" required
                tabindex="3">
    </div>
  </fieldset>
  <fieldset>
    <legend>Booking Information</legend>
    <div class="field">
      <label for="restaurant">Restaurant*:</label>
      <select name="restaurant" id="restaurant" required
                tabindex="8">
        <option>310 West 38th Street, NY</option>
        <option>2450 Broadway, NY</option>
        <option>200 West 44th Street, NY</option>
      </select>
    </div>
    <div class="field">
      <label for="bookingTime">Booking Time*:</label>
      <input type="datetime-local" name="bookingTime"
                id="bookingTime" tabindex="7"
                placeholder="e.g. 2012-09-06 12:14" required>
    </div>
    <div class="field">
      <label for="guests">Number of Guests*:</label>
      <input type="number" name="guests" id="guests" value="2"
                required min="1" max="12" tabindex="6">
    </div>
    <div class="field">
      <label for="marketing">Please tick this box if you
      would like to receive special offers from Joe's
      Pizza Co.</label>
      <input type="checkbox" name="marketing" id="marketing"
                value="1" tabindex="5">
    </div>
    <div class="field">
      <label for="message">Special Requests:</label>
      <textarea name="message" id="message" cols="50" rows="10"
                placeholder="Type your message..."
                maxlength="250" tabindex="4"></textarea>
    </div>
  </fieldset>
  <div class="field">
    <button type="submit" tabindex="9">Request Booking</button>
  </div>
</form>
```

3. Save the `bookings.html` file.

4. Open the `bookings.html` file in your web browser and use the Tab key to cycle through the form fields. You should encounter the following order: Name, Phone, Email, Message, Marketing, Guests, Booking Time, Restaurant, and Submit.

5. Now go back to your text editor and update the `tabindex` attributes so that the values are in a sequential order from 1 to 9.

6. Save the `bookings.html` file.

Check out this video on Treehouse for a quick recap on making your web forms accessible: `http://teamtreehouse.com/library/websites/accessibility/web-apps/forms`.

Making Tables Accessible

In addition to making your web forms accessible, you should ensure that your tables are accessible, too. Assistive technologies such as screen readers should be able to process your tables, but often tabular data does not make much sense unless you first explain what it shows.

You can enhance accessibility in your tables in a number of ways, as demonstrated in this section.

The caption Element

You can place the `<caption>` element at the beginning of a table to describe what that table displays. Screen readers read this text before the tabular data to give the user an understanding of what the table shows before the screen reader gets to the data.

Currently, none of the tables used on the Menu page has captions. Let's change that.

The code for this exercise can be found in folder 2.

Follow these steps:

1. Open the `menu.html` file in your text editor.

2. Find the `<table>` element with the ID `pizzas`.

3. Create a new <caption> element at the top of this table, as in the following code:

```
<table id="pizzas">
  <caption>
    Our fantastic range of pizzas presented here has won us 6
    awards over the past 2 years.
  </caption>
  . . .
</table>
```

4. Find the <table> element with the ID garlic-bread.

5. Create a new <caption> element at the top of this table:

```
<table id="garlic-bread">
  <caption>
    These handmade garlic breads are the best you will find
    anywhere in New York.
  </caption>
  . . .
</table>
```

6. Find the <table> element with the ID sides.

7. Create a new <caption> element at the top of this table:

```
<table id="sides">
  <caption>
    How about trying one of these tasty side dishes with your
    meal?
  </caption>
  . . .
</table>
```

8. Save your menu.html file.

Each of your menu tables should now have a <caption> element that contains text describing the content of the table. If you view the menu page in your browser, you should also see that these captions are displayed to the user, as shown in Figure 9-2.

Now let your screen reader read out the page content. The screen reader should read out the caption before the table data, giving the user more information about what the data in the table represents.

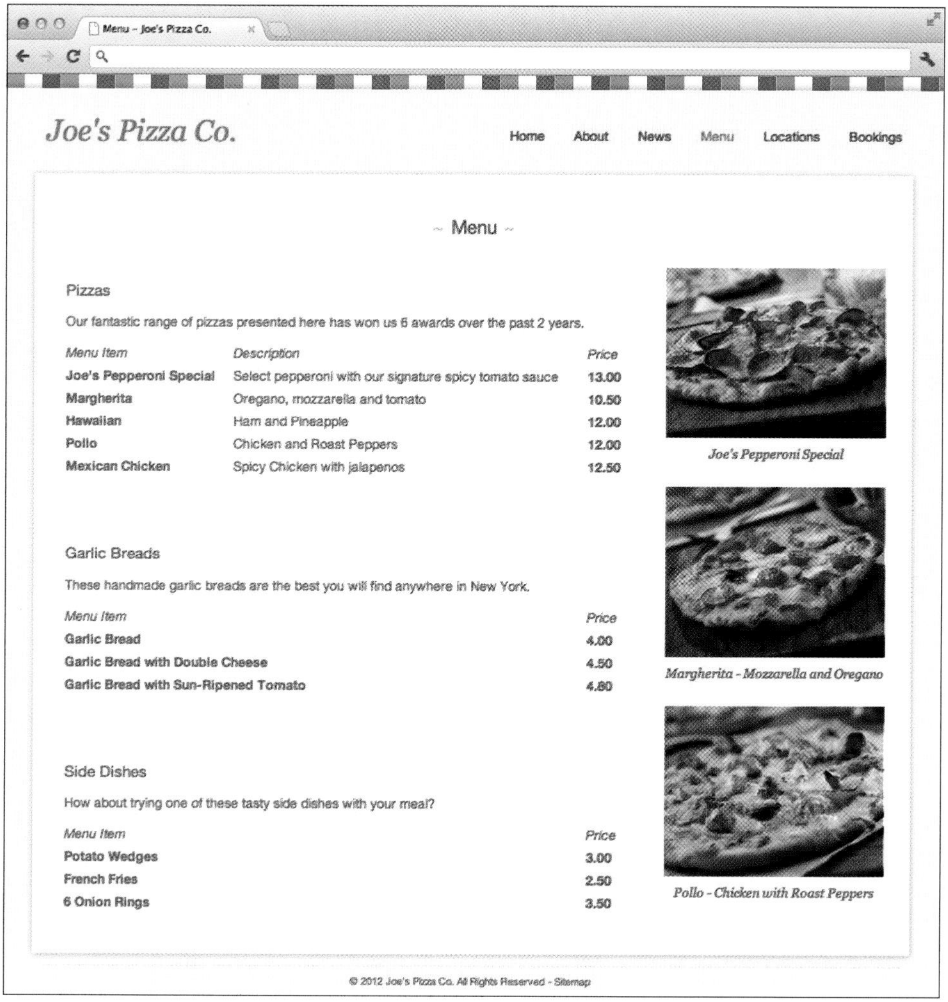

FIGURE 9-2 The menu tables with captions.
Pizza images reproduced by permission of iStockphoto.com/Lauri Patterson

Scoped Table Headers

Using table headers (`<th>` elements) makes it easier for screen readers to identify row and column headings, which is fantastic, but you can even go one step further. You can use the `scope` attribute to indicate whether the table header refers to the content in the same column or the same row as the header.

First, you need to add scopes to the column headers in each of your menu tables.

The code for this exercise can be found in folder 3.

Here are the steps:

1. Open the menu.html file in your text editor.

2. Find the <table> element with the ID pizzas.

3. Apply the scope attribute to each of the <th> elements within the <thead>, and set the values to col.

```
<table id="pizzas">
  <caption>...</caption>
  <thead>
    <tr>
      <th scope="col">Menu Item</th>
      <th scope="col">Description</th>
      <th scope="col">Price</th>
    </tr>
  </thead>
  <tbody>...</tbody>
</table>
```

4. Now repeat Step 3 for the garlic bread and sides menu tables.

```
<table id="garlic-bread">
  <caption>...</caption>
  <thead>
    <tr>
      <th scope="col">Menu Item</th>
      <th scope="col">Price</th>
    </tr>
  </thead>
  <tbody>...</tbody>
</table>

<table id="sides">
  <caption>...</caption>
  <thead>
    <tr>
      <th scope="col">Menu Item</th>
      <th scope="col">Price</th>
    </tr>
```

```
  </thead>
  <tbody>...</tbody>
</table>
```

5. Save the menu.html file.

If you view the menu.html file in your browser, you won't see any visible difference, but screen readers can now get a better understanding of your tables.

Try using the screen reader to read out the table. Close your eyes and try to visualize the table in your head as the screen reader goes through the various table cells. Can you see how using table headers and captions help you build a more complete picture of the table?

In addition to applying scoped column headings to the table, you can go one step further and mark up the first cell in each row to be a table heading. This is because all the data in the rest of the cells in the row relates back to the item named in the first cell. Making this change can help computer programs identify that the data is related. To specify that a table heading is related to the data in that row, you need to set the value of the scope attribute to row.

The code for this exercise can be found in folder 4.

Here are the steps:

1. Open your menu.html file in your text editor again.

2. Find the first row within the <tbody> element in your pizzas table.

3. Change the first <td> element in this row to be a <th> element instead.

4. Now add a scope attribute to this element and set its value to row. Here's how the code for your updated row should look:

```
<tr>
  <th scope="row">Joe's Pepperoni Special</th>
  <td>
    Select pepperoni with our signature spicy tomato sauce
  </td>
  <td>13.00</td>
</tr>
```

5. Now repeat Steps 3 and 4 for each of the rows in all of your menu tables.

6. Save the menu.html file.

The stylesheet I provide does not apply any additional styling to these `<th>` elements, so you should still see what is shown in Figure 9-2. However, your table rows are now a lot more accessible to screen readers.

Throughout this section, you implemented a number of techniques to make your Menu page more accessible. This includes using both `<caption>` elements and scoped table headers. It can sometimes seem like a lot of extra work to add these in. But now you can rest easy knowing your websites are accessible to all those who wish to roam them.

Making Images Accessible

Making images accessible is straightforward. You just need to make sure that you include a good description of the image in the `alt` attribute of each `<img>` element. When screen readers encounter an `<img>` element, they read the contents of the `alt` attribute to the user. However, if you leave this attribute blank or don't include it, the screen reader skips the image. If the image is an important part of your content, this can be confusing to the user.

The following code is one of the `<img>` elements you used on your Menu page. Notice that the value of the `alt` attribute provides a detailed description of the image.

```
<img src="img/pepperoni-pizza.jpeg"
    alt="A pepperoni pizza presented on a wooden chopping board."
    width="240" height="180">
```

Load up your `menus.html` file in your web browser and let your screen reader read through the page content. Notice how the screen reader speaks the text contained within the `alt` attribute when it encounters the image.

Making Links Accessible

You can make your hyperlinks accessible in two ways for users who rely on assistive technologies. You should aim to use both methods whenever possible.

The first method for making your links accessible is to simply use some good anchor text; this is the text contained between the `<a>` element tags. The anchor text should make sense if it was taken out of the context of the page. This means that "Click here" and "Read more" are off limits, I'm afraid. When a screen reader encounters a link, it reads out the anchor text.

The second method is to use the `title` attribute on an `<a>` element to provide a description of the page that you are linking to. Screen readers do not necessarily use this text, but it displays in a tooltip if the user hovers the mouse cursor over the link. That can be useful for giving your users more information about the page at the other end of the link.

Here is an example of how you can make your hyperlinks more accessible using these two methods:

```
<a href="about.html"
   title="Discover more information about Joe's Pizza Co.">
  Find out more about Joe's Pizza Co.
</a>
```

This example uses descriptive text in both the anchor text and the `title` attribute. Notice that even though we don't have any of the page content, this link still makes sense. A simple "More info" link would not have been very useful.

Try navigating the Joe's Pizza Co. home page with your screen reader. Notice that every time a link is encountered, the screen reader says Link or Visited link to let you know that the text about to be read belongs to a link. This behavior may vary slightly depending on which screen reader you are using.

Testing Accessibility

It's great to know these design principles for building an accessible website, but how do you actually test your code? This section shows you a few different ways that you can test your web pages for accessibility.

Testing with Screen Readers

The best way to test your web pages is by using the actual assistive technologies that your users will use. If you haven't already installed at least one screen reader on your computer, now's the time. Make sure you've read the help documentation so that you know how to use the software. You can find a list of popular screen readers and links to user guides at the beginning of this chapter.

Try navigating your pages using the screen reader, paying particular attention to how it deals with forms, tables, links, and images. If you come across any areas that are hard to navigate, think about how you can refactor your code to make the experience easier, based on what you have learned in this chapter.

Testing Markup with WAVE

The Web Accessibility Evaluation Tool (WAVE) is a free tool provided by WebAIM that you can use to test your web pages for any potential accessibility issues. You can access WAVE at `http://wave.webaim.org`.

The tool is similar to the W3C Validator in that it enables you to check your pages in three different ways. You can provide a URL to a live page, upload a file from your computer, or paste your HTML directly into a text area.

Figure 9-3 shows an inaccessible web page that has been tested using WAVE. Recommendations and errors are displayed in yellow and red boxes next to the corresponding elements. As you can see, this test page has a number of errors, including a lack of table headers, form labels, and page structure.

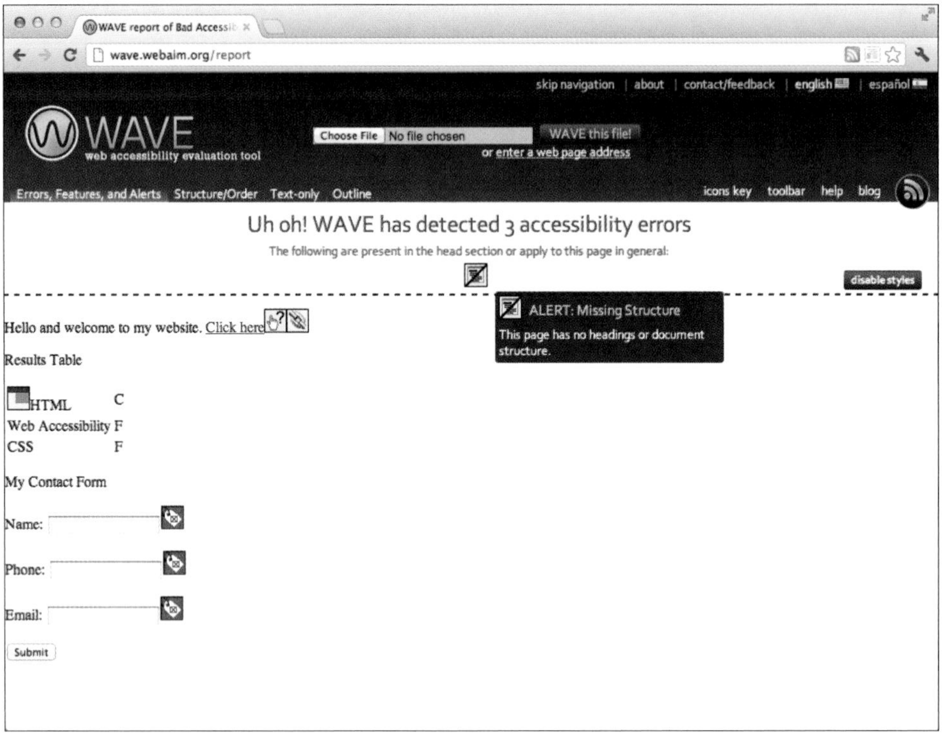

FIGURE 9-3 Testing accessibility using WAVE.

Testing the Visual Design with Spur

Another great tool for testing your web pages is Spur (`http://spurapp.com`). This tool enables you to examine the visual design of your web pages by applying a number of effects such as blur, grayscale, and contrast. This can help to give you a better understanding of how users with low vision or color blindness may view your pages.

Figure 9-4 shows an image of the Google home page that has been converted to grayscale using Spur. Notice how this has affected the contrast between the colors in the logo.

FIGURE 9-4 The Google home page, converted to grayscale using Spur.
2012 © Google

Summary

Creating accessible websites is vital to ensuring that the web stays an open platform that everyone can comfortably use. In this chapter, you learned about a number of different techniques and technologies that you can use to make your websites more accessible.

Images, links, tables, and forms all pose potential problems to users who rely on screen readers to browse the web. You learned how to make use of HTML elements and their attributes to provide more information to these programs, and therefore make it easier for users to interact with your web pages.

As well as looking at the different ways of writing more accessible markup, you also learned how to use tools such as Spur and WAVE to test your pages and identify areas where you can improve accessibility.

In Chapter 10, you learn the basics of JavaScript, a programming language used for writing scripts that interact with web pages. You learn how to write simple JavaScript programs, as well as how to manipulate the content of your web pages. You also learn about jQuery, a JavaScript library that makes writing scripts a breeze.

part 3

Enhancing Web Pages with HTML5 and JavaScript

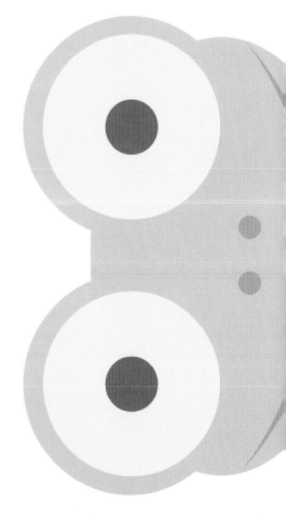

chapter ten
Introducing JavaScript

UP TO THIS point in the book, you focused on how to create web pages using HTML. In the remaining chapters, you are going to be using JavaScript and HTML5 to create interactive features for your Joe's Pizza Co. website. But first, you need to get up to speed about the JavaScript programming language.

The JavaScript programming language is a very large topic, possibly even bigger than HTML and CSS combined. In this chapter I introduce you to the basic concepts of JavaScript so that you can build a foundation on which to enhance your JavaScript knowledge in the future. You will step away from the Joe's Pizza Co. website for a while, and focus instead on building a number of small JavaScript programs. As you progress through each of these exercises you will learn about the key concepts of programming. In the following chapters, you'll return to the Joe's Pizza Co. website and put your new knowledge to use.

You'll start by learning how to add JavaScript to your web pages, by either putting the code inline with your existing HTML or in separate JavaScript files. You will learn how to write your own programs in JavaScript, how JavaScript programs are constructed, and the various tools available to you as a developer. These include control and loop structures as well as how to select and manipulate elements within your pages.

You'll also look at the Document Object Model (DOM), what it is, how it is created, and why it is important. You will also learn about DOM nodes and the relationships between them.

Finally, you will look at a JavaScript library called jQuery and how it can be used to make writing JavaScript programs easier.

Treehouse offers a great JavaScript Foundations course that I recommend you work through in conjunction with this chapter. You can find it at `http://teamtreehouse.com/library/websites/javascript-foundations`.

What is JavaScript?

JavaScript is a general purpose programming language that is used to create dynamic and interactive websites. Brendan Eich originally designed the language while working on the Netscape browser in 1995; he's now the Chief Technology Officer at Mozilla (the non-profit organization that develops, among other things, the Firefox web browser).

So what are *dynamic websites*? JavaScript enables developers to write programs that can change how a website looks and behaves once it has loaded into the user's browser. This means that you could update some of the content in the page without having to reload the page. You can even request new content from a web server and display it on the page without having to refresh it. This is referred to as *Asynchronous JavaScript and XML*, or *AJAX*. Many popular web applications such as Gmail and Facebook make heavy use of AJAX to create fast interfaces.

JavaScript is also very useful for listening for events such as mouse clicks and key presses on the keyboard. Using what are known as *event listeners,* a JavaScript developer can specify some code that should be executed when an event occurs. Remember when you looked at the `<button>` element in Chapter 5 and I said that to make "dumb" buttons smart, you had to use JavaScript? Well, this is how it is done.

An advantage that JavaScript has over other languages is that it runs directly in the user's web browser. This means that the code will often execute very fast. It also helps to lighten the load on the web server that already has enough to deal with, responding to page requests from other users.

Here are some demos of what can now be done using JavaScript and HTML5. Take a look at them—and enjoy:

These demos take advantage of some really advanced HTML5 technologies that are not yet supported in all browsers. I recommend that you view these demos in Google Chrome to ensure that they will work correctly.

- **The Wilderness Downtown by Google**—`http://www.thewildernessdown town.com/`

- **Water/Ocean by OutsideOfSociety**—`http://oos.moxiecode.com/js_webgl/ water_noise/`

- **Rome by Google**—`http://www.ro.me/`

JavaScript Terminology

Throughout this chapter you may encounter some terminology that is new to you. So that you understand what is going on, here are some key terms.

- **variable**—Variables allow you to store pieces of data so that you can use them in your programs. You will look at variables in more detail later in this chapter. The following example creates a variable called `age` and stores in it the integer value `20`.

```
var age = 20;
```

- **function**—A function consists of a block of JavaScript code that is executed when the function is *called*. You call a function by adding the function name to your code at the position which you want the code within the function block to be executed. The following example shows a simple function called `printName`.

```
function printName() {
    document.write("Matt West");
  }
```

You will learn about functions in more detail later in this chapter.

- **object**—A JavaScript *object* consists of a collection of properties and functions. Each of these properties stores some data about the object. A `person` object, for example, might have properties such as `name`, `height`, `age`, and `weight`. This concept is similar to the concept of *microdata items* described in Chapter 8.

  JavaScript objects can also have functions attached to them. Every web browser has a `document` object that has a number of properties containing information about the page. This `document` object also has a number of functions attached to it. These functions are called on an object using the `object. function()` syntax. The benefit of attaching functions to objects is that the function will be able to access all of the object's properties, whereas if the function were not attached to an object the desired properties would have to be passed to the function through parameters.

- **event**—An event is triggered when certain conditions are met. For example, the `onload` event is triggered when the page loads. There are also events for things like mouse clicks, key presses, and form submissions. You can use *event listeners* to attach functions to events so that a function is executed when an event is triggered.

Awesome, aren't they! If you aren't brimming with excitement at what is possible now, don't worry. You soon will be.

So by now you should have a general understanding of the purpose of JavaScript and its position within the web ecosystem. Now it's time to start learning how to use JavaScript so that one day you will be able to create websites as amazing as those demos.

The <script> Element

Before you can start writing JavaScript code, you need to know about a few housekeeping issues. The first of these is where to put your JavaScript code. You have two options: You can either put it inline (embedding it within an HTML file), or you can put it in a completely separate file and link to that file in your HTML. The latter method is generally considered the better approach, and this is how you will be adding JavaScript to the Joe's Pizza Co. website. However, there are times when inline scripts are needed, so in this section I cover both methods. Whichever method you end up using in your projects, you are going to use the <script> element to let the browser know where your JavaScript code is located.

Inline Scripts

JavaScript code that is embedded directly into your HTML page is referred to as *inline* scripts. Inline scripts are best if you have only a short piece of JavaScript; otherwise, it will be easier to maintain your code over the long run if you put it in its own dedicated file.

To embed JavaScript code in your HTML files, you need to place it within a <script> element. Follow these steps:

 The example code used in this chapter is available from the Chapter 10 folder in the download code files.

1. Create a new folder on your desktop called `javascript-examples`.

2. Now create a new file in your text editor.

3. Save this file in the `javascript-examples` folder as `example10-1.html`.

4. Copy the following code into the `example10-1.html` file.

```
<!DOCTYPE html>
<html>
<head>
  <meta charset="utf-8">
  <title>Inline Scripts</title>
</head>
<body>
```

```
    <script>
      window.onload = function() {
        document.write('Hello World!');
      };
    </script>
  </body>
</html>
```

5. Save the file.

Now view this file in your web browser. You should see that `Hello World!` is displayed on the page. Let's dissect this code a little.

JavaScript code will be executed only when you tell the browser to execute it. In this case, you want the code to run as soon as the page has loaded, so you need to tell that to the browser. The first line of your code does this.

JavaScript uses objects to keep track of things like the browser window, document, and HTML elements. When a page finishes loading, the `window` object triggers an event called `onload`. To execute code when the page loads, you need to attach this code to the `onload` event. In the code in the preceding Step 4, you do this by assigning a new function to the `window.onload` event using the = (equals sign) operator. All the code that you place within this function will now be executed when the `onload` event triggers:

```
window.onload = function() {
  document.write('Hello World!');
}
```

To ensure that things are working correctly, you included a line of code that will write the text `Hello World!` onto the screen. To do this, you grabbed the `document` object and used its built-in `write` function. The text that you want to be displayed is placed within the parentheses of the `write` function. You learn more about JavaScript functions later in this chapter.

That's it for inline scripts—pretty straightforward. As you can see, if you had a lot of HTML and JavaScript code in one page, it could be a bit of a pain to maintain, not to mention the fact that if you want to use this code on more than one page you would have to copy and paste it into each page. Then if you wanted to make a change, you would have to make the update in numerous different files. Things can get messy very quickly. This is why it is often better to put your JavaScript code into an external file.

Linking External JavaScript Files

Dedicated JavaScript files should use the `.js` file extension. Make sure that your text editor has syntax highlighting for JavaScript, because this can help to catch any errors (or *bugs*) in your code.

As with external stylesheets, you need to link JavaScript files to your HTML files. You do this using the `<script>` element.

You can use the `src` attribute on the `<script>` element to specify an absolute or relative path to your JavaScript file, in the same way that you do for images.

Unlike the `<img>` element, `<script>` is not a void element and therefore you always have to specify both start and end tags.

The following steps show how to modify `example10-1` to use external JavaScript files instead of inline scripts:

1. Create a new file in your text editor.

2. Save this file in your `javascript-examples` folder as `example10-2.js`.

3. Move the code from your `<script>` element into the new JavaScript file. Don't include the `<script>` element itself.

4. Save the `example10-2.js` file.

5. Now add a `src` attribute to the `<script>` element and set its value to `example 10-2.js`.

   ```
   <script src="example10-2.js"></script>
   ```

6. Save this file as `example10-2.html`.

Load the HTML file in your browser; you should see that the `Hello World!` text is still displayed onscreen. Try changing this text in the JavaScript file to make sure that everything is working properly.

To ensure that your web pages load fast, it's best to always put your `<script>` elements at the end of your HTML file, just before the `</body>` tag.

Now that you know how to get your JavaScript code to run in your web pages, you are going to learn the basics of JavaScript programming.

JavaScript Basics

This section covers the basics of the JavaScript programming language. I explain how to create programs using variables, functions, event listeners, control structures, and loops. These are key programing concepts that will give you the knowledge you need to start using JavaScript with HTML5. As I mentioned before, this is not a comprehensive examination of

JavaScript, but it will give you the skills you need to complete the rest of the exercises in this book and build small JavaScript programs of your own.

A Simple Program

You've already encountered the standard Hello World! program, so let's skip ahead to something a little more interactive. The following program asks users for their names and then displays the input on the screen:

1. Create a new file in your text editor called `example10-3.js`.

2. Copy the following code into this new file.

```javascript
window.onload = function() {
  var name = prompt('Your name please');

  document.write('Hello ' + name + '!');
};
```

3. Save the `example10-3.js` file.

4. Create a new `example10-3.html` file in your text editor.

5. Copy the following code into this HTML file.

```html
<!DOCTYPE html>
<html>
<head>
  <meta charset="utf-8">
  <title>Say Hello</title>
</head>
<body>
  <script src="example10-3.js"></script>
</body>
</html>
```

6. Save the `example10-3.html` file.

Now view the `example10-3.html` file in your browser. You should be prompted for your name. Type this into the text box and click OK (or press Enter). A hello message should display on the screen.

This small program addresses a number of different concepts from JavaScript. First, you declared a variable (name) to hold some data (more on variables soon), and then you told the browser to prompt the user for her name, passing in some text to be displayed in the pop-up window. You then combined the name that you collected with some other text and printed it all out to the screen.

This may seem like a fairly useless little program, but here you have covered the key programming concept of input and output. Next up: taking a closer look at variables.

Variables

Variables are used to store pieces of data so that you can play around with them in your program. Declaring a variable in JavaScript is easy; unlike some other programming languages, you do not need to specify what type of data the variable will hold (for example, a number or text). Programming languages like JavaScript are referred to as *dynamically* typed languages.

To declare a variable, you start by using the JavaScript keyword `var`. This tells the browser that you are creating a new variable. You then add the name of your variable. Variable names should not contain spaces, and you should use *camel-case* to join multiple words together. For example, "guitar stand" becomes `guitarStand`. Note the capital letter of the second word: That's where camel-case gets its name—like the hump on a camel's back.

Once you have declared the name of your variable, you can assign it an initial value. This is known as *initializing* a variable. To do this, you use the equal sign (=) followed by your data. The statement below shows a variable `leafColor` that is initialized with the value `green`.

```
var leafColor = "green";
```

In JavaScript, you add a semicolon to the end of each line to indicate that the statement is finished. A *statement* is a command, such as calling a function or creating a variable.

You will be using variables extensively in the JavaScript programs you build throughout the remainder of this book. For example, in Chapter 11 you will be using variables to store references to buttons on your web page so that you can build custom playback controls for a video.

Reserved Words

There are some words that are *reserved* for the JavaScript language; you should not use them as variable names. If you try to do so, your program likely will not execute correctly.

Here is a list of all the reserved words for JavaScript. Have a quick read so that you are familiar with them.

```
break, case, catch, continue, debugger, default, delete, do, else,
finally, for, function, if, in, instanceof, new, return, switch,
this, throw, try, typeof, var, void, while, with
```

Null and Undefined

When you declare a variable, you do not have to initialize it with a value. You can simply declare a variable, as shown here:

```
var age;
```

Variables that are declared but not initialized are known as *undefined*. Because no value is associated with them, the browser cannot give them a type for you (for example, string or number).

Variables can also be `null`. This is similar to being undefined, but these do have a type. A null variable simply has no value. It is empty, but it does have an implied type that was determined by its value in the past.

Let's write a little program to test the difference between `undefined` variables and `null` variables. Here are the steps:

1. Create a new file in your text editor.

2. Save this file as `example10-4.js`.

3. Copy the following code into this file:

```
window.onload = function() {
  // Undefined variable
  var foo;
  document.write('The foo variable is ' + foo + '<br>');

  // Null variable
  var bar = "Hello";
  bar = null;
  document.write('The bar variable is ' + bar);
};
```

4. Save the `example10-4.js` file.

5. Create a new HTML file called `example10-4.html`.

6. Add the following code to this new HTML file:

```
<!DOCTYPE html>
<html>
<head>
  <meta charset="utf-8">
  <title>Undefined vs Null</title>
</head>
<body>
  <script src="example10-4.js"></script>
</body>
</html>
```

7. Save the `example10-4.html` file.

Now open this file in your browser. You should see the following output:

```
The foo variable is undefined
The bar variable is null
```

Because the foo variable was declared but not initialized, it never actually existed. Therefore, it is undefined. The bar variable, on the other hand, was initialized with the text Hello. However, when you set the bar variable to be empty using the null keyword, it lost its value but still continued to exist. Therefore, when it is written to the screen, the browser sees that it exists but has no value for it, and so displays null.

 Many developers struggle to grasp the difference between undefined and null. Take a look at Jim's video on the Treehouse website, where he explains this in a little more detail: http://teamtreehouse.com/library/websites/javascript-foundations/variables/null-and-undefined.

Functions

Functions (sometimes called *methods*) are code structures that you can use to store code that might be needed several times in your script. Instead of having to write this code out multiple times, you can create a function and then call that function wherever you want the code to run. This makes your code much more maintainable. In Chapter 13 you will be creating a function that uses the GeoLocation API to find the Joe's Pizza Co. restaurant that is nearest to the user.

You can pass inputs to a function using parameters. These are placed within parentheses after the function name.

Take a look at a simple function that will take in a name and write a hello message to the screen.

```
function sayHello(name) {
  document.write("Hello " + name);
}
```

Here you have defined a parameter called name. When the function is called, the browser will create a variable name and initialize it with the content that you pass to the function, as shown here:

```
sayHello("Joe");
```

If all goes to plan, this will output the following on your screen:

```
Hello Joe
```

Let's write a little program that makes use of the sayHello() function. Here you are going to write out a hello message to four different people.

1. Create a new file in your text editor called `example10-5.js`.

2. Copy the following code into this new file:

```javascript
window.onload = function() {
  sayHello('Joe');
  sayHello('Beth');
  sayHello('Steve');
  sayHello('James');
};

// Print out a hello message.
function sayHello(name) {
  document.write('Hello ' + name + '<br>');
}
```

3. Save the `example10-5.js` file.

4. Create a new `example10-5.html` file.

5. Copy the following HTML into this file:

```html
<!DOCTYPE html>
<html>
<head>
  <meta charset="utf-8">
  <title>Say Hello</title>
</head>
<body>
  <script src="example10-5.js"></script>
</body>
</html>
```

6. Save the `example10-5.html` file.

Open the `example10-5.html` file in your browser. You should see the following output on the screen:

```
Hello Joe
Hello Beth
Hello Steve
Hello James
```

In this example, you used the `sayHello()` function that you created to output a hello message to Joe and his friends.

Functions are extremely useful for creating maintainable code. Try to create functions whenever you can; they will make your life much easier as your programs grow.

Event Listeners

You have already encountered event listeners multiple times in this chapter. Event listeners are used to attach functions to a particular event, such as a page load, mouse click, or key press.

There are two ways of creating event listeners. The first is to attach a function to an event that occurs on a JavaScript object, using the following syntax. This should look somewhat familiar to you.

```
window.onload = function() {
  // Do something.
}
```

Here an empty function block is attached to the onload event of the window object. This onload event is called when the page loads. You don't necessarily have to use an empty function block here. If you have defined a function in your JavaScript code you could use that too.

```
window.onload = sayHello("Joe");
```

The second method for creating an event listener is to use the addEventListener() function. This function has two parameters. The first is the event that should trigger the event listener and the second is a function that should be executed when the event is triggered. The addEventListener() function should be called on an object as in the following example.

```
document.getElementById("btn").addEventListener("click",
function(event){
  alert("Boo!");
}};
```

In this example an alert dialog would be displayed to the user when they click the button with the ID btn.

 Note the event parameter that is passed into the function block in the previous example. When the event is triggered, details about the event will be passed to the function block through this parameter. You don't have to define a parameter for the event data; it is optional.

You will be using event listeners many times in the remaining chapters of this book, especially in Chapters 11 and 12 when you will use them to listen for button clicks and form submissions.

Let's write a little program that uses what you have learned here.

1. Create a new file in your text editor.

2. Save this file as example10-6.js.

3. Add the following JavaScript code to this file.

```
window.onload = function() {
  var button = document.getElementById("btn");

  button.addEventListener("click", function() {
    alert("Boo!");
  });
}
```

4. Save the example10-6.js file.

5. Now create a new HTML file called example10-6.html.

6. Copy the following HTML code into this file.

```
<!DOCTYPE html>
<html>
<head>
  <meta charset="utf-8">
  <title>Event Listeners</title>
</head>
<body>
  <button id="btn">Click me!</button>
  <script src="example10-6.js"></script>
</body>
</html>
```

7. Save this file.

Now open up the example10-6.html file in your web browser. If you click the button you should be confronted by an alert dialog that contains the text Boo!

Making Decisions

When writing programs, you will meet scenarios in which you need to make a decision before executing code. Maybe you want to check that the user has provided valid data, or that a number is within a certain range. You can make these decisions in your code using if and else statements.

An if statement should contain a condition that evaluates to either true or false. If the condition evaluates to true, the code within the block is executed; if it is false, the code is skipped. Here is an example of a simple if statement:

```
if(a < b) {
  document.write("a is smaller than b!");
}
```

In this example, the condition would evaluate to `true` if the value of the a variable is smaller than the value of the b variable. This means that the code would execute and the text would be output to the screen.

 You can find a comprehensive list of JavaScript operators that can be used in conditions at `https://developer.mozilla.org/en-US/docs/JavaScript/Guide/ Expressions_and_Operators#Comparison_operators`.

You can also define code that should run if the condition evaluates to `false`. This is done by placing the `else` keyword after the closing curly brace of the `if` statement and then placing the code within two new curly braces. This is shown in the following example.

```
if(a < b) {
  document.write("a is smaller than b!");
} else {
  document.write("a is not smaller than b!");
}
```

This sort of control structure is useful when writing computer programs in any programming language. In later chapters you will be using `if` and `else` statements to check whether a user's web browser supports new technologies like GeoLocation, LocalStorage, and Canvas.

Looping

When coding, you will find that you need to repeat a task multiple times. An example use case would be if you had a collection of structured data about 100 users. The task is to display that data on the page, once for each user. Now you certainly don't want to write out the same code 100 times. This is where loop structures come in. Using them to repeat an action a set number of times can greatly decrease the amount of code you have to write.

There are two types of loop structures, `for` loops and `while` loops. In this section, you learn how to use these in your programs and when you should use one instead of the other.

For Loops

For loops are used when you have a set number of times that you want to execute some code. A `for` loop has three parameters.

The *initialization* parameter comes first. This is usually used to create a counter variable that can track how many times the `for` loop has executed.

Next up is the *condition*. This will be evaluated before each iteration of the loop and should evaluate to either `true` or `false`, just like conditions in `if` statements. It is commonly used to check whether the counter is within a desired range.

The final parameter is the *final-expression*. This expression is executed after each iteration of the loop. This typically is used to increase the value of the counter variable by one.

Let's write a little program that uses a `for` loop:

1. Create a new file in your text editor.

2. Save this file as `example10-7.js`.

3. Add the following code to this file.

```
window.onload = function() {
  for( var i = 0; i < 5; i++ ) {
    document.write(i + '<br>');
  }
}
```

4. Save the `example10-7.js` file.

5. Create a new HTML file called `example10-7.html`.

6. Copy the following code into this file.

```
<!DOCTYPE html>
<html>
<head>
  <meta charset="utf-8">
  <title>For Loops</title>
</head>
<body>
  <script src="example10-7.js"></script>
</body>
</html>
```

7. Save this file.

Here you have first initialized a counter variable `i` and given it the value `0`.

The condition then states that this loop should continue to execute for as long as the counter variable `i` is less than 5.

Finally, you declare that after each iteration of this loop, the counter variable should be increased by one. The `++` syntax here is simply a shorthand way of writing `i=i+1`.

If you run this example in your browser, you should see the following:

```
0
1
2
3
4
```

Notice that the output starts from 0. This is because you initialized the counter variable at 0. In programming, you almost always start counting from 0. This can sometimes lead to the infamous *off-by-one* bug, so be careful to check your numbers if your output is slightly off.

While Loops

While loops are similar to for loops; however, while loops can be used when you don't know how many times you want the loop to iterate. A while loop takes only one parameter, the condition. It will keep iterating until this condition evaluates to true. You want to be sure that it will evaluate to true at some point; otherwise, it will keep iterating until the end of time, or your computer dies, whichever comes first. This is known as an *infinite* loop.

Let's have a bit more fun with while loops. It's time to create a little guessing game. As always, the code below can be found on the book's website in the Chapter 10 folder.

1. Create a new file in your text editor called example10-8.js.

2. Add the following code to this new file:

```
window.onload = function() {
  // Generate random number between 0 and 10.
  var randomNumber = Math.floor(Math.random()*10);

  // Initialize a variable for the guess.
  var guess;

  // Keep asking the user to guess until he gets the number.
  while(guess != randomNumber) {
    guess = prompt('What is your guess?');
  }

  // Let the user know that he guessed correctly.
  alert('Congratulations! You guessed correctly. The number
  was ' +
  randomNumber + '.');
}
```

3. Save the example10-8.js file.

4. Create a new file called example10-8.html.

5. Copy the following code into this new file:

```
<!DOCTYPE html>
<html>
<head>
  <meta charset="utf-8">
  <title>While Loops</title>
</head>
```

```
<body>
  <h1>The Guessing Game</h1>
  <p>
    Guess a number between 0 and 10.
  </p>
  <script src="example10-8.js"></script>
</body>
</html>
```

6. Save the `example10-8.html` file.

Open this example in your browser and give the game a go.

This code is a little more complex than earlier JavaScript you looked at, so I will take you through each part. Lines that begin with `//` are comments.

The objective of this game is for the user to guess a random number that is generated by the program. This number will be between 0 and 10.

First you need to generate the random number. To do this, you initialize a new variable `randomNumber`. You use JavaScript's built-in `Math` library to help generate the number. Let's take a closer look at this segment.

```
Math.floor(Math.random()*10)
```

Here you first use the Math library's `random` function to generate a decimal number between 0 and 1. Your program needs a number between 0 and 10, though, so you multiply this random number by 10 to make it larger. Finally, you only want that random number as an integer so you can use the `floor` function to round your decimal number to the closest integer. The example below shows how the random number is calculated:

```
Math.random()   = 0.4382
Math.random()*10 = 4.382
Math.floor(Math.random()*10) = 4
```

Okay, I'm sorry about the math lesson, but it couldn't be avoided. Moving on . . .

Now that you have your `randomNumber`, you create another variable, `guess`, to store the user's latest attempt to beat the game.

The next step is to create the `while` loop that will check to see if the user's guess is correct and prompt her to make another guess if it is not.

```
while(guess != randomNumber) {
  guess = prompt('What is your guess?');
}
```

The condition of the `while` loop compares the `guess` variable to the `randomNumber` variable using the not-equal operator (`!=`). If the guess is correct, it will continue to execute the rest of the JavaScript. However, if it is incorrect, then you will prompt the user to make another guess and store this new attempt in the `guess` variable. The next time the `while` loop condition evaluates, it will check against the new guess.

You may have noticed that you enter the `while` loop before the user has made a guess at all. Because you have declared the `guess` variable but not initialized it with a value, it will be `undefined`. This means that when the `while` loop compares it to `randomNumber`, the result will be false and the user will be prompted to make a guess. This eliminates the need to duplicate the code for the prompt outside of the `while` loop.

Once the user guesses correctly, the rest of the code will be executed, and therefore you add a little congratulations message to let the user know that she won.

```
alert('Congratulations! You guessed correctly. The number was ' +
  randomNumber + '.');
```

Here you have used the `alert` function. This will display the text in a pop-up similar to the one displayed by the `prompt` function.

That's it for loops. Hopefully, you now understand how you can use `for` and `while` loops to make your code much more maintainable by reducing the amount of code that you have to write.

The Document Object Model (DOM)

The Document Object Model (or DOM for short) is a structural representation of a web page. The DOM is generated by taking all your HTML code and all your CSS code and putting them together to create a master blueprint of the page (the DOM). This is then presented on the screen by the browser. As a developer, you can then manipulate the DOM (and therefore the page that is displayed) using JavaScript.

The DOM Tree

The DOM tree consists of all the elements that you have defined in your HTML code. These elements are converted to what are known as *nodes*. Each node represents an object, and these objects are what you will interact with in your JavaScript programs. Remember all of those attributes that you were placing on your HTML elements? These have now become properties of the new DOM objects.

The DOM tree follows the same structure as your HTML document, and therefore elements that are nested in your markup will appear as children of their parent element in the DOM.

This parent-child relationship is important to the way that the DOM tree works. Let's look at an example.

The following code example shows a `<div>` element that contains an unordered list, which in turn contains a number of list items.

```
<div>
    <ul id="fruits">
      <li>Apples</li>
      <li>Oranges</li>
      <li>Bananas</li>
    </ul>
</div>
```

When the DOM is generated, it first creates an element node for the `<div>` element. As the unordered list is nested within this element, it would become a child node of the `<div>` element node. This `<ul>` element also has an id attribute. This would become a property of the unordered list node. Each list item then becomes a child node of the unordered list node. Figure 10-1 shows how this segment of the DOM tree would be visualized (not including properties).

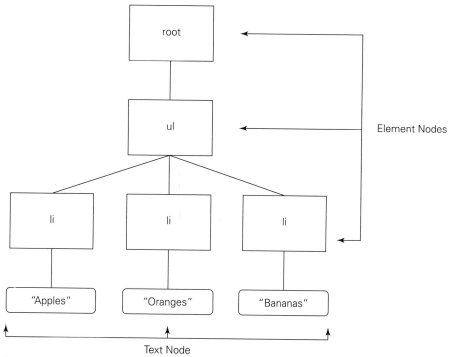

FIGURE 10-1 A visual representation of a segment from the DOM tree.

As you can see in this diagram, there is more than one type of node. The main two types that you will need to worry about are element nodes and text nodes. As the names suggest, *element nodes* are created for HTML elements and *text nodes* are created for the text contained within HTML elements.

Selecting Page Elements

In this section, you discover how to select elements in the DOM using JavaScript. You can use a number of different functions to select elements. Here you are going to look at the four main ones. You use what you learn here in Chapter 11 when building custom playback controls for a video, and in Chapter 12 when you store data entered into a web form.

Up to now, you haven't made much use the developer tools that you installed at the beginning of the book. That's going to change. You could do this work in JavaScript files, as you have done up to now, but I want you to get used to using the JavaScript console that comes with your developer tools. The skills that you learn here will be very useful when it comes to debugging your JavaScript programs in the future.

Debugging refers to the process of examining your code to find and correct errors (or *bugs*) that are causing your program to behave in a way that it was not intended to.

The following examples use the developer tools supplied with Google Chrome, but feel free to use other tools if you are more familiar with them.

Before starting, you need to set up a test page from which you can select elements. Create a new file using the following code, or alternatively you can use the `example10-9.html`, which can be found in the Chapter 10 folder of the downloadable code resources.

```
<!DOCTYPE html>
<html>
<head>
  <meta charset="utf-8">
  <title>Selectors Test Page</title>
</head>
<body>
  <header>
    <h1>This is a test page</h1>
  </header>

  <section id="text">
    <h1>A Text Section</h1>
    <p id="firstParagraph" class="paragraph">
      This text is within the first paragraph element.
    </p>
```

```
      <p class="paragraph">
        This text is in the second p element.
      </p>
  </section>

  <section id="form">
    <h1>A Web Form</h1>
    <form id="webForm" action="#" method="post">
      <p>
        <label for="name">Name</label>
        <input type="text" id="name" name="name">
      </p>
      <p>
        <label for="email">Email</label>
        <input type="email" id="email" name="email">
      </p>
      <p>
        <button type="submit">Submit</button>
      </p>
    </form>
  </section>
</body>
</html>
```

Load this page in your web browser and launch the developer tools. Not sure how to do this? They usually can be found in the Tools menu within your browser. Alternatively, take a quick look at Chapter 1, where I cover the most popular developer tools. Once you have them open, you need to launch the console view. In Chrome, this is done by selecting the Console tab.

Good to go? Awesome.

getElementById()

The first selector function that you are going to look at is `getElementById()` (note the lowercase d in Id). This function takes the ID of your element and will return that element's object in the DOM. You call this function on the `document` object.

Let's use this function to select the `<section>` element with the ID `text`. In your console, type the following and then press Enter:

```
document.getElementById("text");
```

Figure 10-2 shows what should be displayed in your console window.

FIGURE 10-2 Selecting an element getElementById().

Executing this function will return the target element and all its child elements.

getElementsByClassName()

The `getElementsByClassName()` function can be used to simultaneously select multiple elements based on a class that has been assigned to them. This function will return an array of element objects. An *array* is very much like a list, where each item is separated by a comma. Arrays are enclosed within square brackets, as shown in the following example:

```
["red", "green", "blue"]
```

Try using the `getElementsByClassName()` function to select all elements that have the class `paragraph`.

```
document.getElementsByClassName("paragraph");
```

This should return an array of two element objects. These are the paragraphs from the text section. Figure 10-3 shows the output in the console window.

FIGURE 10-3 Selecting elements using getElementsByClassName().

 Note that the `getElementsByClassName()` function is not supported in Internet Explorer 6 to 8.

getElementsByTagName()

There may also be scenarios in which you would like to select a number of elements by their tag name. For such occasions, you can use the getElementsByTagName() function.

Try selecting all the paragraph elements on the page:

```
document.getElementsByTagName("p");
```

Figure 10-4 shows the expected output for this selection. In this figure I have expanded the final three elements so that you can see their contents by clicking the little gray triangle next to the element in the output.

FIGURE 10-4 Selecting Elements Using getElementsByTagName().

getElementsByName()

Remember those name attributes that you were specifying on form fields? You can also select elements based on those. The getElementsByName() function takes in a name and returns an array of all the elements that have that name.

Try selecting the e-mail field using getElementsByName():

```
document.getElementsByName("email");
```

This should return an array with one object, the <input> element for the e-mail field, as shown in Figure 10-5.

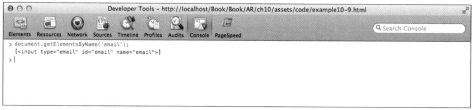

FIGURE 10-5 Selecting elements using getElementsByName().

Interacting with Page Elements

Now that you understand how to select elements using JavaScript, let's look at how you can manipulate their content and attributes.

Manipulating Text Content

First try changing the text of the first <p> element. To do this, select the element and update its innerHTML property to This text was changed using JavaScript.

```
document.getElementById("firstParagraph").innerHTML = "This text
    was changed using JavaScript";
```

Execute this in your console. You now should see the text on the page change.

What if you wanted to just add more text after what is already there? To do this, you could simply use the += operator instead of =. Here's an example:

```
document.getElementById("firstParagraph").innerHTML += " This text
    was added to the end of the current text.";
```

Manipulating Attributes and Properties

To inspect all the properties that an element has, you can use the dir() function in the developer tools console. This will show you a list of all the element's properties as well as its child elements.

Take a look at the properties of the email input by selecting it using getElementById.

```
dir(document.getElementById("email"));
```

This should display a really long list of properties. You can ignore most of them at this stage, but the key properties are those that link to the element attributes, such as id, class, placeholder, and value.

Let's update the value of this field. To do this, select the <input> element, specify the property you would like to change, and then assign it a value. Oh, by the way: Did I mention that you can create variables in the console? Let's also create a variable to store the email field so that you don't have to type the selection code every time.

```
var emailField = document.getElementById("email");
emailField.value = "test@example.com";
```

You should now see that the value of the email field has been updated to the e-mail address you specified.

Throughout the remainder of this book, you will write a lot of JavaScript code that interacts with page elements, updating content and properties based on user input and events.

JavaScript Libraries

JavaScript libraries are collections of code that you can use to make writing JavaScript programs easier by enabling you to write less code. Some of these libraries address cross-browser compatibility issues, and some give you easy ways to create interactive widgets for your pages. Some even do both.

To use a JavaScript library, all you need to do is to include the library script in your HTML file using a `<script>` element. Make sure that you include this script before your JavaScript files, because the browser will load scripts in the order in which it discovers them. You need the library to be seen first so that you can use the functions that it provides.

In this section, you learn some of the basics about the popular JavaScript library called jQuery. You look at some of the ways the jQuery simplifies writing JavaScript programs and how it can differ from writing programs in pure JavaScript.

I strongly recommend that you learn pure JavaScript before getting too involved in libraries like jQuery. That way you have a better understanding of what JavaScript itself is responsible for and what the library is doing to help you out.

jQuery Basics

Before you can use jQuery, you need to download the library and include it in your HTML file. Let's set up another test file so that you can get familiar with jQuery. Follow these steps:

1. Download the latest version from the jQuery website (`http://jquery.com`). At the time of writing this, the latest version is 1.8.1

2. Place this file in your `javascript-examples` folder.

3. Create a new file in your text editor.

4. Save this file as `example10-10.html`.

5. Add the following code to this file:

```
<!DOCTYPE html>
<html>
<head>
  <meta charset="utf-8">
  <title>jQuery Test Page</title>
</head>
<body>
```

```
<header>
  <h1>This is a test page</h1>
</header>

<section id="text">
  <h1>A Text Section</h1>
  <p id="firstParagraph" class="paragraph">
    This text is within the first paragraph element.
  </p>
  <p class="paragraph">
    This text is in the second p element.
  </p>
</section>

<section id="form">
  <h1>A Web Form</h1>
  <form id="webForm" action="#" method="post">
    <p>
      <label for="name">Name</label>
      <input type="text" id="name" name="name">
    </p>
    <p>
      <label for="email">Email</label>
      <input type="email" id="email" name="email">
    </p>
    <p>
      <button type="submit">Submit</button>
    </p>
  </form>
</section>

<script src="jquery-1.8.1.js"></script>
</body>
</html>
```

6. Save the file.

Now that you have a test page set up, let's look at some of the ways that using jQuery can make writing JavaScript programs easier.

Executing Code on Page Load

In pure JavaScript, you can tell the browser to execute some code when the page loads by attaching a function to the window.onload event. The following code shows how this would be done:

```
window.onload = function() {
    // Do something here.
}
```

jQuery provides an alternative way of doing this, as shown here:

```
$(function() {
    // Do something here.
});
```

The dollar ($) symbol at the beginning of this code represents the jQuery object. This object provides a number of helper functions that can take care of common tasks, such as selecting elements and updating the content of those elements.

Many developers (including me) prefer to use the jQuery method of executing code when the page has loaded, even though the syntax itself does not make much sense to humans.

Selecting Elements

The jQuery library provides a simpler way of selecting page elements that is very popular with developers. Instead of using the `getElementsBy...` functions, you can simply pass a selector to the jQuery object and it will return the page element or an array of page elements. If you are familiar with CSS, jQuery uses the same syntax as CSS selectors for referring to IDs and classes. Let me show you some examples comparing the pure JavaScript selectors to jQuery selectors. Load your new test page and try these out in the developer tools console.

To select an element by its ID in jQuery, you use the # sign followed by the ID:

```
// Select an element by its ID.
document.getElementById("text"); // Pure JavaScript
$("#text"); // jQuery
```

Using jQuery, you can select all elements within a certain class by placing a period before the class name:

```
// Select all elements with a class.
document.getElementsByClassName("paragraph"); // Pure JavaScript
$(".paragraph"); // jQuery
```

To select elements by their tag name, simply use the name of the tag. No special characters are needed:

```
// Select elements by their tag name.
document.getElementsByTagName("p"); // Pure JavaScript
$("p"); // jQuery
```

jQuery has other nifty selectors that you can use, too. You can find a full list of these on the jQuery website: `http://api.jquery.com/category/selectors/`.

Other Benefits of Using jQuery

As well as providing handy ways to select elements, jQuery offers a lot of other useful functions. There are functions for easily updating the properties and content of elements as well as manipulating CSS styling. There are even functions available to help you add effects such as fades and animations to your web pages. The jQuery library also provides a series of functions that make it easier to set up event listeners.

One of the biggest benefits of using jQuery is that the library accounts for the inconsistencies in browsers so that you don't have to. As explained earlier in this book, some browser vendors decided to implement technologies slightly differently, whether it is a variation in how a particular function is named or whether a browser vendor decided to include a function at all. This means that it is often necessary to write multiple variations of the same code in order to ensure that it will work in all web browsers. The jQuery library takes care of a lot of these inconsistencies for you so that you can just focus on writing your programs.

That concludes the brief tour of jQuery. If you like the look of jQuery's simpler syntax, check out the documentation on the jQuery website (`http://jquery.com`).

Summary

Congratulations! You just learned the basics of a new programming language.

JavaScript is one of the most important languages for creating modern web applications, especially if you want to take advantage of the awesome new features introduced in HTML5.

In this chapter, you learned the basics of JavaScript and created a number of programs of varying complexity. You also learned how the DOM works and what happens to your HTML and CSS code when the browser processes it. You were introduced to a number of key programming concepts in this chapter, but it takes months (if not years) to truly master all that JavaScript has to offer. Now that you have the basic foundations in place I recommend that you explore JavaScript some more by getting a book on the subject or completing the JavaScript courses on Treehouse. You might want to start with the *JavaScript Foundations* course at `http://teamtreehouse.com/library/websites/javascript-foundations`.

In the next chapter, you dig into some slightly more advanced HTML5 features, starting with native video and audio. You learn how to embed videos and audio clips into your web pages and how to use the new skills that you acquired in this chapter to create custom controls to manage playback.

chapter eleven
Adding Video and Audio

THE WEBSITE YOU have been building for Joe's Pizza Co. looks pretty good so far, but it would look even better if it included a video. In this chapter, you update the About page, adding a short video with some custom playback controls that you build yourself. When the video is in place, you learn how you can make video and audio content more accessible by adding subtitles to your multimedia content.

Until recently, embedding video and audio within a web page required the use of a third-party plug-in, such as Adobe Flash or Microsoft Silverlight. The result was a fragmented ecosystem of plug-ins that users had to install, manage, and upgrade, often confusing less tech-savvy individuals. This approach also meant that developers had less control over their video content.

The capability to create custom playback controls or special effects required the use of proprietary software such as Adobe Flash Professional. Even when developers did take the leap and purchase this considerably expensive software, they still had to learn a whole new programming language, ActionScript, in order to achieve what they desired.

Fortunately, HTML5 introduces a new way of embedding video and audio into web pages. Using the new <video> and <audio> elements, developers can now add multimedia content to their websites as easily as they can add images or text. Hurray!

Converting Video and Audio Files

Before you can start adding video and audio to your web pages, you first need to make sure browsers will be able to play your multimedia files. In this section, you learn about the various video and audio formats that are natively supported by modern web browsers. (*Natively* means there is no need for a plug-in.) You also create the video files you will use in the Joe's Pizza Co. website.

Video File Formats

Three main video formats are used for HTML5 video: WebM, MP4, and OGV. Unfortunately, the browser vendors each had their own opinions on which format should become the standard; therefore, no one format is supported by all modern web browsers. This means you must convert your video file into all three formats to ensure that everyone can see it. I cover how to detect whether a browser supports a certain video format later in this chapter.

Table 11-1 shows browser support for the three main video formats. Notice that by using the WebM and MP4 formats, you can cover all modern web browsers. MP4 files, however, are usually quite large, so it is often useful to provide an OGV file, too, because OGV files are much smaller and take less time to download.

Table 11-1   Video Codec Support in Modern Browsers

	WebM (VP8 codec)	MP4 (H.264 codec)	OGV (Ogg Theora codec)
Chrome	Yes	Yes	Yes
Firefox	Yes	No	Yes
Opera	Yes	No	Yes
Safari	No	Yes	No
IE9 +	Yes	Yes	No

For WebM to work in IE and Safari, the user has to manually install the WebM codec. You can download the installer here: `https://tools.google.com/dlpage/webmmf`.

Browser support for these codecs may change over time. You can check the latest browser support for these codecs using the following links:

- **WebM** - `http://caniuse.com/#feat=webm`
- **MP4** - `http://caniuse.com/#feat=mpeg4`
- **OGV** - `http://caniuse.com/#feat=ogv`

Audio File Formats

Just like with video formats, not a single accepted audio format is supported in all browsers. This means that, once again, you must convert your audio file into a number of different formats to ensure that everyone can enjoy it.

Table 11-2 lists the four main audio formats. The best way to cover all modern web browsers is to provide your audio in MP3, M4A (AAC), and WAV formats.

Table 11-2   Audio Codec Support in Modern Browsers

	OGG (Vorbis codec)	MP3	M4A (AAC codec)	WAV
Chrome	Yes	Yes	No	Yes
Firefox	Yes	No	No	Yes
Opera	Yes	No	No	Yes
Safari	No	Yes	Yes	Yes
IE 9 +	No	Yes	Yes	No

Converting the Video File

Now that you know about the various audio and video formats supported by modern web browsers, it's time to prepare the video files for the Joe's Pizza Co. website. In this section, you use a free tool called Firefogg to convert an MP4 file to OGV and WebM.

If you have trouble converting these video files, you can find copies of the converted files in the `videos` subfolder within folder 1 of the download code for Chapter 11.

To save you from having to download multiple copies of these video files (one set for each code folder), I placed the videos in folder 1 of the download files. If you need to view the About page from any of the other code folders in your browser, please copy the video files from folder 1 into the desired code folder; otherwise the video will not load.

Also, I have a confession to make. The video file you will use is actually a sketch involving Mike the Frog, the mascot from TeamTreehouse.com. Ideally, when you create websites for businesses in the wider world, you will use a more relevant video. This one, however, is just fine for teaching you all about HTML5 video.

Here are the steps to convert an MP4 file:

1. Create a new folder in your project directory and name it `videos`.

2. Download the `mikethefrog.mp4` file from this book's website at `http://wiley.com/go/treehouse/html5foundations` (video courtesy of © Treehouse Island, Inc.). You can find the file in the `chapter11/1/videos` folder of the download files.

3. Place the `mikethefrog.mp4` file in the `videos` folder that you created within your project directory.

4. The Firefogg converter requires that you are using Firefox. If you do not already have Firefox installed, you can download it from `http://www.mozilla.org/en-US/firefox/new/`.

5. Open Firefox and go to `http://firefogg.org`.

6. Click the button that reads Install Firefogg. This will install a Firefox extension. Click Allow and Install Now on the dialogs that appear. You may need to restart Firefox when the installation is complete.

7. Navigate to `http://firefogg.org/make/index.html` using Firefox.

8. Click Select File and select the `mikethefrog.mp4` file from your `videos` folder.

9. On the page that loads, make sure WebM (VP8/Vorbis) is selected in the format drop-down menu. Select the 1080p option from the preset drop-down.

10. Click the Encode button and save the video file in the `videos` folder as `mikethe-frog.webm`. Firefogg may take a little while to encode the new file. Once Firefogg completes the encoding, you should be presented with the video; the application also saves a copy of the new video in your videos folder.

11. Repeat Steps 7 to 10, this time selecting the Ogg (Theora/Vorbis) option from the format drop-down menu.

12. Check that the two new video files (`mikethefrog.webm` and `mikethefrog.ogv`) are in your `videos` folder; then close Firefox.

You now have all the video files you need for the rest of this chapter. In the next section, you embed these video files into your About page.

Adding a Video to the About Page Using the `<video>` Element

The new HTML5 `<video>` element has become very popular recently, with many companies implementing support for HTML5 video within their websites. At the time of this writing, YouTube is running a trial where you can opt-in to being shown HTML5 video (you can sign up at `http://youtube.com/html5`). Vimeo has a similar scheme running. Treehouse also uses HTML5 video to display the lessons on its website.

The `<video>` element, in its simplest form, is similar to the `<img>` element in that it uses a `src` attribute to specify a path to the video.

```
<video src="videos/mikethefrog.webm"></video>
```

Also note that the `<video>` element has a complete set of start and end tags. You can place some content between these tags that should be displayed if the browser does not support HTML5 video (more on this in the "Ensuring Compatibility" section coming up).

In this chapter, you mainly use the `<video>` element; however, the `<audio>` element is nearly identical. What you learn in this chapter can be transferred to the `<audio>` element when embedding audio content.

Adding the `<video>` Element

In this section, you add a basic `<video>` element to your About page. To start, you use only one video file, the WebM file. It's best, therefore, to use a browser that supports this format (such as Google Chrome). In the next section, you learn how to provide your video in multiple formats to ensure that everyone can view it.

The code for this exercise can be found in folder 2.

Follow these steps to add a `<video>` element:

1. Open the `about.html` file in your favorite text editor.

2. Between the main page heading (`<h1>`) and the page text, add a new `<div>` element with the ID `video`. This element will contain your `<video>` element as well as the controls that you build later in this chapter.

   ```
   <div id="video"></div>
   ```

3. Now add a `<video>` element to this new `<div>`.

   ```
   <video></video>
   ```

4. Set the `src` attribute on the `<video>` element to point to the `mikethefrog.webm` file in your `videos` folder.

   ```
   <video src="videos/mikethefrog.webm"></video>
   ```

5. Set the `width` attribute to 400 and the `height` attribute to 225.

   ```
   <video src="videos/mikethefrog.webm" width="400" height="225">
   </video>
   ```

6. Add an `id` attribute to the `<video>` element and set its value to `myVideo`.

```
<video src="videos/mikethefrog.webm" id="myVideo"
       width="400" height="225">
</video>
```

7. Now add a `controls` attribute to the `<video>` element. This prompts the browser to display its default video controls. Later in this chapter, you will replace these with your own custom controls.

```
<video src="videos/mikethefrog.webm" id="myVideo" width="400"
       height="225" controls>
</video>
```

8. Save the `about.html` file.

If you load up the About page in your web browser, you should see that your video appears to the left of the page text, as shown in Figure 11-1. Click the Play button to ensure that the video will start playing.

FIGURE 11-1 The About page with video.

Styling for the default browser controls has not been standardized, so these controls may look slightly different depending on which browser the video is being viewed in.

Ensuring Compatibility

As I mention earlier in this chapter, there is no single universal video format. If you were to open your About page in a browser that doesn't support the WebM format (such as Safari), you would see that the video never loads. You can solve this problem by providing multiple video files to the browser. The browser then chooses the one it can play and ignores the rest.

You provide multiple file formats using <source> elements. These elements go inside the <video> element and should have src and type attributes.

```
<video id="myVideo" width="400" height="225" controls>
  <source src="videos/mikethefrog.webm" type="video/webm">
  <source src="videos/mikethefrog.ogv" type="video/ogv">
  <source src="videos/mikethefrog.mp4" type="video/mp4">
  <p>
    Your browser doesn't support HTML5 video.
    <a href="videos/mikethefrog.mp4">Download</a> the video
    instead.
  </p>
</video>
```

You can also add some fallback content to the <video> element that will display if the browser does not support HTML5 video (such as the <p> element in the preceding example). This fallback content should usually include a link for the user to download the video file directly.

The <video> element is not supported in Internet Explorer versions 8 and earlier. You can check cross-browser support for this element here: http://caniuse.com/#feat=video.

Now it's time to modify your About page and add the other video files you created earlier in this chapter. You also add in some fallback content.

The code for this exercise can be found in folder 3.

Here are the steps for modifying your About page to add other video files:

1. Open the about.html file in your text editor.

2. Remove the src attribute from the `<video>` element.

3. Add a `<source>` element for the WebM file within the `<video>` element.

   ```
   <source src="video/mikethefrog.webm" type="video/webm">
   ```

4. Now add a `<source>` element for the OGV file.

   ```
   <source src="video/mikethefrog.ogv" type="video/ogv">
   ```

5. Finally, add a `<source>` element for the MP4 file.

   ```
   <source src="video/mikethefrog.mp4" type="video/mp4">
   ```

6. Now add some fallback content.

   ```
   <p>
      Your browser doesn't support HTML5 video.
      <a href="videos/mikethefrog.mp4">Download</a> the video
      instead.
   </p>
   ```

7. Save the about.html file.

Now, if you open the About page in Safari, you would see that the video plays perfectly. This is because the browser chooses a file that it can play from the source options you give it.

You also added some fallback content, just in case the user's browser doesn't support HTML5 video. Figure 11-2 shows how the page looks if the fallback content is displayed instead of the video.

Adding a Poster Image

Depending on your browser, you might have noticed that when the page first loads the video is displayed as a solid black box (refer to Figure 11-1). This may not be the same in all browsers, but there is a way that you can make sure that this black box does not appear.

The `<video>` element has a poster attribute that can be used to specify a path to an image file that should be displayed in the video's place until the user clicks the Play button.

FIGURE 11-2 How the About page appears if the user's browser does not support HTML5 video.

In this section, you add a poster image to the video on the About page.

The code in this exercise can be found in folder 4.

Follow these steps to add a poster image:

1. First, download the `poster.png` file from the book's website and place it in your `img` folder. You can find this file in the `chapter11/4/img` folder of the download files.

2. Open the `about.html` file in your text editor.

3. Add a `poster` attribute to your `<video>` element and set its value to `img/poster.png`.

```
<video id="myVideo" width="400" height="225" controls
       poster="img/poster.png">
  ...
</video>
```

4. IE9 contains a bug that prevents the browser from using the poster image. To work around this bug, you need to add a `preload` attribute to the `<video>` element and set its value to none.

```
<video id="myVideo" width="400" height="225" controls
       poster="img/poster.png" preload="none">
   ...
</video>
```

5. Save the about.html file.

Now, if you take a look at the About page in your web browser, you should see a nice image of Mike the Frog, as shown in Figure 11-3.

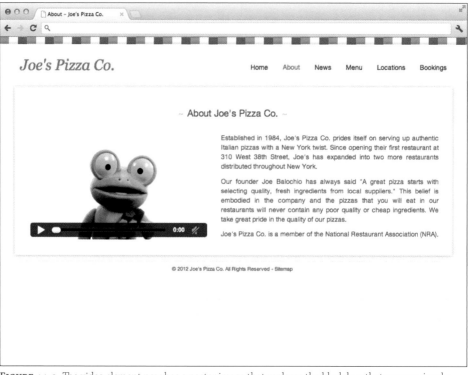

FIGURE 11-3 The video element now has a poster image that replaces the black box that was previously displayed.

The fallback content displays only if a browser does not support HTML5 video at all. If the browser does support HTML5 video but you haven't provided a file in a format it can play, the browser just shows an empty black box.

Other <video> Attributes

In addition to the `poster` attribute, you can use a few other attributes on the `<video>` element. You won't be using the following attributes in the example website, but they are useful to know about.

The `autoplay` attribute tells the browser to start playing the video as soon as the page finishes loading. This is a *Boolean* attribute; it has no value because its presence alone is enough to prompt an action by the browser.

```
<video src="." width="." height="." autoplay></video>
```

Be sure to use the `autoplay` attribute wisely. It can be annoying for users if your video starts playing on its own. If you are going to use the `autoplay` attribute, consider using the `muted` attribute too. The `muted` attribute simply mutes the audio track of the video. Again this is a Boolean attribute.

```
<video src="." width="." height="." muted></video>
```

> The `muted` attribute is not supported in Safari and IE9 (and earlier versions).

The `loop` attribute causes a video or audio clip to repeat itself every time it finishes. This attribute is particularly useful when applied to `<audio>` elements.

```
<audio src="." width="." height="." loop></audio>
```

Creating Custom Controls Using JavaScript

So far in this chapter, you have relied on the browser's default controls for controlling playback. In this section, you get rid of these default controls and build your own custom controls that allow the user to play, pause, seek, and mute your video as well as control the volume.

The `<video>` and `<audio>` elements both have the same underlying interface, `HTMLMedia Element`. This interface allows you to interact with the video and audio content in your pages using JavaScript. As you progress through this chapter, you learn about the various methods and properties that you can use to control your media content. Again, in this section, you focus on video—but everything you learn here applies to audio, too.

Before you can start building your custom playback controls, you first need to add a JavaScript file to your project. This file contains all the JavaScript code that controls the video.

 The code for this exercise can be found in folder 5.

Here are the steps for adding a JavaScript file:

1. Create a folder named `js` in the root of your project folder.

2. Within this new `js` folder, create a new file called `video.js`.

3. Open the `video.js` file in your text editor.

4. Copy the following code into this file. Here you create a variable (`video`) that contains a reference to the `<video>` element on the page.

    ```
    window.onload = function() {
      // Get the video.
      var video = document.getElementById("myVideo");
    }
    ```

5. Save the `video.js` file.

6. Open the `about.html` file in your text editor.

7. Add the following `<script>` element just before the `</body>` tag. This tells the browser to load the `video.js` file into the About page.

    ```
    . . .
    <script src="js/video.js"></script>
    </body>
    ```

8. Remove the `controls` attribute from the `<video>` element.

9. Save the `about.html` file.

That's it! Everything is set up, and you're ready to start building those custom controls. Let's get started.

Debugging Your JavaScript Code

If you encounter any problems when building the controls in this chapter, try using your browser's developer tools to help you find any bugs that might be in your code.

Most modern web browsers have a JavaScript console as part of their developer tools. If the browser encounters an error when trying to execute your JavaScript code, it prints the error message to this console. To access the JavaScript console, click the Console tab in your developer tools.

When something is not working as you want it to, check this console for any errors. The errors can help you to pinpoint the problem with your code. It is often something as simple as a misspelling in a method name or a missing semicolon from the end of a line.

Creating the Play Button

To start playing a video, you can call the `play()` method on the `<video>` element through JavaScript.

The Play button uses a `<button>` element that hooks up to an event listener in your JavaScript code. When the button is clicked, the event listener calls the `play()` method on your `<video>` element.

The code for this exercise can be found in folder 6.

Start by adding the new Play button to your HTML code. Follow these steps:

1. Open the about.html file in your text editor.

2. Underneath the `<video>` element, create a new `<div>` with the ID video-controls.

```
<video id="myVideo" width="400" height="225"
       poster="img/poster.png" preload="none">
  ...
</video>
<div id="video-controls"></div>
```

3. Within this new <div> element, create a <button> element. Set the type to button and the ID to playBtn.

```
<div id="video-controls">
  <button type="button" id="playBtn">Play</button>
</div>
```

4. Save the about.html file.

Next, you need to set up an event listener that fires when the Play button is clicked:

1. Open the video.js file in your text editor.

2. Create a new variable called playBtn and initialize it by fetching the Play button in your HTML.

```
window.onload = function() {
  // Get the video.
  var video = document.getElementById("myVideo");

  // Get the buttons.
  var playBtn = document.getElementById("playBtn");
}
```

3. Now create an event listener on the Play button that fires when the click event occurs.

```
window.onload = function() {
  ...
  // Add an event listener for the play button.
  playBtn.addEventListener("click", function(e) {

  });
}
```

4. Within the function block of this event listener, add a statement that calls the play() method on the video variable.

```
// Add an event listener for the play button.
playBtn.addEventListener("click", function(e) {
  // Play the video.
  video.play();
});
```

5. Save the video.js file.

Open the About page in your web browser. If all went according to plan, a Play button should be beneath the video, as shown in Figure 11-4. Click the button and the video should start playing. Success!

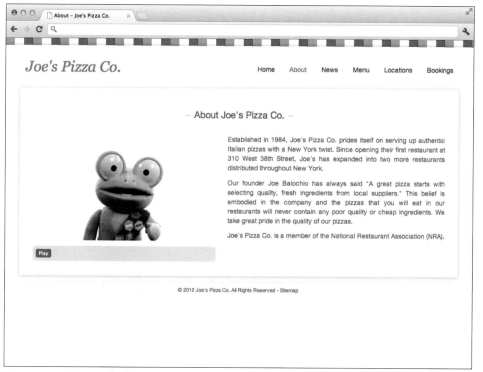

FIGURE 11-4 The new Play button.

If clicking the Play button doesn't start your video, check your code against the files in folder 6 of the download code. There is probably a typo or a missing semi-colon somewhere.

There is one problem: You don't have a way to stop the video yet. Let's fix that.

Creating the Pause Button

The `<video>` and `<audio>` elements have a method you can call that causes playback to pause. This is the `pause()` method.

In this section, you follow a process similar to the one you used when you created the Play button.

The code for this exercise can be found in folder 7.

Start by adding the new Pause button to your HTML code:

1. Open the about.html file in your text editor.

2. Create a new <button> element underneath the Play button. Set the type to button and the ID to pauseBtn.

```
<div id="video-controls">
  <button type="button" id="playBtn">Play</button>
  <button type="button" id="pauseBtn">Pause</button>
</div>
```

3. Save the about.html file.

Now, you need set up an event listener that fires when the Pause button is clicked:

1. Open the video.js file in your text editor.

2. Create a new variable called pauseBtn and initialize it by fetching the Pause button in your HTML.

```
window.onload = function() {
  ...
  // Get the buttons.
  var playBtn = document.getElementById("playBtn");
  var pauseBtn = document.getElementById("pauseBtn");
}
```

3. Create an event listener on the Pause button that fires when the click event occurs. You should add this below the event listener you created for the Play button.

```
window.onload = function() {
  ...
  // Add an event listener for the pause button.
  pauseBtn.addEventListener("click", function(e) {

  });
}
```

4. Within the function block of this event listener, add a statement that will call the pause() method on the video variable.

```
// Add an event listener for the pause button.
pauseBtn.addEventListener("click", function(e) {
  // Pause the video.
  video.pause();
});
```

5. Save the video.js file.

Open the About page. You should see your new Pause button, as shown in Figure 11-5. Try playing the video and then using the Pause button to pause playback. If the Pause button doesn't work, try using your browser's developer tools to diagnose what is causing the problem.

FIGURE 11-5 The new Pause button.

Seeking by Using a Slider

You can now control the basic playback of your video, but it would be kind of cool if you could also seek through the video. To do this, you create a Seek bar using a range slider that's hooked up to an event listener. Every time the user moves the Seek bar, the action manipulates the video's `currentTime` property, which moves playback to the desired point.

> The code for this exercise can be found in folder 8.

Let's start by adding the range slider to your HTML:

1. Open the about.html file in your text editor.

2. Create a new <input> element below the Pause button. Set its type to range, its ID to seekBar, and its value to 0.

```
<input type="range" id="seekBar" value="0">
```

3. Save the about.html file.

Next, you need to hook this range slider up to the video using an event listener:

1. Open the video.js file.

2. Create a new variable called seekBar and initialize it by fetching the <input> element you just created.

```
window.onload = function() {
  ...
  var pauseBtn = document.getElementById("pauseBtn");
  var seekBar = document.getElementById("seekBar");
  ...
}
```

3. Create a new event listener on the seekBar that listens for the change event.

```
window.onload = function() {
  ...
  // Add an event listener for the seek bar.
  seekBar.addEventListener("change", function(e) {

  });
}
```

4. Within the function block of this event listener, you first need to calculate the time the video must be moved to. You do this by multiplying the duration of the video by the value of the Seek bar divided by 100. You access the video's duration property to get the video duration.

```
// Add an event listener for the seek bar.
seekBar.addEventListener("change", function(e) {
  // Calculate the time in the video that playback
  // should be moved to.
  var time = video.duration * ( seekBar.value / 100 );
});
```

5. Now that you have the `time` variable calculated, you need to update the video's `currentTime` property.

```
// Add an event listener for the seek bar.
seekBar.addEventListener("change", function(e) {
  // Calculate the time in the video that playback
  // should be moved to.
  var time = video.duration * ( seekBar.value / 100 );

  // Update the current time in the video.
  video.currentTime = time;
});
```

6. Save the `video.js` file.

Now if you open the About page and play the video, you can skip to different parts of the video using the new Seek bar. Great work so far! There are still a few little problems, however. As you drag the bar, the video continues to attempt to play, causing jerky playback. The position of the slider handle also does not move along the slider as the video plays.

Later, we address the problem of jerky playback. First, let's fix the Seek bar so that the position of the slider handle updates as the video plays:

1. In the `video.js` file, create a new event listener on the `video` variable (yes, videos fire events too!) that listens for the `timeupdate` event. This event is fired repeatedly as the video plays.

```
window.onload = function() {
  ...
  // Update the seek bar as the video plays.
  video.addEventListener("timeupdate", function(e) {

  });
}
```

2. Calculate the correct position for the slider handle relative to the playback of the video. To do this, you divide the video duration by 100 and then multiply the result by the current time in the video.

```
// Update the seek bar as the video plays.
video.addEventListener("timeupdate", function(e) {
  // Calculate the slider value.
  var value = ( 100 / video.duration ) * .
  video.currentTime;
});
```

3. Update the slider value using the `value` variable you just created. This moves the slider handle along the slider.

```
// Update the seek bar as the video plays.
video.addEventListener("timeupdate", function(e) {
  // Calculate the slider value.
  var value = ( 100 / video.duration ) *
  video.currentTime;

  // Update the slider value.
  seekBar.value = value;
});
```

4. Save the `video.js` file.

Open the About page again and click the Play button. You should now see that the slider handle moves along the slider as the video plays. Awesome!

Let's fix that problem with jerky playback as you seek the video.

To fix this problem, you use two event listeners. The first event listener pauses the video when the user clicks the slider handle; the second event listener plays the video when the user releases the mouse button. This prevents the video from trying to play as the user moves the slider handle. Follow these steps:

1. Create a new event listener on the `seekBar` that listens for the mousedown event, and place a statement inside its function block that will pause the video.

```
window.onload = function() {
  ...
  // Pause playback when the user starts seeking.
  seekBar.addEventListener("mousedown", function(e) {
    video.pause();
  });
}
```

2. Create the other event listener that starts the video playing again when the user releases the mouse button (the mouseup event).

```
window.onload = function() {
  ...
  // Continue playback when the user stops seeking.
  seekBar.addEventListener("mouseup", function(e) {
    video.play();
  });
}
```

3. Save the `video.js` file.

That's it! You're all done with the Seek bar.

Open the About page and play around a bit with the Seek bar. You should see that the video pauses when you start to drag the slider handle and then starts playing again when you release it. The frame displayed in the video still changes as you drag the handle to show where you are moving to in the video. Figure 11-6 shows how your page should look with the new Seek bar.

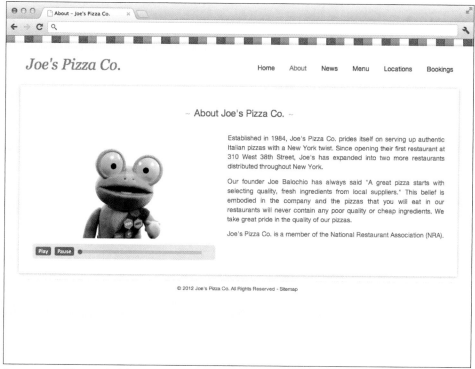

FIGURE 11-6 The new Seek bar.

Next, you tackle the volume control.

Creating the Volume Control

The Volume control also uses a slider. This time it is hooked up to an event listener that manipulates the video's `volume` property. The value of the `volume` property should be a number between 0 and 1.

The code in this exercise can be found in folder 9.

Here are the steps for creating a volume control:

1. Open the about.html file.

2. Add an <input> element and <label> below the Seek bar. Note the attributes on the <input> element.

```
<label for="volume">Volume: </label>
<input type="range" id="volume" min="0" max="1" step="0.1"
       value="1">
```

3. Save the about.html file.

4. Open the video.js file.

5. Create a new variable volumeControl and initialize it by fetching the volume slider in your HMTL.

```
window.onload = function() {

   . . .
   var seekBar = document.getElementById("seekBar");
   var volumeControl = document.getElementById("volume");

   . . .
}
```

6. Create a new event listener on volumeControl that listens for the change event.

```
window.onload = function() {

   . . .
   // Add an event listener for the volume control.
   volumeControl.addEventListener("change", function(e) {

   });
}
```

7. Inside the function block of this event listener, update the video's volume property using the current value of the volumeControl.

```
// Add an event listener for the volume control.
volumeControl.addEventListener("change", function(e) {
   // Update the videos volume property.
   video.volume = volumeControl.value;
});
```

8. Save the video.js file.

Open the About page and start playing the video. As you drag the volume slider, the volume changes. Figure 11-7 shows how your new Volume control should look.

FIGURE 11-7 The new Volume control.

Creating a Mute Button

The volume slider you just created works great, but sometimes it can be useful to have a Mute button, too. You can mute the audio for your video by setting the `muted` property to `true`.

You should always use the `muted` property rather than just setting the volume to 0. That way, you do not have to write code that remembers the volume level before you mute and retrieves that value when you unmute.

> The code for this exercise can be found in folder 10.

Here are the steps for creating a Mute button:

1. Open the `about.html` file in your text editor.

2. Create a new `<button>` element below the volume slider and give it the ID `muteBtn`.

   ```
   <button type="button" id="muteBtn">Mute</button>
   ```

3. Save the about.html file.

4. Open the video.js file in your text editor.

5. Add a variable for the Mute button called muteBtn.

```
window.onload = function() {

  . . .
  var volumeControl = document.getElementById("volume");
  var muteBtn = document.getElementById("muteBtn");
  . . .
}
```

6. Create a new event listener for muteBtn that listens for the click event.

```
window.onload = function() {

  . . .
  // Add an event listener for the mute button.
  muteBtn.addEventListener("click", function(e) {

  });
}
```

7. Inside the function block of this event listener, you use an if/else statement to check whether the video is currently muted. If it is, you set the muted property to false and update the button text to Mute; otherwise, set the muted property to true and the button text to Unmute.

```
// Add an event listener for the mute button.
muteBtn.addEventListener("click", function(e) {
  // Toggle the muted value.
  if (video.muted == true) {
    video.muted = false;
    muteBtn.textContent = "Mute";
  } else {
    video.muted = true;
    muteBtn.textContent = "Unmute";
  }
);
```

8. Save the video.js file.

Open the About page in your web browser. If you start playing the video and then click the Mute button, the audio is muted. Click the button again and the audio comes back. Figure 11-8 shows how the Mute button should look in your browser.

FIGURE 11-8 The Mute button.

You've now created all your custom video controls. The CSS stylesheet you added in Chapter 2 takes care of styling them appropriately. Next, you find out how to make your video more accessible by adding subtitles.

Making Your Video Accessible

It's important to remember that not everyone is lucky enough to experience the rich media that the web has to offer. HTML5 has been designed with this in mind. A number of technologies are available that you can use to ensure that people with disabilities can enjoy your multimedia content. In this section, you learn about the different types of subtitles and how you can use the HTML5 <track> element to add subtitles to your video and audio content.

You can package subtitles with your videos in two ways. The first method, *in-band* subtitles, involves embedding the subtitle file within the video file itself. The MP4 file format, for example, is a container for an H.263 video component and an AAC audio component. This format also has the facility for you to store more metadata files within it (including subtitle files). After a subtitle file has been embedded within a file, it is still up to the media player (read: browser) to find it and put it to use.

The second method you can use to add subtitles to a video is *out-of-band* subtitles. These are not directly packaged within the media file; instead, they are provided as separate .VTT files. The new `<track>` element can be used to associate these files with a video.

Later in this section you use the HTML5 `<track>` element to add subtitles to your video. First, however, take a quick look at some of the attributes of the `<track>` element:

- **src**—This attribute provides a path to the subtitles file.

- **kind**—This attribute describes what kind of content the file referenced in the `src` attribute contains. We will be using `subtitles`, but other possible values are `captions`, `descriptions`, `chapters`, and `metadata`.

- **label**—The attribute should be used to provide a title for the track. If you have more than one `<track>` element, the browser may present a list of subtitles for the user to choose from; this label will appear in that list.

- **srclang**—This attribute specifies the content language of the subtitles file. Browsers may try to select the correct subtitle's file based on the value of this attribute and the user's preferences.

- **default**—This attribute sets the current track to be used as default unless the user's browser preferences specify otherwise.

I think you've learned enough about the `<track>` element now. Let's add some subtitles to your video.

 The code for this exercise can be found in folder 11.

Follow these steps to add subtitles:

1. Download the subtitle's file (`subtitles_en.vtt`) from the book's website and place it in your `videos` folder. You can find it in the `chapter11/11/videos` folder.

2. Open the `about.html` file in your text editor.

3. Underneath the last `<source>` element, add the following `<track>` element.

```
<video id="myVideo" width="400" height="225"
        poster="img/poster.png" preload="none">
  <source src="videos/mikethefrog.webm" type="video/webm">
  <source src="videos/mikethefrog.ogv" type="video/ogv">
  <source src="videos/mikethefrog.mp4" type="video/mp4">
```

```
<track kind="subtitles" label="English subtitles"
       src="videos/subtitles_en.vtt" srclang="en"
       default>
</track>

<p>
  Your browser doesn't support HTML5 video.
  <a href="videos/mikethefrog.mp4">Download</a> the
  video instead.
</p>
</video>
```

4. Save the `about.html` file.

To test out the subtitles, you need to install a local development server on your computer. If you do not feel comfortable doing this, you can skip the remainder of this section and trust me when I say the subtitles will work. Figure 11-9 shows how the page looks when subtitles are enabled.

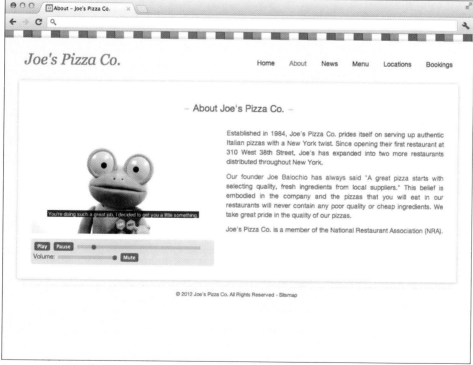

FIGURE 11-9 The About page with video subtitles.

Browser support for the <track> element is still lacking a bit, so I recommend that you test your About page in Google Chrome. To enable support for the <track> element in Chrome, type **chrome://flags** into the address bar and press Enter; then enable the Enable <track> Element option.

At the time of this writing, the <track> element still does not work unless the website is on a web server. So far in this book, you have been accessing the web pages directly from your hard drive using the file:// protocol. (Take a look at the address bar in your browser; it's there.) If you want to test the subtitles, you need to install a local development server using a tool such as XAMPP (http://www.apachefriends.org/en/xampp.html). When you have a local development server installed, make sure that your project files are in a folder accessible by the web server (such as the xampp/htdocs folder if using XAMPP on Mac) and open the About page to test your subtitles.

Summary

Native video and audio are some of the nicest new features of HTML5. In this chapter, you learned how to convert and embed video files into your web pages. You also learned about the available file formats and which browsers support them.

You put your JavaScript skills to the test in this chapter, creating custom controls for controlling the playback of the video you embedded on the About page of Joe's Pizza Co.'s website—learning all about the HTMLMediaElement interface in the process.

Finally, you took steps to make your video more accessible by adding subtitles using the new <track> element. This element can help people understand the video, even if they are hearing impaired or do not speak the language you are using for your website.

In Chapter 12, you learn how to store data on a user's computer by using the new client-side storage APIs introduced in HTML5.

chapter twelve
Storing Data

ALMOST ALL APPLICATIONS involve storing data of some kind. This can be data about users, products, videos, or even page visits. Used correctly, this data can be a powerful tool in the decision-making process. That's why companies like Google and Facebook try to collect as much data as they can about their users and their behaviors.

Web applications that handle a lot of data have traditionally used databases for storage. These databases are stored on servers that are often hundreds, if not thousands, of miles away from the user (hence the term *server-side* storage). An alternative option is *client-side* storage. Storing data on the client side means that it is stored on the user's computer or device—the *client*—as opposed to being stored on a web server. In this chapter, you learn about the strengths and weaknesses of using client-side storage. You explore two new technologies that HTML5 introduces for storing data on the client side and learn how these technologies can be used in modern web applications and websites to boost performance and make websites function offline.

More pros and cons of using client-side storage are discussed in the last portion of this chapter.

Why Use Client-Side Storage?

There are many reasons why you might want to store data on the client. In this section, I explore some of the most important, such as the following:

- **Performance**—With a traditional website, every time an application wants to fetch some data, it has to send a request to the server, wait for it to respond, and then download the response. This all takes time and can slow down the user's browsing experience. If you store data on the client, it can be accessed much more quickly because there is no need to make lengthy HTTP requests. Just to clarify: By lengthy, I mean 200 to 400 milliseconds (more on mobile devices). This might not sound like a lot, but it all adds up.

- **Offline access**—The capability to access your data offline is another reason why many developers prefer to keep data on the client side. This is especially prudent for web applications built for mobile phones; these devices are more likely to be without a stable Internet connection at some point in the day. If the data is stored on the device, it can be accessed without having to talk to a web server.

- **No cookies**—Before HTML5 came along, most client-side data was stored using *cookies*, small pieces of data stored in the browser. Cookies have several problems that make them unsuitable for storing a relatively large quantity of data. The first problem is that cookies are limited in size—to be specific, 4096 bytes. That's not much space for storing data. The other big drawback is that cookies are sent with every request your browser makes to the web server, whether needed or not. This increases the amount of time each request takes to complete, and therefore affects your application's performance.

HTML5 introduces two new APIs that you can use to store data on a client: LocalStorage and SessionStorage. In the next few sections, you learn how to use LocalStorage and SessionStorage to store data on a client.

 Note that when I refer to client-side storage in this chapter, I am referring to LocalStorage and SessionStorage, not IndexedDB, which is also classed as a client-side storage API but is a little too advanced for this book.

LocalStorage

LocalStorage is a simple way of storing data using key/value pairs. The LocalStorage API consists of an object that provides several functions to store, access, and delete data from the client. You access the API using JavaScript.

All the data that your web application stores is placed in a datastore that is accessible only through your application. This means that the data your application saves cannot be accessed by other applications, and vice versa. Applications are identified by their domain names. If you have sub-domains, such as `a.example.com` and `b.example.com`, they are treated as separate applications and are each given their own datastore.

Using Key/Value Pairs

The concept of key/value pairs is explained in Chapter 5, which examines how form data is passed via parameters in a URL.

If you want to store a simple piece of data, such as a user's name, you create a key that describes the data (in this case, `name`) and then use the data (that is, a specific user's name) as that key's value. This mechanism is good for storing simple unstructured data; however, if you want to store data about multiple users at once, you might be better off utilizing a system that supports structured data, such as a database.

The technical term for assigning datastores to specific domains is *sandboxing*.

To start using LocalStorage, you first need to get familiar with the `localStorage` object and its associated functions. Fire up your developer tools console; you're going to need it in this section. After you work through the examples in the next few pages, you use what you learn here to add LocalStorage capabilities to the bookings form on the Joe's Pizza Co. website.

setItem(key, value)

The `setItem()` function has two parameters. The first parameter, `key`, is used to assign the name by which you access the data. The second, `value`, is where you put the data you want to save.

Try saving some data. Start by opening up a blank HTML file in your browser and naming it `test.html`. Next, fire up the console in your developer tools and enter the following code:

```
localStorage.setItem("name", "Joe Balochio");
```

If all went well, that data should now be stored in the datastore that the browser created for your domain.

Next let's retrieve your data.

getItem(key)

The `getItem()` function has just one parameter, the `key` that is used to identify your data in the datastore.

Try retrieving the data you saved in the preceding example. Enter the following code into your console:

```
localStorage.getItem("name");
```

You should see that the data you stored is displayed in the console window, as shown in Figure 12-1.

FIGURE 12-1 Retrieving data in localStorage using the getItem() function.

The data that you store in LocalStorage is *persistent*. This means that if you close your browser window and then reopen it, the data is still there. Try closing your browser and then loading the same HTML file again. Can you still access the data?

removeItem(key)

Naturally you need to be able to remove the data that you place in LocalStorage. This is done using the `removeItem()` function, passing in the `key` of the data you want to remove.

Try removing the data you saved in the previous example and then attempt to fetch it again. If all goes well, it should be gone.

```
localStorage.removeItem("name");
localStorage.getItem("name");
```

You should see that the console returns `null` when you try to fetch the data. This is shown in Figure 12-2.

FIGURE 12-2 Removing data using the removeItem() function.

key(index)

The `localStorage` object also has a function you can use to retrieve the name of a key from the datastore. This function is called `key()`, and it takes an integer that represents the position of a key in the key index. The order in which keys are stored in this index varies between browsers. This means that you cannot really rely on this function for finding a specific key, but it does come in handy when trying to retrieve all of the data in LocalStorage; as you will see in the next example.

Try storing a few key/value pairs and then retrieving all the keys in LocalStorage. Enter each line in the code listing below into your console. You need to type the entire `for` loop into the console on one line.

```
// Store some data.
localStorage.setItem("name", "Joe Balochio");
localStorage.setItem("phone", "012-345-6789");
localStorage.setItem("email", "joe@example.com");

// Retrieve the keys for your data.
for (var i = 0; i < localStorage.length; i++) {
console.log(localStorage.key(i)) };
```

The `for` loop in this example will iterate through each piece of data stored in LocalStorage and print the keys to the console, as Figure 12-3 shows.

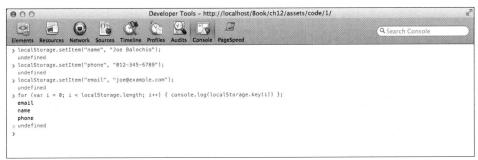

FIGURE 12-3 Finding key names using the key() function.

clear()

To clear all the data stored in your application's datastore, you can use the `clear()` function. This deletes every key/value pair associated with your application.

Try deleting all the data you have stored up to now. Enter the following into your console window:

```
localStorage.clear();
```

Now try to retrieve some data. You should find that the `getItem()` function returns `null`, as shown in Figure 12-4.

FIGURE 12-4 Using the clear() function to delete all the stored data.

length

You can find out how many key/value pairs have been stored by accessing the `length` property of the `localStorage` object.

Store some key/value pairs and access the length in your console.

```
localStorage.length;
```

Note that this is a property, not a function, so it has no parentheses or parameters.

Saving Customer Data from the Bookings Form

A use case that suits LocalStorage particularly well is saving the data that a user commonly inputs into a web form. In this section, you use the LocalStorage API to store data from the bookings form on the Joe's Pizza Co. website. You then add some JavaScript code that attempts to pre-load the form with this stored data when the page loads. Specifically, you are storing data from the Name, Phone, and Email fields of the form.

The code for this exercise can be found in the download code for Chapter 12, folder 1.

Here are the steps for saving user data:

1. Open the bookings.html file in your text editor.

2. Load the storage.js file (you create this shortly) into the Bookings page by adding a new <script> element just above the closing tag of the <body> element.

```
<script src="js/storage.js"></script>
</body>
```

3. Locate the <form> element and add an id attribute to it with the value bookings Form.

4. Save and close the bookings.html file.

5. Create a new file in your text editor called storage.js and save it in the js folder.

6. Attach an empty function to the onload event of the window, as you did for the video.js file in Chapter 11.

```
window.onload = function() {

}
```

7. Check that LocalStorage is supported by the user's web browser. To do this, create an if statement that looks for the presence of the localStorage object. Remember, lines that start with // are comments.

```
window.onload = function() {
    // Check for LocalStorage support.
    if (localStorage) {

    }
}
```

8. Create a new variable called form and initialize it by fetching the <form> element from your Bookings page using its ID.

```
window.onload = function() {
    // Check for LocalStorage support.
    if (localStorage) {
        // Get the form
        var form = document.getElementById("bookingsForm");
    }
}
```

9. Set up an event listener on the form that is executed when the form is submitted (or the submit event is fired).

```
// Get the form
var form = document.getElementById("bookingsForm");

// Event listener for when the bookings form is submitted.
form.addEventListener("submit", function(e) {

});
```

10. Inside the function block of this event listener, add a call to saveData(form). You create this function in the next step.

```
form.addEventListener("submit", function(e) {
  saveData(form);
});
```

11. At the bottom of the storage.js file, create a new function called saveData().

```
window.onload = function() {
  ...
}

// Save the form data in LocalStorage.
function saveData() {

}
```

12. You now need to get the values from the Name, Phone, and Email <input> elements. Within the saveData() function, create three new variables (name, phone, and email), and initialize them by fetching the <input> elements using their IDs.

```
function saveData() {
  // Fetch the input elements.
  var name = document.getElementById("name");
  var phone = document.getElementById("phone");
  var email = document.getElementById("email");
}
```

13. Now that you have references to the <input> elements, you can get their values and store them in LocalStorage. Use the setItem() function to store the values.

```
function saveData() {
  // Fetch the input elements.
  var name = document.getElementById("name");
  var phone = document.getElementById("phone");
```

```
    var email = document.getElementById("email");

    // Store the values.
    localStorage.setItem("name", name.value);
    localStorage.setItem("phone", phone.value);
    localStorage.setItem("email", email.value);
}
```

14. You have now added all the code needed to store a user's contact details when the form is submitted. Save the `storage.js` file and try submitting some data using the bookings form. If you go back to the Bookings page, you can use the developer tools console to check that data is being stored correctly. Use the `localStorage.getItem(key)` function you learned about earlier in this chapter to retrieve the data.

15. Write code to populate the form fields with the data in LocalStorage when the page loads. Create a new function called `populateForm()` below the `saveData()` function:

```
// Attempt to populate the form using data stored in
LocalStorage.
function populateForm() {


}
```

16. Copy the code that you used to fetch the form fields in your `saveData()` function to the new `populateForm()` function.

```
// Attempt to populate the form using data stored in
LocalStorage.
function populateForm() {
    // Fetch the input elements.
    var name = document.getElementById("name");
    var phone = document.getElementById("phone");
    var email = document.getElementById("email");
}
```

17. Set the `value` property of each of these three inputs using the data stored in LocalStorage. You can use the `getItem(key)` function to retrieve data from the datastore. If no contact data has been saved yet, the `getItem()` function returns `null`. Most browsers recognize that `null` is not the desired value and won't update the value of the input. However, Internet Explorer will populate the fields with the string `null`. This means that you need to first check that the result of `getItem()` is not null before updating an input's value. Use multiple `if` statements to do this.

```
// Attempt to populate the form using data stored in
LocalStorage.
function populateForm() {
```

```
// Fetch the input elements.
var name = document.getElementById("name");
var phone = document.getElementById("phone");
var email = document.getElementById("email");

// Retrieve the saved data and update the values of the
// form fields.
if (localStorage.getItem("name") != null) {
  name.value = localStorage.getItem("name");
}

if (localStorage.getItem("phone") != null) {
  phone.value = localStorage.getItem("phone");
}

if (localStorage.getItem("email") != null) {
  email.value = localStorage.getItem("email");
}
}
```

18. To finish up, add a call to the populateForm() function at the top of the window. onload event listener.

```
window.onload = function() {
  // Check for LocalStorage support
  if (localStorage) {
    // Populate the form fields
    populateForm(form);

    . . .

  }
}
```

19. Save the storage.js file.

That's it! You have now successfully implemented LocalStorage into your website.

Try opening up the Bookings page and entering some data into the form. When you click the Request Booking button, the contact details will be saved. Go back to the Bookings page and you should see that the Name, Phone, and Email fields are already populated when the page loads. Figure 12-5 shows how this looks in your web browser.

Using the LocalStorage API to enhance your web forms in this way can be beneficial to users. In the next section, you learn how to store more complex data in LocalStorage, such as JavaScript objects and arrays.

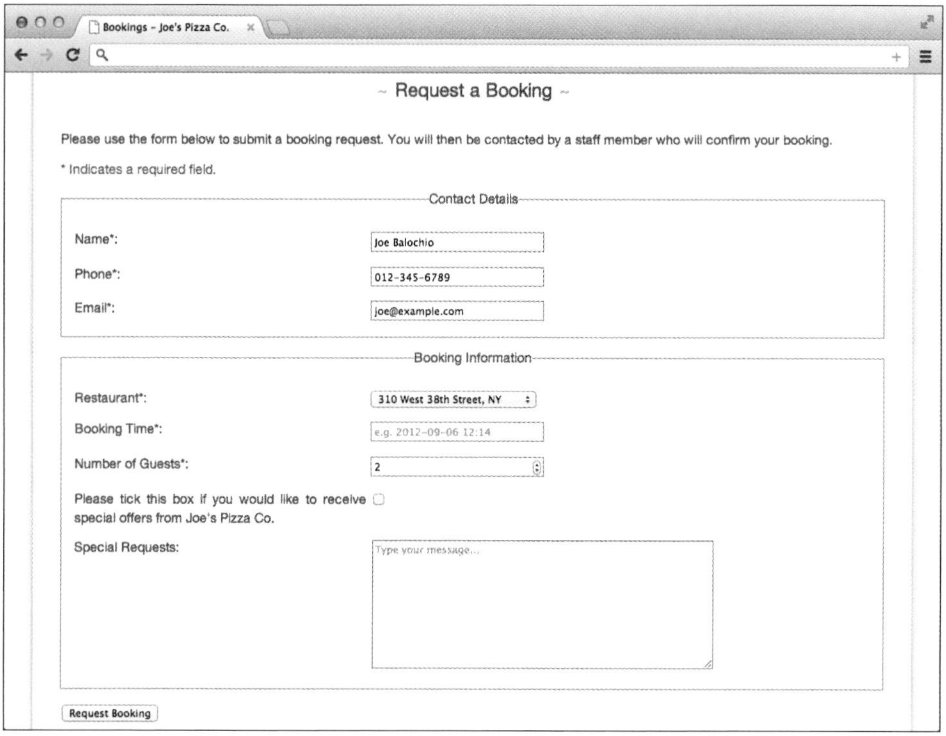

FIGURE 12-5 The Name, Phone, and Email fields are populated from data stored in LocalStorage.

Storing Objects and Arrays

Until now, you looked only at how to store text and numbers using LocalStorage. In this section, let's look at how you can store more complex data such as objects and arrays.

A key component in storing these types of data is the use of a data interchange format called JSON.

Introducing JSON

JavaScript Object Notation, or *JSON*, is a lightweight data interchange format used to transmit data over a network. It uses a human-readable, standardized syntax to define data objects that can be parsed by many computer programs.

Here is an example of how to define a simple JavaScript object in JSON.

```
{
    "name": "Joe Balochio",
    "age": "28",
    "gender": "male"
}
```

You define a new object in JSON using curly braces {} and then use key/value pairs to define the object's properties. A colon is used to separate a key from its value, and commas separate each of the properties in the object.

JSON objects can easily be serialized and parsed by libraries present in many programming languages. *Serialization* is the process of taking an object in your code and converting it to a JSON object, like the one in the example above. *Parsing* is the opposite; it takes a JSON object and converts it to an object that can be used in your JavaScript code.

The JSON Object

Many programming languages have built-in libraries that provide support for JSON. In JavaScript, you can use the JSON object to make use of the JSON library present in most browsers (excluding IE7 and below). This object has several available functions that you can use to help handle JSON data.

stringify(object)

The first function that we are going to look at is `stringify()`. This function converts an object (or objects) into a JSON object(s) and then returns that JSON as a string. Let's test this out.

Open your console and create a new JavaScript object by entering the following statements:

```
var person = {};
person.name = "Joe Balochio";
person.age = 28;
person.gender = "male";
```

Now that you have created a JavaScript object, use the `stringify()` function to convert it to JSON.

```
var jsonPerson = JSON.stringify(person);
```

This converts the `person` object to JSON and saves the result to the `jsonPerson` variable. You can output the JSON by inspecting the `jsonPerson` variable in the console (just type `jsonPerson` and press Enter). Figure 12-6 shows the expected output for this example.

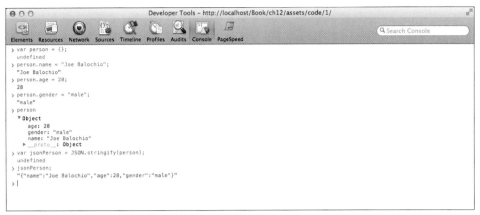

FIGURE 12-6 Converting a JavaScript object to JSON.

parse(json)

Now that you know how to convert JavaScript objects to JSON, let's look at how you can convert JSON back to JavaScript objects. This is done using the `parse()` function. Simply pass this function your JSON, and it will return your object(s).

Try converting the JSON you have stored in the `jsonPerson` variable back to a JavaScript object. Enter the following into your console.

```
JSON.parse(jsonPerson);
```

This outputs an object into the console. You could also initialize a new variable to hold this object if you so desired. Figure 12-7 shows the JavaScript object that has been parsed from the JSON.

FIGURE 12-7 Converting a JSON string to a JavaScript object.

Objects in LocalStorage

More complex types of data such as JavaScript objects cannot be stored in the same way as text and numbers. If you tried to store a normal JavaScript object, it would be converted to a string and saved. The problem is that you cannot easily get this data back to an object once it has been saved. This is where JSON comes in. Using JSON, you can convert a JavaScript object to a JSON string and then save that. Then when you want to retrieve your object, you simply retrieve the JSON and parse it.

Storing Objects

Storing your objects using JSON is fairly simple. The following example shows how to do it. Fire up your console and give it a go.

```
// Create an object.
var myObject = {};
myObject.name = "book";
myObject.color = "green";
myObject.pages = 292;

// Convert the object to JSON.
var json = JSON.stringify(myObject);

// Store the JSON using localStorage.
localStorage.setItem("myObject", json);
```

In this example, you created a new JavaScript object, converted it to JSON, and then saved it on the client using LocalStorage.

Retrieving Objects

So that's great: You have your JavaScript object converted to JSON and safely stored in LocalStorage. But what if you want to retrieve that object? This is where the JSON.parse() function comes in handy.

The example below shows how you can retrieve your object by retrieving the JSON from the datastore and converting it to a JavaScript object.

```
// Get the JSON from the datastore.
var retrievedJson = localStorage.getItem("myObject");

// Convert the JSON to a JavaScript Object.
var myNewObject = JSON.parse(retrievedJson);
```

Now, if you inspect the myNewObject variable in the console, you should see that your JavaScript object is back! This is shown in Figure 12-8.

FIGURE 12-8 Retrieving and parsing an object from LocalStorage.

Arrays in LocalStorage

Arrays can be stored in the same way that objects are. First you must convert the array to JSON, and then you can store it as a string. To retrieve your array, you just need to parse the JSON that has been stored. The following example code shows how you could store and retrieve arrays using LocalStorage:

```
// Create an array.
var myArray = ["Mike", "Jim", "Becky", "Jo", "Steph"];

// Convert the array to JSON.
var myJsonArray = JSON.stringify(myArray);

// Store the JSON.
localStorage.setItem("myArray", myJsonArray);
```

. . . . and to retrieve the array:

```
// Retrieve the JSON.
var retrievedJson = localStorage.getItem("myArray");

// Parse the JSON.
var myNewArray = JSON.parse(retrievedJson);
```

Using JSON allows you to maintain your data structures when using a simple datastore such as LocalStorage. You should consider, however, whether you are using this facility correctly. LocalStorage is designed only to hold simple data. If you want to store multiple objects that have the same structure, you are better off using a database.

HTML5 does introduce a way of maintaining a client-side database through the IndexedDB API, which isn't covered in this book. If you're interested, I encourage you to look into it. You can find a great tutorial on how to use IndexedDB on HTML5Rocks at `http://www.html5rocks.com/en/tutorials/indexeddb/todo/`.

SessionStorage

As I mention earlier in this chapter, LocalStorage is persistent. The data you save stays there when you close your browser. This is exactly what you want for most applications; but there may be instances when you want to temporarily store some data, such as session IDs (what applications use to identify different users). It can be a pain to remember to remove all this from LocalStorage when the user leaves your page and ends the session.

SessionStorage was developed to solve this problem. This API has the exact same functions as LocalStorage (under the hood, it uses the same basic `Storage` object), but the data you save in SessionStorage is wiped by the browser when the user closes the window and ends his or her session on your website.

To use SessionStorage, you simply call your functions on the `sessionStorage` object instead of `localStorage`, as shown in the following examples:

```
sessionStorage.setItem("name", "Joe Balochio");
sessionStorage.getItem("name");
sessionStorage.key(0);
sessionStorage.removeItem("name");
sessionStorage.clear();
```

Additional Considerations on Using Client-Side Storage

The new client-side storage APIs introduced in HTML5 are truly wonderful things, but you should carefully consider whether using them adds value to your web application. For some applications, using client-side storage is a no-brainer; for others, you may be better off storing your data on a web server as people have done for the last few decades. The purpose of client-side storage is to enhance the user experience. Be careful that you don't become too eager to use it and end up diminishing it.

Browser vendors have already done a lot of work to help make client-side storage secure; however, it is important that you understand what has and has not been taken care of for you, so that you can build secure applications. In the following sections, you explore some of the factors to consider when using client-side storage in your applications.

Storage Limits

How much data will your application require? With client-side storage, all that data will be taking up valuable space on the user's hard drive, and you don't want to allow websites to store gigabytes of data and fill up your user's drive.

To prevent this problem, browser vendors have imposed a limit on the amount of storage space that each application can use. The official specification outlines that 5 megabytes is an acceptable level of storage space; ultimately, however, it is up to the browser vendor to decide how much storage space to make available. In reality, browsers currently allow between 2.5 and 5 megabytes of data to be stored. You have to think worst-case in these sorts of scenarios, so that means you can only rely on 2.5 megabytes being available. Design your applications with this in mind.

You can use the Web Storage Support Test tool to track the amount of storage available in various browsers, as well as test the amount available in the one you are using. You can find this tool at `http://dev-test.nemikor.com/web-storage/support-test/`.

User Tracking

User tracking refers to the practice of tracking what a user is doing on a website (for example, the pages and products the person views). This data is often used by a third party to carry out targeted advertising. This practice is commonplace today and is achieved by placing a unique identifier in a cookie that can then be used to track a user as he or she navigates the website.

However, some privacy concerns surround this sort of activity. User tracking can also be carried out using the LocalStorage API. Learning from the lessons of the past, the standards organizations have begun to think about how this sort of use case can be handled in a way that is more respectful of the user's privacy.

The WebStorage specification published by the W3C makes recommendations that browser vendors should follow to help protect the privacy of their users. These include making it easier for users to delete data that has been stored on the client and allowing them to blacklist websites that they do not want to have access to client-side storage. The W3C is also considering the suggestion that these blacklists should be combined so that all the browser vendors can see which sites are abusing client-side storage and take necessary precautions to protect their users.

Sensitive Data

Client-side storage is a big bonus for web applications that need to work offline and boost performance. Many of these applications, however, store personal information about users and therefore you should carefully consider how secure this data is on the client.

The job of securing data once it has been saved falls more in the realm of browser vendors because as a developer, you don't really have much control over what's "under the hood." One of the best things that browser vendors can do, and in most cases are doing, is to ensure that when you delete data from LocalStorage, it is also promptly deleted from the underlying system storage (such as the hard drive).

Cross-Directory Attacks

Assigning datastores to individual domains does wonders to stop websites from accessing each other's data. It falls down, however, when it comes to websites like the now deceased geocities.com that allowed people to create their own customized pages. All these pages were under the same domain name and, therefore, would have shared the same datastore on the client. This means that everyone could access, change, or delete the data stored by everybody else's pages. This is known as a *cross-directory attack*. At the moment, there is no way to protect against it. It is recommended that you don't use client-side storage if you are building an application that enables users to create customized web pages under the same domain.

Summary

As HTML5 matures and more companies come on board, we are going to see more and more web applications leverage both the performance boost and added offline capabilities that the new storage APIs provide. Google, for example, has already taken advantage of these APIs to build a version of Gmail that works offline.

In this chapter, you learned how to use the new storage APIs in order to save data on the client-side rather than sending it up to a server to be stored in a database. You updated the Joe's Pizza Co. website, adding some JavaScript code that saves users' contact details when they first submit the bookings form and then automatically populates the Name, Phone, and Email fields for them when they use the form in the future.

You also explored some of the privacy and security concerns surrounding client-side storage and learned what browser vendors have done to make client-side storage more secure.

Chapter 13 introduces you to the GeoLocation API. Although this is not strictly part of HTML5, it's awesome—and so I have included it in this book. You learn all about how to use the API to pinpoint your user's location and how you can use the information to personalize your websites.

part 4

Advanced HTML5 Technologies

Using Geolocation

FOR MANY YEARS now, devices such as mobile phones have had built-in GPS locators that allow native applications to get the geographic location of the device at any given time. This functionality can now be accessed by your web applications too, using the new GeoLocation API. Although this API is not strictly part of HTML5, it is fun to play around with and so I have included it in this book.

In this chapter, you learn how to use the GeoLocation API to request a user's location. You will be modifying the Locations page so that it highlights the restaurant location that is closest to the user. To do this, you will be using the GeoLocation API and a small JavaScript library that I have provided. Figure 13-1 shows how your Locations page will look by the time you complete this chapter.

FIGURE 13-1 Using the GeoLocation API to highlight the nearest restaurant on the Locations page.
Map data 2012 © Google

Getting the User's Location

The GeoLocation API is remarkably simple to use. Browsers that support geolocation expose a `geolocation` interface that has a number of methods (kind of like how you call `getElementById()` on the document object).

The main method that you will be using in this chapter is `getCurrentPosition()`. This will return a `GeoPosition` object that has a number of properties, including `coords`. The `coords` property contains data such as the `latitude` and `longitude` of the user's position. Later in this chapter, you will be using these latitude and longitude coordinates to calculate the distance between the user and each of the Joe's Pizza restaurants. Then you will write some code that compares the results to find the closest restaurant.

Setting Up Your JavaScript Files

Before you can dive into writing code that interacts with the GeoLocation API, you first need to add two new JavaScript files to your project. The first of these contains a small JavaScript library to help you out when calculating distances; the second file is where you will place all of the code you are going to write.

The code for this exercise can be found in the download files for Chapter 13, folder 1.

Here are the steps:

1. Download the `geo.js` file from the book's website and place it in the `js` folder within your project directory. The `geo.js` file can be found in the following folder: `chapter13/1/js`.

2. Create a new file in your `js` folder and call it `geolocation.js`.

3. Open the `locations.html` file in your text editor.

4. Add the following two new `<script>` elements just before the end tag for the `<body>`, one for each of the JavaScript files. Make sure that the `geo.js` file is first.

   ```
   <script src="js/geo.js"></script>
   <script src="js/geolocation.js"></script>
   </body>
   ```

5. Save the `locations.html` file.

Requesting the User's Location

Now you have the admin stuff out of the way, and it's time to start working with the GeoLocation API. In this section, you learn how to request the user's location.

First you need to write some code that detects whether the user's browser supports the GeoLocation API. To do this, you use an `if` statement that checks whether the `geolocation` interface is available. This is how the code would look:

```
if (navigator.geolocation) {
  // geolocation is supported.
}
```

The `navigator` object contains information about the browser such as its version number and the browser vendor. Browsers that support the GeoLocation API will have a `geolocation` property on this `navigator` object.

If you wanted you could also add an `else` statement here that displays a message to the user informing him that his browser does not support geolocation and therefore your application may not function correctly. However, for the Locations page, you are going to stick with a simple `if` statement. Users who have browsers that don't support geolocation will still be able to use the page; they will just have to figure out the nearest restaurant on their own.

Once you have determined that the user's browser supports geolocation, you can request his location using the getCurrentPosition() function.

```
navigator.geolocation.getCurrentPosition(function(position) {
    // Do something with the location data
});
```

As you can see, getCurrentPosition() takes a function (this is similar to how event listeners work). In the example, a GeoPosition object will be passed into the function you create through the position variable. You can then obtain the user's latitude and longitude coordinates by examining this GeoPosition object.

To get the latitude coordinate, you need to first select the coords property and then the latitude property, as I have done here:

```
position.coords.latitude;
```

The same goes for obtaining the longitude coordinate:

```
position.coords.longitude;
```

Now let's put this all together. Time to add some JavaScript code that will get the user's location.

The code for this exercise can be found in folder 2.

Here are the steps:

1. Open the geolocation.js file in your text editor.

2. Add an empty function block that will execute when the window.onload event is fired.

   ```
   window.onload = function() {

   }
   ```

3. Inside this function block, create an if statement that will check to see if the user's browser supports the GeoLocation API.

   ```
   window.onload = function() {
       // Check to see if the user's browser supports GeoLocation.
       if (navigator.geolocation) {
   ```

```
        }
    }
```

4. Now call the `getCurrentPosition()` method on the `geolocation` object by adding an empty function block between the parameters of the method call. Note the presence of the `position` parameter in the function block below.

```
if (navigator.geolocation) {
    navigator.geolocation.getCurrentPosition(function(position) {

    });
}
```

5. Use the `alert()` function to display the latitude and longitude coordinates to the user. You will replace this code later, but for now it is useful for checking that everything is working correctly.

```
navigator.geolocation.getCurrentPosition(function(position) {
    alert("Latitude: " + position.coords.latitude + " " +
            "Longitude: " + position.coords.longitude);
});
```

6. Save the `geolocation.js` file.

How Does GeoLocation Work?

The GeoLocation API is somewhat of a black box from a developer's point of view. You can easily request a user's location using the `getCurrentPosition()` method, but how does the device know where it is?

For devices like mobile phones, the answer is fairly intuitive. If the device has GPS, the browser can get the location data from the GPS receiver. However, not all devices have built-in GPS.

Devices like desktop and laptop computers can use network information such as Wi-Fi triangulation to make a guess at where they are in the physical world. This is not as accurate as the data obtained using GPS, but it will generally return a fairly accurate location. Using network information is also a good backup when the device is in an area where obtaining a good GPS signal can be difficult, such as indoors or in built-up areas. The IP address of a device may also be used to determine its location, but this is notoriously inaccurate and will often return only the nearest city.

You don't need to worry too much about the specifics of how the GeoLocation API obtains the location data you will be using. Just be aware that the accuracy of this data can vary depending on the type of device being used.

To test out GeoLocation, you will need to access the page from your local development environment (or a web server). Refer back to the section "Making Your Video Accessible" in Chapter 11 for more information on how to set up a local development environment.

Now open the Locations page in your web browser. I recommend using Google Chrome for testing out GeoLocation. You should see a permissions dialog appear at the top of the screen just below the URL bar, as shown in Figure 13-2. This important privacy feature gives the user the option to either allow or block your website from using his or her location data, and so cannot be overridden.

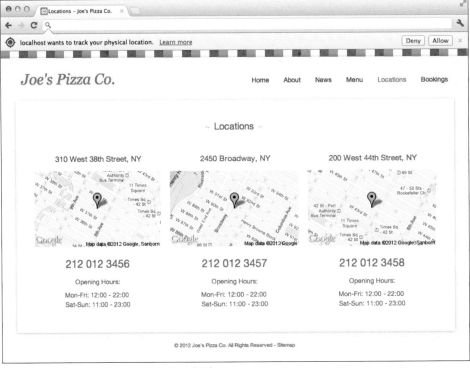

FIGURE 13-2 Location permissions in Google Chrome.
Map data 2012 © Google

Once you allow the page to use your location data, you should see an Alert dialog containing the latitude and longitude coordinates for your current location as shown in Figure 13-3. This Alert dialog is generated by the code you added in Step 5.

FIGURE 13-3 An alert dialog showing my current position.
Map data 2012 © Google

Calculating the Distance Between Two Sets of GPS Coordinates

Now that you can successfully capture a user's location data, it's time to write code that will calculate the distance between the user and each restaurant location.

To calculate the distance between two sets of GPS coordinates, you use the Haversine formula. This formula calculates the distance between two points on the earth's surface, taking into account the curvature of the earth (which makes a big difference for two points that are far away from each other). The geo.js file that you included earlier in this chapter contains a JavaScript function that calculates distances using an implementation of the Haversine formula. This function takes four parameters: the latitude and longitude values of the two locations.

```
haversine(lat1, lon1, lat2, lon2);
```

This function returns a distance in miles, rounded to two decimal points.

The Haversine formula would usually return a distance in kilometers but for the purposes of this book I have altered it to return a distance in miles. This is all taken care of in the geo.js file.

You will use this function to calculate the distance between the user and each of the restaurant locations. Once you have the distances, you will update the Locations page, adding a distance label under each of the locations.

Updating the Locations Page

First you need to add an element that will hold the distance label for each location, using the following steps.

The code for this exercise can be found in folder 3.

1. Open the locations.html file in your text editor.

2. Underneath the opening hours for location 1, create a new `<div>` element with the ID location1distance.

```
<h2>Opening Hours:</h2>
<p>
  <time itemprop="openingHours"
        datetime="Mo-Fr 12:00-22:00">
    Mon-Fri: 12:00 - 22:00
  </time><br>
  <time itemprop="openingHours"
        datetime="Sa,Su 11:00-23:00">
    Sat-Sun: 11:00 - 23:00
  </time>
</p>
<div id="location1distance"></div>
</section>
```

3. Now do the same for location 2, this time using the ID location2distance.

```
<div id="location2distance"></div>
```

4. Finally, add a `<div>` element for location 3 with the ID location3distance.

```
<div id="location3distance"></div>
```

5. Save the locations.html file.

Your HTML now includes three `<div>` elements to which you will add content using JavaScript.

Calculating Distances for Each Location

In this section, you are going to create a new function called `findNearest` that will take in the latitude and longitude coordinates of the user and calculate the distances for each of the restaurant locations. The function will then add these distances to the `<div>` elements you previously added. Later in this chapter, you will add more code to this function that handles finding the nearest location.

> The code for this exercise can be found in folder 4.

First you need to calculate the distances. The following steps show you how to do this.

1. Open the `geolocation.js` file.

2. At the bottom of the file, create a new function, `findNearest()`. It should have two parameters: `lat` and `lon`. These parameters will be used to pass the user's location details to the function.

   ```
   // Find the restaurant that is nearest to the user's location.
   function findNearest(lat, lon) {

   }
   ```

3. Within this new function, use the `haversine()` function to calculate the distance between the user and the first location. Initialize a new variable named `d1` using the result.

   ```
   function findNearest(lat, lon) {
     // Calculate the distances.
     var d1 = haversine(lat, lon, 40.755018, -73.992556); // 310
     West 38th Street
   }
   ```

4. Now do the same for location 2, this time creating a new variable named `d2`. Note that the last two parameters in the `haversine()` call have changed. This is because these are the coordinates of the restaurant location.

   ```
   function findNearest(lat, lon) {
     // Calculate the distances.
     var d1 = haversine(lat, lon, 40.755018, -73.992556); // 310
     West 38th Street
     var d2 = haversine(lat, lon, 40.791121, -73.973971); // 2450
     Broadway
   }
   ```

5. Finally, create a variable, `d3`, and initialize it with the result of the `haversine()` call for the third location.

```
function findNearest(lat, lon) {
  // Calculate the distances.
  var d1 = haversine(lat, lon, 40.755018, -73.992556); // 310
  West 38th Street
  var d2 = haversine(lat, lon, 40.791121, -73.973971); // 2450
  Broadway
  var d3 = haversine(lat, lon, 40.757498, -73.986654); // 200
  West 44th Street
}
```

Now that you have all three distances, you need to update the <div> elements that you added to the Locations page earlier.

6. Update the distance <div> for the first location by getting the element using its ID (location1distance) and then setting its textContent property to Distance: n miles (where *n* is the distance value).

```
function findNearest(lat, lon) {

  ...
  // Add text to the distance labels.
  document.getElementById("location1distance").textContent =
  "Distance: " + d1 + " miles";
}
```

7. Now do the same for locations 2 and 3. Don't forget to update the IDs of the elements and variables being used for the distance value.

```
function findNearest(lat, lon) {

  ...
  // Add text to the distance labels.
  document.getElementById("location1distance").textContent =
  "Distance: " + d1 + " miles";
  document.getElementById("location2distance").textContent =
  "Distance: " + d2 + " miles";
  document.getElementById("location3distance").textContent =
  "Distance: " + d3 + " miles";
}
```

That completes the findNearest() function for now. All that is left to do is to call this function when you get the user's location.

8. Remove the call to the alert() function that you added in the previous code exercise. (It can be found in the function block of your getCurrentPosition() call).

```
navigator.geolocation.getCurrentPosition(function(position) {
  alert("Latitude: " + position.coords.latitude + " " +
        "Longitude: " + position.coords.longitude);
});
```

9. Add a call to the findNearest() function where your original alert() call was, passing in the latitude and longitude coordinates obtained from the GeoPosition object.

```
navigator.geolocation.getCurrentPosition(function(position) {
    // Pass the location data to the findNearest method.
    findNearest(position.coords.latitude,
    position.coords.longitude);
});
```

10. Save the geolocation.js file.

Load the Locations page in your web browser. You now should see some text displayed below the opening hours for each location, as shown in Figure 13-4. This tells the user how far away the restaurant is. Remember: This will work only if you are using a local development server. If you aren't, you will not see any distance labels (but nothing will look broken either, which is always good).

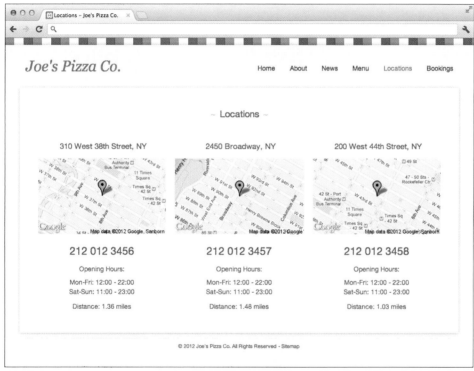

FIGURE 13-4 The Locations page with distance labels.
Map data 2012 © Google

Finding the Nearest Restaurant

In this section, you are going to write an algorithm that can find the restaurant location that is nearest to the user. You will then apply a class to the relevant location <section> element that will cause the element to be styled slightly different than the others, highlighting the location nearest to the user.

The code for this exercise can be found in folder 5.

Here are the steps:

1. Make sure that you have the `geolocation.js` file open in your text editor.

2. Create an `if` statement at the bottom of your `findNearest()` function and set the condition to: `d1 <= d2 && d1 <= d3`. The purpose of this is to determine whether the distance to location 1 is the smallest of the three distances. The condition checks first to see if the value of d1 (location 1) is smaller or equal to the value of d2 (location 2). If it is, it will also check to see if the value of d1 is smaller or equal to the value of d3 (location 3). Both conditions need to be met in order for the complete statement to evaluate to true.

```
function findNearest(lat, lon) {
  ...
  // Find the smallest distance.
  if (d1 <= d2 && d1 <= d3) {

  }
}
```

3. Within this `if` block, add code that will add the class `nearest` to the `<section>` element with the ID `location1`.

```
function findNearest(lat, lon) {
  ...
  // Find the smallest distance.
  if (d1 <= d2 && d1 <= d3) {
    // Location 1
    document.getElementById("location1").className = "nearest";
  }
}
```

4. Now add an `else if` condition to the `if` statement. This time, you are going to be checking to see if location 2 is the nearest, so you want to use the following condition: `d2 <= d1 && d2 <= d3`.

```
function findNearest(lat, lon) {
  ...
  // Find the smallest distance.
  if (d1 <= d2 && d1 <= d3) {
    // Location 1
    document.getElementById("location1").className = "nearest";
  } else if (d2 <= d1 && d2 <= d3) {
```

```
      }
    }
```

5. Add code to this new block that will add the `nearest` class to the `<section>` element with the ID `location2`.

```
function findNearest(lat, lon) {
  ...
  // Find the smallest distance.
  if (d1 <= d2 && d1 <= d3) {
    // Location 1
    document.getElementById("location1").className = "nearest";
  } else if (d2 <= d1 && d2 <= d3) {
    // Location 2
    document.getElementById("location2").className = "nearest";
  }
}
```

6. Finally, add an `else` clause to the end of your `if` statement that contains some code that adds the `nearest` class to the `<section>` element with the ID `location3`. If d1 and d2 are not the smallest, you can assume that d3 (location3) is your winner, so there is no need for another condition here.

```
function findNearest(lat, lon) {
  ...
  // Find the smallest distance.
  if (d1 <= d2 && d1 <= d3) {
    // Location 1
    document.getElementById("location1").className = "nearest";
  } else if (d2 <= d1 && d2 <= d3) {
    // Location 2
    document.getElementById("location2").className = "nearest";
  } else {
    // Location 3
    document.getElementById("location3").className = "nearest";
  }
}
```

7. Save the `geolocation.js` file.

That's it! Your Locations page is now complete. Open it in your web browser and take a look. The stylesheet will take care of adding some styling to the nearest location, as shown in Figure 13-5.

FIGURE 13-5 The finished Locations page with geolocation built in.
Map data 2012 © Google

Summary

The new GeoLocation API is helping to bridge the gap between native applications and web applications. In this chapter, you learned how to take advantage of this new API in order to enhance the Locations page on the Joe's Pizza Co. website.

Additionally, you learned how to obtain a user's location and how the device goes about gathering this information. With a little help from an external JavaScript library, you wrote code that can find the restaurant location that is nearest to the user. Your program then highlights this location to make it more visible to the user as well as adding distance labels to each of the restaurant locations on the Locations page.

In Chapter 14, you will learn about the new <canvas> element. Combined with a bit of JavaScript, the Canvas API enables you to draw pictures directly in the browser.

chapter fourteen

Using Canvas to Create Online Ads

ONE OF THE most important new features of HTML5 is the new Canvas API (*Application Programming Interface*). The Canvas API allows you to programmatically draw graphics using JavaScript. You can use the Canvas API to do many tasks, including creating diagrams, charts, graphs, animations, advertisements, and interactive drawing applications. Using Canvas instead of regular images can also help to reduce the time it takes for your web pages to load. Why, you ask? Because the browser does not have to issue HTTP requests to fetch image files and then download those files.

In this chapter, you use the Canvas API to create an online advertisement for Joe's Pizza Co. (see Figure 14-1). This advertisement would be placed on other websites to help raise awareness of the Joe's Pizza Co. brand and hopefully encourage more customers to eat at Joe's.

FIGURE 14-1 The advertisement you are going to create.
Pizza image reproduced by permission of iStockphoto.com/Lauri Patterson

Setting Up Your Canvas

To create a canvas, you use the <canvas> element. The default size of a canvas is 300 pixels wide and 150 pixels high. You can, however, change these default dimensions by adding height and width attributes to the <canvas> element, like so:

```
<canvas width="600" height="150" id="adCanvas"></canvas>
```

Your <canvas> element should also have an id attribute. The ID that you set here will be used to get a reference to the canvas in your JavaScript code.

The advertisement that you will be creating is separate from your existing Joe's Pizza Co. website, and so you will want to create a new folder for the files used in this mini-project.

 The code in this exercise can be found in folder 1 of the Chapter 14 download files.

Here are the steps to set up your canvas:

1. Create a new folder on your computer called canvas-ad. This is where you will put all your files related to the Joe's Pizza advertisement.

2. Open your text editor and create a new file called advert.html. Make sure that you save this in your ad-canvas folder.

3. Add the following HTML code to your advert.html file.

```
<!DOCTYPE html>
<html lang="en">
<head>
  <meta charset="utf-8">
  <title>Joe's Pizza Co. Advert</title>
</head>
<body>
  <script src="adscript.js"></script>
</body>
</html>
```

4. Save the advert.html file.

5. Now create a file called adscript.js and open it in your text editor. This is where you write all the code that draws on the canvas.

6. Attach an empty function to the `window.onload` event.

```
window.onload = function() {

}
```

7. Save the `adscript.js` file.

Now that you have your file structure set up, it's time to add the `<canvas>` element to your HTML.

Canvas is not yet supported in all browsers, and so it is a good idea to provide some fallback content whenever you use it. As with the `<video>` element, any content that you place between the tags of the `<canvas>` element will be displayed if the browser does not support the Canvas API. In this example, you are going to add an image that will be displayed if Canvas is not supported.

The code in this exercise can be found in folder 2.

Follow these steps:

1. Open the `advert.html` file in your text editor.

2. Create a `<canvas>` element above the `<script>` element that is 600 pixels wide and 150 pixels high. Give this element the ID `adCanvas`.

```
<canvas id="adCanvas" width="600" height="150"></canvas>
<script src="adscript.js"></script>
```

3. Download the `fallback.png` file from the book's website and place it in your `canvas-ad` folder. You can find this file in folder 2.

4. Create a new `<img>` element within the `<canvas>` element for the fallback image.

```
<canvas id="adCanvas" width="600" height="150">
  <img src="fallback.png" alt="Joe's Pizza Co. Advert"
       width="600" height="150">
</canvas>
```

5. Save the `advert.html` file.

That covers all the HTML code that you will be writing in this chapter. Now you need to get a reference to the canvas in your JavaScript code, using the following steps.

The code in this exercise can be found in folder 3.

1. Open the `adscript.js` file in your text editor.

2. Within the empty function block that you created earlier, create a new variable called `adCanvas` and initialize it by fetching the canvas from your HTML.

```
window.onload = function() {
  var adCanvas = document.getElementById("adCanvas");
}
```

3. Now you need to check to see if the user's browser supports the Canvas API. Do this by creating an `if` statement that checks to see whether your new `adCanvas` variable has a `getContext` method. This is similar to how you checked for geolocation support in Chapter 13.

```
window.onload = function() {
  var adCanvas = document.getElementById("adCanvas");

  if (adCanvas.getContext) {

  }
}
```

4. Finally, you need to get a 2D drawing context. You will use this to draw onto the canvas. Create a new variable called `ctx` and initialize it by calling `getContext("2d")` on your `adCanvas` variable. The `d` must be lowercase for this function to work correctly. You will call methods on this context in order to draw onto the canvas.

```
window.onload = function() {
  var adCanvas = document.getElementById("adCanvas");

  if (adCanvas.getContext) {
    // Initialize a 2d drawing context.
    var ctx = adCanvas.getContext("2d");
  }
}
```

5. Save the `adscript.js` file.

Congratulations! You now have your canvas set up and you're ready to start drawing on it.

The *context* holds all the information about your canvas, such as the objects that you will be drawing and any styling that you might add. It also provides the functions that you need to draw and paint on the canvas. The `2d` value that is passed to the `getContext()` function signals that you want to use the 2D drawing API.

Creating the Background

In this section, you will add a rectangle to your canvas that will make up the advertisement's background. However, before you get to that, you need to know a few things about how Canvas works.

Think of a canvas as a big grid in which each square represents a single pixel on the screen. When you draw using the Canvas API, you need to specify where on the canvas you want the object to be drawn. You do this using x and y coordinates relative to the origin of the grid. The origin (0, 0) is in the top-left corner of the canvas (see Figure 14-2). Although it is possible to change this origin point, you won't need to in this project.

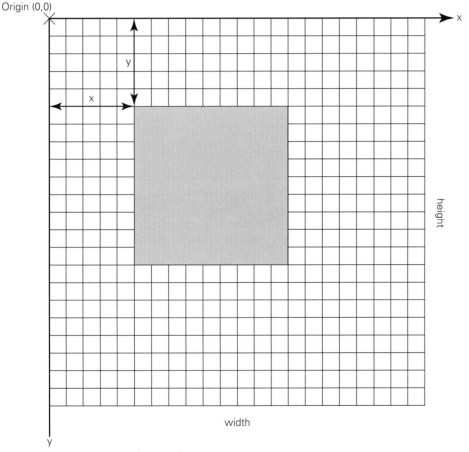

FIGURE 14-2 The canvas coordinate grid.

Every time that you draw on a canvas, you create a new layer. This means that if you need something to appear above everything else, it should be the last thing that you draw on the canvas.

Now that you've covered some of the theory behind how the Canvas API works, you can start drawing on your canvas.

The first object that you are going to draw is a rectangle. To do this, you use the `fillRect()` function:

```
fillRect(x,y,width,height)
```

The `fillRect()` function has four parameters. The x and y parameters specify the position of the rectangle on the canvas grid. These will be the coordinates for the top-left corner of the rectangle (see Figure 14-2). The `width` and `height` parameters specify the rectangle's size.

To set the fill color of your rectangle, you set the `fillStyle` property on the context to the desired color. This color should be specified using a standard color format, such as a hexadecimal, rgb (red, green, blue), or rgba (red, green, blue, alpha) color code. You can also use color keywords such as `red`, `blue`, and `green`.

```
ctx.fillStyle = "rgba(0,0,0,0.4)";
```

Here the fill color has been set to a semitransparent black. The alpha value controls the opacity. Setting the alpha value to 1 will cause the color to be opaque whereas setting it to 0 will cause it to be fully transparent.

 The code in this exercise can be found in folder 4.

Here are the steps to draw your rectangle:

1. Open the `adscript.js` file in your text editor.

2. Create a new function called `drawAdvert()` underneath the `if` statement that checks for Canvas support. This is where you are going to write all the code that draws on the canvas. The reason for putting this code in its own function will become clear toward the end of this chapter.

```
window.onload = function() {
  var adCanvas = document.getElementById("adCanvas");

  if (adCanvas.getContext) {
    // Initialize a 2d drawing context.
    var ctx = adCanvas.getContext("2d");
  }
```

```
   function drawAdvert() {

     }
   }
```

3. Call this `drawAdvert()` function after you initialize the `ctx` variable.

```
if (adCanvas.getContext) {
  // Initialize a 2d drawing context.
  var ctx = adCanvas.getContext("2d");

  drawAdvert();
}
```

4. Within the `drawAdvert()` function, set the `fillStyle` to use the color: `rgba(0,0,0,0.4)`.

```
function drawAdvert() {
  // Create the Background Rectangle
  ctx.fillStyle = "rgba(0,0,0,0.4)";
}
```

5. Now use the `fillRect()` function to draw the rectangle on the canvas. You want the rectangle to fill the whole canvas, so set the x and y parameters to 0, the `width` to 600, and the `height` to 150.

```
function drawAdvert() {
  // Create the Background Rectangle
  ctx.fillStyle = "rgba(0,0,0,0.4)";
  ctx.fillRect(0,0,600,150);
}
```

6. Save the `adscript.js` file.

Now if you open the `advert.html` file in your web browser, you should see a rectangle that looks like the one shown in Figure 14-3.

Later in this chapter, you will be taking advantage of Canvas layers to add an image underneath this rectangle—hence the need for it to be semitransparent.

FIGURE 14-3 The canvas with a semitransparent black rectangle.

Other Functions for Drawing Rectangles

In addition to the `fillRect()` function, two other functions can be used for drawing rectangles. These are `strokeRect()` and `clearRect()`.

The `strokeRect(x, y, width, height)` function is used to draw the outline of a rectangle. This has a similar effect to adding a border to an HTML element using CSS.

The `clearRect(x, y, width, height)` function clears a rectangular area on the canvas. Anything that has already been drawn on the canvas that falls within the area of this new rectangle will effectively be deleted.

Adding Text

The next job to complete is to add the text to your canvas. In this section, you are going to focus on adding the "New York's Best Pizza" and "Joe's Pizza Co." text, shown earlier in Figure 14-1.

You draw text onto a canvas using the `fillText()` function:

```
fillText(text, x, y);
```

This function has three parameters: the `text` that you want to draw and the `x` and `y` coordinates specifying where you want to place that text.

You can specify the font, font style, and size using the contexts `font` property:

```
ctx.font = "Bold 32px Georgia";
```

The text alignment can be set using the `textAlign` property:

```
ctx.textAlign = "center";
```

For the text color, use the `fillStyle` property you learned about earlier in this chapter.

Now that you know the basics of how to add text to your canvas, let's write some more code.

 The code in this exercise can be found in folder 5.

Follow these steps to add the text:

1. Open the `adscript.js` in your text editor.

2. Set the font to `Bold 32px Georgia`.

   ```
   function drawAdvert() {
     ...

     // Add the text styling
     ctx.font = "Bold 32px Georgia";
   }
   ```

3. Set the text alignment to `center`.

   ```
   function drawAdvert() {
     ...

     // Add the text styling
     ctx.font = "Bold 32px Georgia";
     ctx.textAlign = "center";
   }
   ```

4. Set the text color to `#FFFFFF` (white).

   ```
   function drawAdvert() {
     ...

     // Add the text styling
     ctx.font = "Bold 32px Georgia";
     ctx.textAlign = "center";
     ctx.fillStyle = "#FFFFFF";
   }
   ```

5. Now you need to calculate the x and y coordinates for the text. For the x coordinate, divide the canvas width by two to get the center point and then subtract 80 in order to move everything slightly to the left. Initialize a new variable called `textX` with the result:

   ```
   function drawAdvert() {
     ...

     // Add the text styling
     ctx.font = "Bold 32px Georgia";
     ctx.textAlign = "center";
     ctx.fillStyle = "#FFFFFF";

     // Calculate the positions for the text
     var textX = (adCanvas.width / 2) - 80;
   }
   ```

6. To calculate the y coordinate, divide the canvas height by 2. Create a variable called texty and initialize it with the result:

```
function drawAdvert() {
  ...

  // Add the text styling
  ctx.font = "Bold 32px Georgia";
  ctx.textAlign = "center";
  ctx.fillStyle = "#FFFFFF";

  // Calculate the positions for the text
  var textX = (adCanvas.width / 2) - 80;
  var textY = (adCanvas.height / 2);
}
```

7. Now add the New York's Best Pizza text using the fillText() function. You need the text to be slightly higher than the middle of the canvas, so subtract 10 from the texty variable to get the value for the y parameter:

```
function drawAdvert() {
  ...

  // Add the text styling
  ctx.font = "Bold 32px Georgia";
  ctx.textAlign = "center";
  ctx.fillStyle = "#FFFFFF";

  // Calculate the positions for the text
  var textX = (adCanvas.width / 2) - 80;
  var textY = (adCanvas.height / 2);

  // Add the "New York's Best Pizza" text
  ctx.fillText("New York's Best Pizza", textX, textY - 10);
}
```

8. Change the font property to Italic 22px Georgia.

```
function drawAdvert() {
  ...

  // Add the text styling
  ctx.font = "Bold 32px Georgia";
  ctx.textAlign = "center";
  ctx.fillStyle = "#FFFFFF";

  // Calculate the positions for the text
  var textX = (adCanvas.width / 2) - 80;
```

```
    var textY = (adCanvas.height / 2);

    // Add the "New York's Best Pizza" text
    ctx.fillText("New York's Best Pizza", textX, textY - 10);

    // Update the font and add the "Joe's Pizza Co." text
    ctx.font = "Italic 22px Georgia";
}
```

9. Add the `Joe's Pizza Co.` text using the `filltext()` function. This time you want the text to be drawn just below the center, so add 25 to the `textY` variable.

```
function drawAdvert() {
    ...

    // Add the text styling
    ctx.font = "Bold 32px Georgia";
    ctx.textAlign = "center";
    ctx.fillStyle = "#FFFFFF";

    // Calculate the positions for the text
    var textX = (adCanvas.width / 2) - 80;
    var textY = (adCanvas.height / 2);

    // Add the "New York's Best Pizza" text
    ctx.fillText("New York's Best Pizza", textX, textY - 10);

    // Update the font and add the "Joe's Pizza Co." text
    ctx.font = "Italic 22px Georgia";
    ctx.fillText("Joe's Pizza Co.", textX, textY + 25);
}
```

10. Save the `adscript.js` file.

Now open up the `advert.html` file in your web browser. You should see that the text is positioned just to the left of the center point on the canvas, as shown in Figure 14-4.

FIGURE 14-4 Drawing text onto a canvas.

Drawing Lines

The next thing that you need to draw on your canvas is the separator line that goes between the two lines of text (refer to Figure 14-1).

When using the Canvas API, you can draw lines by creating paths. To create a path, you start with the `beginPath()` function. A path consists of any number of points. These points are added using the `moveTo()` and `lineTo()` functions.

The `moveTo(x,y)` function doesn't actually draw anything on the canvas but will move the cursor to another location. Think of it as lifting your pencil off a piece of paper and moving it to another spot on the paper. The `x` and `y` parameters specify the coordinates for the new starting point.

The `lineTo(x,y)` function is similar to `moveTo()`, but this one draws on the canvas. The `x` and `y` parameters specify the coordinates for the endpoint of the line. The start point is the last point that was added to the path.

If your path has more than one point and you want the path to form a closed shape, you need to call the `closePath()` function when you are done adding your points. This will attempt to close the path by drawing a straight line between the last point you specified and the start of the path.

Once you have your path created, you can use the `fill()` function to fill in the area that the path outlines or the `stroke()` function to paint a line along the parts of the path that were drawn using the `lineTo()` function.

It is important to note that, unlike when drawing rectangles, your path will not be displayed on the canvas until you call either `fill()` or `stroke()`. This "draw first, render later" process is key to the way that the Canvas API works.

To set the color of the line, you can use the `strokeStyle` property:

```
ctx.strokeStyle = "rgba(255,255,255,0.4)";
```

The line width can be set using the `lineWidth` property:

```
ctx.lineWidth = 1.0;
```

Now that you understand how to create paths and draw lines, you can add the line to your canvas using the following steps.

The code in this exercise can be found in folder 6.

1. Open the adscript.js file in your text editor.

2. First you need to create some variables that will make it easier to calculate the positions for your path. Create a variable called lineLength and initialize it with the value 360.

```
function drawAdvert() {
  ...
  // Add the separator line
  var lineLength = 360;
}
```

3. Now you need to calculate the vertical position of the line. To do this, divide the height of the canvas by 2 and then add 0.5. Initialize a new variable called lineY with the result.

```
function drawAdvert() {
  ...
  // Add the separator line
  var lineLength = 360;
  var lineY = (adCanvas.height / 2) + 0.5;
}
```

Adding 0.5 here will ensure that the line is crisp. If your lines ever appear blurry, it may be because pixels are only being partially painted. This is caused by the way that lines are drawn on the canvas.

For information on how to fix this issue, check out Mozilla's Canvas documentation here: https://developer.mozilla.org/en-US/docs/Canvas_tutorial/Applying_styles_and_colors - Line_styles.

4. Now call the beginPath() function to create a new empty path.

```
function drawAdvert() {
    ...
    // Add the separator line
    var lineLength = 360;
    var lineY = (adCanvas.height / 2) + 0.5;

    ctx.beginPath();
}
```

5. Set the start point of your line using the moveTo() function. The x parameter should be 40 and the y should use the value of the lineY variable.

```
function drawAdvert() {
    ...
    // Add the separator line
    var lineLength = 360;
    var lineY = (adCanvas.height / 2) + 0.5;

    ctx.beginPath();
    ctx.moveTo(40, lineY);
}
```

6. Use the lineTo() function to draw the line. The x parameter should be the value of the lineLength plus 40 (because the starting point of the line is 40 pixels from the left of the canvas). The y parameter should be the value of the lineY variable.

```
function drawAdvert() {
    ...
    // Add the separator line
    var lineLength = 360;
    var lineY = (adCanvas.height / 2) + 0.5;

    ctx.beginPath();
    ctx.moveTo(40, lineY);
    ctx.lineTo((lineLength + 40), lineY);
}
```

7. Now set the line width to be 1.0.

```
function drawAdvert() {
    ...
    // Add the separator line
    var lineLength = 360;
    var lineY = (adCanvas.height / 2) + 0.5;

    ctx.beginPath();
    ctx.moveTo(40, lineY);
    ctx.lineTo((lineLength + 40), lineY);
```

```
    ctx.lineWidth = 1.0;
}
```

8. Set the line color to rgba (255, 255, 255, 0.4), which is semitransparent white:

```
function drawAdvert() {
    ...
    // Add the separator line
    var lineLength = 360;
    var lineY = (adCanvas.height / 2) + 0.5;

    ctx.beginPath();
    ctx.moveTo(40, lineY);
    ctx.lineTo((lineLength + 40), lineY);
    ctx.lineWidth = 1.0;
    ctx.strokeStyle = "rgba(255,255,255,0.4)";
}
```

9. Finally, stroke the path using the stroke() function.

```
function drawAdvert() {
    ...
    // Add the separator line
    var lineLength = 360;
    var lineY = (adCanvas.height / 2) + 0.5;

    ctx.beginPath();
    ctx.moveTo(40, lineY);
    ctx.lineTo((lineLength + 40), lineY);
    ctx.lineWidth = 1.0;
    ctx.strokeStyle = "rgba(255,255,255,0.4)";
    ctx.stroke();
}
```

10. Save the adscript.js file.

Now if you open up the advert.html file in your web browser, you should see a line between the two lines of text, as shown in Figure 14-5.

FIGURE 14-5 Drawing lines onto a canvas.

Drawing Circles

The Canvas API only provides native functions for creating rectangular shapes. To create circles, you actually need to create a circular path that you can then stroke and/or fill, depending on your requirements. To create a circular path, use the `arc()` function:

```
arc(x,y,radius,startAngle,endAngle,anticlockwise);
```

The `arc()` function takes five parameters. The `x` and `y` parameters specify the position of the circle's center. The `radius` parameter explains itself. The `startAngle` and `endAngle` parameters are used to specify the start and endpoint of the arc. These values should be given in radians, not degrees. The `anticlockwise` parameter takes a Boolean value that specifies whether the arc should be drawn anticlockwise (`true`) or clockwise (`false`).

To convert degrees to radians in JavaScript, use the following statement:

```
var radians = (Math.PI / 180) * degrees;
```

As you are creating a path, you need to make sure that you call the `beginPath()` function before you draw your arc. Here is a small example of how you might draw a circle using the `arc()` function (this assumes that you have already set up the canvas and a 2D drawing context):

```
ctx.beginPath();
ctx.arc(50, 50, 50, 0, Math.PI*2, true);
ctx.fill();
```

This code would draw a circle like the one shown in Figure 14-6.

Here I have used `Math.PI*2` for the `endAngle` parameter. This is effectively the same as writing `(Math.PI/180)*360` but requires less typing.

FIGURE 14-6 A simple circle drawn using Canvas.

You can also draw a segment of a circle.

```
ctx.beginPath();
ctx.arc(50, 50, 50, 0, Math.PI*1.5, true);
ctx.fill();
```

Figure 14-7 shows the result of this code.

FIGURE 14-7 Drawing a segment of a circle.

Here the `arc()` function draws a curved path between the start and end points. When the `fill()` function is called the start and end points of the path are joined, creating a segment.

To draw a sector of a circle (that is, a pie-shaped part of a circle) you need to draw a line to the center of the circle after you have created your arc. The following example shows how this would be done.

```
ctx.beginPath();
ctx.arc(50, 50, 50, Math.PI*1.75, Math.PI*1.5, true);
ctx.lineTo(50, 50);
ctx.fill();
```

Figure 14-8 shows the sector that this code will produce.

FIGURE 14-8 Drawing a sector of a circle.

Now that you understand how to draw arcs and circles on a canvas, you can continue with your advertisement using the following steps:

The code in this exercise can be found in folder 7.

1. Open the adscript.js file in your text editor.

2. Create a new path at the end of your drawAdvert() function using the begin-Path() function.

```
function drawAdvert() {
  . . .
  // Draw the offer circle
  ctx.beginPath();
}
```

3. Now draw the circle using the arc() function. The circle should be positioned to the right of the canvas, so set the x parameter to 525 and the y parameter to 75. You want the circle to be slightly bigger than the canvas so that the whole of the circle is not showing (refer to Figure 14-1). To do this set, the radius to 80. This will be a complete circle, so set the startAngle to 0 and the endAngle to Math.PI*2. Set the anticlockwise parameter to true; however, this doesn't really matter because you are drawing a full circle.

```
function drawAdvert() {
  . . .
  // Draw the offer circle
  ctx.beginPath();
  ctx.arc(525, 75, 80, 0, Math.PI*2, true);
}
```

4. Set the fill style to be #009A00.

```
function drawAdvert() {
  . . .
  // Draw the offer circle
  ctx.beginPath();
  ctx.arc(525, 75, 80, 0, Math.PI*2, true);
  ctx.fillStyle = "#009A00";
}
```

5. Fill the circle.

```
function drawAdvert() {
  . . .
  // Draw the offer circle
  ctx.beginPath();
  ctx.arc(525, 75, 80, 0, Math.PI*2, true);
```

```
        ctx.fillStyle = "#009A00";
        ctx.fill();
    }
```

6. Save the `adscript.js` file.

You should now have a green circle displayed on the right side of your canvas, as shown in Figure 14-9. Notice how the edges of the circle go beyond the boundaries of the canvas.

FIGURE 14-9 Drawing a circle on your canvas.

Creating Gradients

The circle that you just drew onto your canvas looks good, but it would look even better if it used a gradient for the fill instead of just a solid color. In this section, you learn how to create linear gradients. To do this, use the `createLinearGradient()` function:

```
createLinearGradient(x1, y1, x2, y2);
```

This function will return a `canvasGradient` object and includes four parameters. These are the starting point (`x1` and `y1`) and the endpoint (`x2` and `y2`) of the gradient.

Once you have created your `canvasGradient` object and stored it in a variable, you need to add the colors to your gradient. You do this using the `addColorStop()` function:

```
myGradient.addColorStop(position, color);
```

This function has two parameters: the position of the color in the gradient (this should be a value between 0 and 1) and the color.

After you have added all of your color stops, you apply your gradient to an object on the canvas by setting the `fillStyle` property to your gradient variable. The following example code shows how to create a simple gradient and apply it to a rectangle.

```
var linGrad = ctx.createLinearGradient(0,0,0,160);
linGrad.addColorStop(0, "#009A00");
linGrad.addColorStop(1, "#085A00");

ctx.rect(0,0,200, 160)
ctx.fillStyle = linGrad;
ctx.fill();
```

This code would draw a rectangle on the canvas and fill it with the gradient shown in Figure 14-10.

FIGURE 14-10 A simple canvas gradient.

 The rect() function used in this example is very similar to the fillRect() function that you encountered earlier in this chapter. The difference is that the rect() function will draw a rectangle but will not initiate a fill.

Now that you understand how Canvas gradients work, let's add a gradient to the circle that you created in the previous section.

 The code in this exercise can be found in folder 8.

Here are the steps:

1. Open the adscript.js file.

2. Create a new variable in your drawAdvert() function called linGrad and initialize it by creating a new canvasGradient object using the createLinearGradient() function. Set the x1, y1, and x2 parameters to 0 and the y2 parameter to 160. This is because your circle is 160 pixels high. Place this code before the code that you wrote to draw the circle.

```
function drawAdvert() {
  ...

  // Create a Linear Gradient for the Circle
  var linGrad = ctx.createLinearGradient(0,0,0,160);

  // Draw the offer circle
  ...
}
```

3. Add a color stop at position 0 that uses the color #009A00.

```
function drawAdvert() {
  ...

  // Create a Linear Gradient for the Circle
  var linGrad = ctx.createLinearGradient(0,0,0,160);
  linGrad.addColorStop(0, "#009A00");

  // Draw the offer circle
  ...
}
```

4. Add another color stop at position 1 that uses the color #085A00.

```
function drawAdvert() {
  ...

  // Create a Linear Gradient for the Circle
  var linGrad = ctx.createLinearGradient(0,0,0,160);
  linGrad.addColorStop(0, "#009A00");
  linGrad.addColorStop(1, "#085A00");

  // Draw the offer circle
  ...
}
```

5. Change the fillStyle property of the circle to use your gradient.

```
function drawAdvert() {
  ...

  // Create a Linear Gradient for the Circle
  var linGrad = ctx.createLinearGradient(0,0,0,160);
  linGrad.addColorStop(0, "#009A00");
  linGrad.addColorStop(1, "#085A00");
```

```
// Draw the offer circle
ctx.beginPath();
ctx.arc(525, 75, 80, 0, Math.PI*2, true);
ctx.fillStyle = linGrad;
ctx.fill();

}
```

6. Save the adscript.js file.

Now open the advert.html file in your web browser and admire your lovely new gradient.
It should look like the one in Figure 14-11.

FIGURE 14-11 Adding a gradient to your canvas.

Adding Shadows

One more styling addition would look good on that circle: a shadow.

You can add a shadow to an object on your canvas by setting the shadowOffsetX, shadowOffsetY, shadowBlur, and shadowColor properties on your context.

Use the shadowOffsetX and shadowOffsetY properties to position the shadow. By
default, the shadow will be positioned directly underneath any objects that are drawn on the
canvas after the shadow properties are set. The shadowOffsetX property allows you to
move the shadow to the left and right (use negative values to go left), and the shadowOffsetY property allows you to move the shadow up and down (use negative values to go up).

```
ctx.shadowOffsetX = 10;
ctx.shadowOffsetY = 10;
```

The shadowBlur property specifies the size of the blur effect:

```
ctx.shadowBlur = 15;
```

If you set this to 0 (the default) there will be no blur at all.

Finally, the `shadowColor` property allows you to set the color of the shadow:

```
ctx.shadowColor ="rgba(0,0,0,0.8)";
```

Here is an example of how you could create a shadow for a simple rectangle:

```
ctx.shadowOffsetX = 10;
ctx.shadowOffsetY = 10;
ctx.shadowBlur = 15;
ctx.shadowColor = "rgba(0,0,0,0.8)";

ctx.fillStyle = "#CC0000";
ctx.fillRect(15,15,100,100);
```

This code would create the shadow shown in Figure 14-12. Notice how the shadow is positioned down and to the right of the rectangle.

FIGURE 14-12 A simple shadow.

Now that you understand how to add shadows to the objects that you draw on your canvas, let's update your advertisement.

The code in this exercise can be found in folder 9.

1. Open the `adscript.js` file in your text editor.
2. Set the `shadowOffsetX` and `shadowOffsetY` properties to 0. This will position the shadow directly behind the rectangle so that only the blurred edges are visible. Put this code underneath the code that creates the gradient.

```
function drawAdvert() {

  ...

  // Set a shadow
  ctx.shadowOffsetX = 0;
  ctx.shadowOffsetY = 0;

  // Draw the offer circle
  ...
}
```

3. Set the shadowBlur property to 10.

```
function drawAdvert() {

  ...

  // Set a shadow
  ctx.shadowOffsetX = 0;
  ctx.shadowOffsetY = 0;
  ctx.shadowBlur = 10;

  // Draw the offer circle
  ...
}
```

4. Set the shadowColor property to rgba(0,0,0,0.8).

```
function drawAdvert() {

  ...

  // Set a shadow
  ctx.shadowOffsetX = 0;
  ctx.shadowOffsetY = 0;
  ctx.shadowBlur = 10;
  ctx.shadowColor = "rgba(0,0,0,0.8)";

  // Draw the offer circle
  ...
}
```

5. Save the adscript.js file.

That should have added a shadow to your circle. Open up the advert.html file in your text editor and check. You should see a subtle shadow around the circle, like the one shown in Figure 14-13.

FIGURE 14-13 Adding a shadow to your canvas.

Adding the Offer Text

If you look back at Figure 14-1, you will see three lines of text inside the circle. Unfortunately, there is no easy way to wrap text onto multiple lines using the Canvas API, so you will need to add each line of text to the canvas separately.

You've already learned how to add text to a canvas, so let's dive right in.

The code in this exercise can be found in folder 10.

1. Open the `adscript.js` file.

2. Create a new variable called `offerTextX` and initialize this with the statement `(adCanvas.width - 75)`. Creating a variable to store this value will save you writing this statement three times, thus reducing the chance of introducing a bug in your code. Place this code at the end of your `drawAdvert()` function.

```
function drawAdvert() {
  . . .

  // Add the Offer Text
  var offerTextX = (adCanvas.width - 75);
}
```

3. Set the `fillStyle` property to #FFFFFF (white).

```
function drawAdvert() {
  . . .

  // Add the Offer Text
  var offerTextX = (adCanvas.width - 75);
  ctx.fillStyle = "#FFFFFF";
}
```

4. Set the `font` property to `24px Georgia`.

```
function drawAdvert() {

  . . .

  // Add the Offer Text
  var offerTextX = (adCanvas.width - 75);
  ctx.fillStyle = "#FFFFFF";
  ctx.font = "24px Georgia";
}
```

5. Draw the first line of text using the `fillText()` function. Use the `offerTextX` variable for the x parameter and set the y parameter to 55.

```
function drawAdvert() {

  . . .

  // Add the Offer Text
  var offerTextX = (adCanvas.width - 75);
  ctx.fillStyle = "#FFFFFF";
  ctx.font = "24px Georgia";
  ctx.fillText("10% OFF", offerTextX, 55);
}
```

6. Draw the next line of text. Again, use the `offerTextX` variable for the x parameter but set the y parameter to 84.

```
function drawAdvert() {

  . . .

  // Add the Offer Text
  var offerTextX = (adCanvas.width - 75);
  ctx.fillStyle = "#FFFFFF";
  ctx.font = "24px Georgia";
  ctx.fillText("10% OFF", offerTextX, 55);
  ctx.fillText("your first", offerTextX, 84);
}
```

7. Draw the final line of text. Once again, use the `offerTextX` variable but set the y parameter to 113.

```
function drawAdvert() {

  . . .

  // Add the Offer Text
  var offerTextX = (adCanvas.width - 75);
  ctx.fillStyle = "#FFFFFF";
  ctx.font = "24px Georgia";
  ctx.fillText("10% OFF", offerTextX, 55);
```

```
    ctx.fillText("your first", offerTextX, 84);
    ctx.fillText("meal", offerTextX, 113);
}
```

8. Save the adscript.js file.

Now if you open the advert.html file, you should see that the text appears within the circle, as shown in Figure 14-14.

FIGURE 14-14 Drawing the offer text on your canvas.

There is one problem here, however. Because you have set the shadow parameters on the context, there is a subtle shadow on the text as well as the circle. The text would look better without a shadow. You are going to fix this in the next section.

Saving and Restoring State

You set the shadow for the purpose of the circle, but didn't really intend for a shadow to be put on the text. To cancel out the shadow, you could reset all the shadow properties so that the shadow would not be visible, but this involves writing quite a bit of code—and if your drawing was more complex, this could also cause a headache. Luckily, there is an easier solution.

You can save the state of your context at any point by using the save() function. This will create and save a snapshot of all your styles. You are then free to manipulate the styles as you wish. When you want to get your original styles back, just call the restore() function: All the styles from the snapshot you saved are retrieved.

Here is example code that shows how this works:

```
ctx.fillStyle = "red";
ctx.fillRect(0,0,50,50);

ctx.save();
```

```
ctx.fillStyle = "blue";
ctx.fillRect(60,0,50,50);

ctx.restore();

// Back to red again.
ctx.fillRect(120,0,50,50);
```

In this example, you set the fillStyle to red and draw the first square. You then call the save() function, which takes a snapshot of your current styles and saves them in memory. You then change the fillStyle to blue and draw another square. Then you call the restore() function, which retrieves your saved styles (setting fillStyle back to red). Just to prove that everything is working correctly, you draw another square that should come out red. Figure 14-15 shows how this would look on the canvas.

FIGURE 14-15 Saving and restoring state.

You can use the save() and restore() functions to solve the text shadow problem. If you call the save() function before you set the shadow styles and then the restore() function before you draw the offer text, the text will have no shadow.

 The code in this exercise can be found in folder 11.

Here are the steps:

1. Open the adscript.js file.

2. Add a call to the save() function just before you set the shadow styles.

   ```
   function drawAdvert() {
     ...

       // Save the context
       ctx.save();
   ```

```
  // Set a shadow
  ...
}
```

3. Now add a call to the restore() function before you draw the offer text.

```
function drawAdvert() {

  ...

  // Restore the saved context
  ctx.restore();

  // Add the Offer Text

  ...
}
```

4. Save the adscript.js file.

Problem solved! Open your advert.html file now; you should see that the text no longer has a shadow, as shown in Figure 14-16. The save() and restore() function can be extremely useful when using the Canvas API, especially when you go on to create more complex drawings.

FIGURE 14-16 Using the save() and restore() functions to remove the text shadow.

Adding Images

The final thing that you need to add to your canvas is the background image. There are a number of ways to draw an image onto the canvas, but I'm just going to show you the most popular (and easiest!) way.

You draw images onto a canvas using the drawImage() function:

```
drawImage(image, x, y);
```

This function takes three parameters. The `image` parameter should be an `Image` object, not just a path to an image (more on this shortly), and the `x` and `y` parameters are used for positioning the image on the canvas. Although it is possible to resize images on the canvas, by default images will be drawn to their native dimensions.

To create an `Image` object to pass into the `drawImage()` function, you can use the following statement:

```
var img = new Image();
```

Once you have created your new `Image` object, you can load your image file by setting the object's `src` property, like so:

```
img.src = "myImage.png";
```

There is one caveat when drawing images onto a canvas. The JavaScript code that you write to draw onto your canvas will likely execute before your image has finished loading. If you call the `drawImage()` function when the image is still loading, nothing will happen, and so your image won't appear on your canvas. To get around this, you need to attach a function to the `onload` event of your `Image` object and call the `drawImage()` function from there. Here is an example:

```
var img = new Image();
img.onload = function() {
  ctx.drawImage(img,0,0);
}
img.src = "myImage.png";
```

For your advertisement, you need the image to be drawn first so that all the other objects appear above it on the canvas. However, as I mention earlier, the JavaScript code that you previously wrote that draws the objects on the canvas will execute before the image has loaded, causing the image to be drawn on top of everything else, not below it. You need some way of telling the browser to only start drawing on your canvas after the image has loaded. Well, you just learned how to do this by attaching a function to the `onload` event of your `Image` object. Now you just need a way of calling the rest of your drawing code once the image has been drawn. Lucky that you put all your drawing code into that `drawAdvert()` function then, isn't it?

You could just copy all your drawing code inside the event listener, but using a function makes it much easier to manage your code in the long run.

Add the background image to your canvas with the following steps:

> The code in this exercise can be found in folder 12.

1. Open the `adscript.js` file in your text editor.

2. Download the `background.png` file from the book's website and place it in your `canvas-ad` folder. You can find this image in folder 12.

3. Go to the top of the `adscript.js` file and delete the call to the `drawAdvert()` function that is below where you initialize the `ctx` variable.

    ```
    if (adCanvas.getContext) {
      // Initialize a 2d drawing context.
      var ctx = adCanvas.getContext("2d");

      drawAdvert();
    }
    ```

4. In its place, create a new variable called `img` and initialize it by creating a new empty `Image` object.

    ```
    if (adCanvas.getContext) {
      // Initialize a 2d drawing context.
      var ctx = adCanvas.getContext("2d");

      // Draw on the Canvas
      var img = new Image();
    }
    ```

5. Attach a function to the `onload` event of the `Image` object.

    ```
    if (adCanvas.getContext) {
      // Initialize a 2d drawing context.
      var ctx = adCanvas.getContext("2d");

      // Draw on the Canvas
      var img = new Image();
      img.onload = function() {

      }
    }
    ```

6. Inside this function, write a call to the `drawImage()` function that will add your image to the canvas.

```
if (adCanvas.getContext) {
  // Initialize a 2d drawing context.
  var ctx = adCanvas.getContext("2d");

  // Draw on the Canvas
  var img = new Image();
  img.onload = function() {
    ctx.drawImage(img,0,0);
  }
}
```

7. Underneath `drawImage()`, add the call to your `drawAdvert()` function.

```
if (adCanvas.getContext) {
  // Initialize a 2d drawing context.
  var ctx = adCanvas.getContext("2d");

  // Draw on the Canvas
  var img = new Image();
  img.onload = function() {
    ctx.drawImage(img,0,0);
    drawAdvert();
  }
}
```

8. After the event listener, set the `src` property of your `Image` object to `background. png`.

```
if (adCanvas.getContext) {
  // Initialize a 2d drawing context.
  var ctx = adCanvas.getContext("2d");

  // Draw on the Canvas
  var img = new Image();
  img.onload = function() {
    ctx.drawImage(img,0,0);
    drawAdvert();
  }
  img.src = "background.png";
}
```

9. Save the `adscript.js` file.

You're now at the moment of truth. Open your `advert.html` file in your web browser and take a look at your finished advertisement. If all is well, it should look like the one in Figure 14-17.

FIGURE 14-17 The finished HTML5 Canvas advertisement.
Pizza image reproduced by permission of iStockphoto.com/Lauri Patterson

To distribute the advertisement on partner websites, you need to send the JavaScript file (`adscript.js`) and the two images (`fallback.png` and `background.png`) to the websites' developers. The developers on the other end would then need to add the `<canvas>` element onto the websites where they want the advertisement to appear. If you want to be really helpful, you could create a text file called README with some instructions for the other websites' developers to follow.

Summary

In this chapter, you have learned about one of the biggest new features in HTML5, the Canvas API. You've used this API to generate an online advertisement using just JavaScript and a few images. The beauty of being able to use JavaScript to draw in the browser is that you can create your graphics on the fly, maybe even using real-time data from some of the other new APIs (like GeoLocation) to personalize these graphics.

The Canvas API is massive and there's a lot of stuff that I could not cover in this chapter, including cool things like animation. If you are interested in learning more about the Canvas API, I recommend that you check out the developer docs on the Mozilla Developer Network (`https://developer.mozilla.org/en-US/docs/HTML/Canvas`). The site has loads of great information and tutorials that dive deeper into the inner workings of the Canvas API.

The end of this chapter also brings the Joe's Pizza Co. project to a close. In just a few hundred pages, you have managed to build a website using technologies that even many professional website designers are only just beginning to understand. Through the course of this book, you have learned two new languages, the HTML markup language and the programming language JavaScript. Combined with CSS, these three languages make up the backbone of front-end development for the modern-day web. Whether you want to freelance, join a studio, or design websites as a hobby, you now have the foundation you need to go out and build some really awesome websites.

Every day, I wake up and feel privileged to work in an industry that is truly making the world a better place. The web industry is one of the most exciting places to work right now. So much is evolving that it is completely possible to be faced with a new challenge every single day. This industry also has the best community in the world (I'm probably biased, but I really believe this is true). There is always someone happy to support you with the challenges that you will inevitably encounter as you put your new skills into practice—and that includes me (@MattAntWest on Twitter).

The web is always evolving, and so are the technologies that the web is built upon. Innovation in this industry is moving at such a staggering pace that it can sometimes feel like a full-time job just keeping up. Sit back and let your curiosity guide you. No one person knows everything about web development. As in life, you will always be learning—and that is exactly the way it should be.

Additional HTML Markup for Text

THROUGHOUT THIS BOOK, you have learned about several HTML elements that can be used for layout and content markup. In this appendix, I cover some additional HTML elements that can be used to mark up your text content.

Indicating Importance

The `<strong>` element is used to signify that a piece of text is important and should be noted. Browsers will usually display the content as bold text; however, it is important to understand that by putting text within a `<strong>` element you are also altering its semantic meaning. You should not use it purely for styling purposes. (In those cases, you should use the `<span>` element and CSS, as discussed later in this appendix.)

```
<p>
  <strong>Do not cross the bridge</strong>, as the support
  structure has been weakened.
</p>
```

In the preceding example, I use the `<strong>` element to indicate that the instruction is more important than the explanation.

Emphasizing Text

The `<em>` element is used to place emphasis on a particular word or phrase. This element can be used to change the meaning of a sentence and indicates that the content should be read with a different mood or voice. The following example conveys the tone that someone is very passionate about HTML5.

```
<p>HTML5 <em>rocks</em>!</p>
```

This would appear in most browsers as "HTML5 *rocks!*"

Browsers will usually style text within the `<em>` element in italics, but again, it should not be used purely for styling purposes. Using a `<span>` element with CSS would be more appropriate.

Strikethrough

The `<s>` element is used to identify text that is no longer relevant, but which continues to be displayed. The following line is an example of how the `<s>` element can be used to signal that the maintainer of a web page has been updated.

```
<p>This page is maintained by <s>Joe Balochio</s> Matt West.</p>
```

Browsers will often apply a strikethrough style to the contents of `<s>` elements. Figure A-1 shows how this example would be displayed.

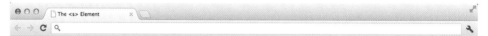

FIGURE A-1   The `<s>` element, as displayed in Google Chrome.

Inserts

As well as being able to mark up text that is no longer relevant, you can also mark up text that has been added to the page by using the `<ins>` element.

Building on the preceding example, here is how you could use the `<ins>` element to mark up new content.

```
<p>This page is maintained by <s>Joe Balochio</s> <ins>Matt West</ins>.</p>
```

Browsers will often apply an underline to text content contained within an `<ins>` element. This can of course be overridden using CSS. Figure A-2 shows how this example would be displayed in Google Chrome.

This page is maintained by ~~Joe Balochio~~ <u>Matt West</u>.

FIGURE A-2 The <ins> element, as displayed in Google Chrome.

The <span> Element

The <span> element has no meaning itself, but can be used to apply attributes such as class or id to a specific part of text. The element can then be used to apply styling to a section of text that does not have any semantic meaning and therefore should not use the <em>, <strong>, <s>, or <ins> elements. Here's an example showing the use of the <span> element.

```
<span class="big-text">Style me!</span>
```

The <address> Element

The <address> element is used to mark up contact information related to a particular article or a web page as a whole. (You should not use it to mark up postal addresses unless that information is directly relevant; best practice is to use the <p> element for that use case.) Here's an example that uses the <address> element to mark up contact information within a press release.

```
<article>
  <h1>Press Release</h1>
  <p>...</p>
  <address>
    For more information, contact
    <a href="mailto:joe@example.com">Joe Balochio</a>.
  </address>
</article>
```

Defining Terms

You may want to define new terms when you first introduce them in your text.

You can use the <dfn> element to identify the term that is being defined to computer programs. The <dfn> element should contain either the word or phrase that is being defined or an <abbr> element. The following example shows how you might use the <dfn> element when defining the term *Internet*.

```
<p>The <dfn>Internet</dfn> is a vast computer network linking
smaller computer networks worldwide.</p>
```

You could also use the `<dfn>` and `<abbr>` elements together when defining an acronym:

```
<p>The <dfn><abbr title="World Wide Web Consortium">W3C</abbr>
  </dfn> is the main standards body for the World Wide Web.</p>
```

Most browsers will apply an italic font style to the text within a `<dfn>` element. However, this is not standardized and therefore can vary between browsers.

Line Breaks

You may need to use line breaks to format your content. A good example is addresses, where each line of the address needs to be presented on a new line in the browser. You can achieve this using the `<br>` element. Here's an example of an address that uses the `<br>` element to separate each line.

```
<p>
  B. Obama<br>
  The White House<br>
  1600 Pennsylvania Avenue NW<br>
  Washington, DC 20500
</p>
```

Why not just use the `<p>` element for each line and make them separate paragraphs? I have placed this address within a single `<p>` element because all the text content is related. Using individual `<p>` elements for each line of the address would imply that the text content is not directly related.

You must only use the `<br>` element when line breaks are actually part of the content—in poems and addresses, for example. You should never use the `<br>` element to create extra space between elements, or for other styling purposes; that is a job for CSS.

Meter Elements

The `<meter>` element, new in HTML5, is useful for displaying data relative to a scale, such as temperature readings.

You can use six attributes on the `<meter>` element: min, max, low, high, optimum, and value. The only attribute that you **must** specify is value; the rest are optional.

The min attribute specifies the minimum value on the scale. If you do not specify this attribute, the value 0 will be used. The max attribute is used to specify the maximum value on the scale. The default for this attribute is 1.

The `low` attribute is used to mark the upper boundary of the *low* section of the scale. If you were using a `<meter>` element to present the temperature in a room, this `low` attribute could be set to the lowest temperature that humans would be comfortable in. The `high` attribute is simply the opposite of `low`. It defines the lower boundary of the *high* section on the scale. To use the temperature analogy again, this would be the highest temperature that humans would be comfortable working in.

You guessed it! The `optimum` attribute would be used to define the optimum temperature for humans to work in. Not too hot and not too cold.

The `value` attribute is used to set your actual measurement.

Here is a code snippet that shows how you could mark up the temperature example.

```
<meter min="-20" low="5" max="30" high="20" optimum="15"
value="-10"></meter>
```

Browsers that support the `<meter>` element will display a bar graphic that represents your value in the scale, as shown in Figure A-3.

Meter:

FIGURE A-3 A `<meter>` element, as displayed in Google Chrome.

Some browsers will even change the color of the bar depending on where the value lies on the scale you set. Google Chrome, for example, will show a yellow bar if the `value` is above the `high` point or below the `low` point, and a green bar if it is between these two points. If you take a look at Figure A-4 you can see this variation in color.

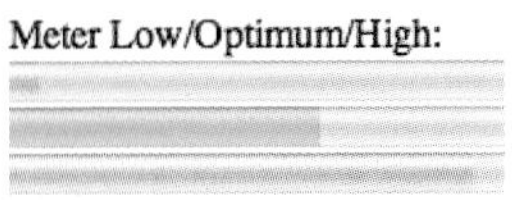

Meter Low/Optimum/High:

FIGURE A-4 A series of `<meter>` elements, showing the variations in color states.

Progress Bars

Also new in HTML5, the `<progress>` element is similar to the `<meter>` element; however, this element should be used to represent a value that is changing instead of a value that has already been measured. This element is commonly used in applications such as file upload forms where you want to let the user track the progress of the upload.

The `<progress>` element only has two attributes: a `max` and a `value`.

The `max` attribute is used to specify how much work a task needs to complete in total. For a file upload form, this could be the size of the file in kilobytes.

The `value` attribute is then used to specify how much of the job has been completed. In our file upload example, this could be the number of kilobytes that have been uploaded.

The browser will automatically calculate the percentage of the task that has been completed and display that percentage using a bar graph, as shown in Figure A-5.

Progress: [▓▓▓▓   ]

FIGURE A-5 A `<progress>` element, as displayed in Google Chrome.

Here is an example of how you can create a `<progress>` element.

```
<progress max="1145" value="203"></progress>
```

appendix b
HTML Elements Index

THIS APPENDIX CONTAINS a list of the most commonly used HTML elements with definitions and examples for each of these elements. Note that I cover only the basic attributes for each of the elements here. For an exhaustive list of elements and their attributes check out the HTML5 specifications that can be found here:

- WHATWG Specification - `http://developers.whatwg.org/`

- W3C Specification - `http://www.w3.org/TR/html5/`

Element	Definition
`<a>`	The `<a>` element is used for creating hyperlinks to other pages on the web or to a section in the current page. The location of the target page is specified in the `href` attribute. The *anchor text* between the tags will be shown to the user. `<a href="http://html5foundations.com">HTML5 Foundations</a>`
`<abbr>`	The `<abbr>` element is used to markup an abbreviation or acronym. An optional `title` attribute may be used to specify an expansion of the abbreviation. `<abbr title="World Wide Web Consortium">W3C</abbr>`

continued

339

Element	Definition

`<address>`	The `<address>` element should contain contact information for a section or page.
	
	`<address>`
	 `<a href="mailto:matt.west@developercity.co.uk">`
	  `Email Matt`
	 `</a>`
	`</address>`

`<article>`	The `<article>` element is used to define a section on a page that contains an independent piece of content such as a blog post or newspaper article.
	
	`<article>`
	 `<h1>Blog Post Title</h1>`
	 `<p>Blog post content...</p>`
	`</article>`

`<aside>`	If the `<aside>` element is used within an `<article>` element, it should contain content that is related to the article, but that could also be considered separate from it. In this context the `<aside>` element is similar to the purpose of a sidebar in a printed book or magazine article.
	If the `<aside>` element is not used within an `<article>` element it should contain content that is related to the page, but that again, could be considered separate from it. For example, this could be a sidebar containing links to related websites.
	
	`<article>`
	 `<h1>HTML5 Elements</h1>`
	 `<p>Some content goes here...</p>`
	 `<aside>`
	  `<h1>Sidebar Title</h1>`
	  `<p>Content related to the article.</p>`
	 `</aside>`
	`</article>`

`<audio>`	The `<audio>` element is used to embed audio content within a web page. A path to the audio file can be specified either using the `src` attribute or by using `<source>` elements. Multiple `<source>` elements can be used to provide additional versions of an audio file.
	Content placed between the start and end tags of this element will be displayed if the user's browser does not support HTML5 audio.
	
	`<audio src="path/to/audio/file.mp3">`
	 `<p>Your browser does not support HTML5 audio :(</p>`
	`</audio>`

`<base>`	The `<base>` element allows the developer to specify a base URL from which all relative URLs will resolve. For example, using a base URL of `http://html5foundations.com/test/` would mean that the relative URL `img/photo.png` would resolve to `http://html5foundations.com/test/img/photo.png`. This element should be placed in the document `<head>`. `<base href="http://html5foundations.com/test/">`

Element	Definition
`<blockquote>`	The `<blockquote>` element should contain content that is quoted from another source. `<blockquote>To be or not to be.</blockquote>`

`<body>`	The `<body>` element should contain the main content of the document.
	
	`<!DOCTYPE html>`
	`<html lang="en">`
	`<head>`
	` <meta charset="utf8">`
	` <title>Document Title</title>`
	`</head>`
	`<body>`
	` Content goes here...`
	`</body>`
	`</html>`

` `	The ` ` element represents a line break. This element should be used only where a line break is a natural part of the content (such as postal addresses) and should not be used for styling purposes. `The White House ` `1600 Pennsylvania Avenue NW ` `Washington, DC 20500`
`<button>`	The `<button>` element represents a clickable button. Buttons can be used to submit (or reset) forms. `<button type="submit">Send Form</button>`

`<canvas>`	The `<canvas>` element is used to create a bitmap canvas that can be used to render graphics on the fly. The content placed between the tags of the `<canvas>` element will be displayed if the user's browser does not support the Canvas API.
	`<canvas width="500" height="500" id="myCanvas">`
	` <p>Your browser does not support canvas :(</p>`
	`</canvas>`

`<caption>`	The `<caption>` element is used to define the title of a `<table>` element.
	
	`<table>`
	` <caption>Exam Results</caption>`
	` ...`
	`</table>`

`<cite>`	The `<cite>` element is used to mark up the title of a piece of work (such as a book, song, poem, article, or sculpture). `I recently read <cite>HTML5 Foundations</cite> by Matt West.`

Element	Definition

`<code>`	The `<code>` element is used to mark up a piece of computer code that is to be displayed in the page content. This could be a computer program or even a filename.
	
	`<code>`
	 `function boo() {`
	  `alert("Boo");`
	  `}`
	`</code>`

`<datalist>`	The `<datalist>` element is used to define a list of options that can be mapped to an `<input>` element. When the user starts typing into the input field, the browser will attempt to match the text input to the options in the datalist and will display any matches in a drop-down menu underneath the `<input>` element.
	
	`<input type="text" list="drinks">`
	`<datalist id="drinks">`
	 `<option>Coffee</option>`
	 `<option>Tea</option>`
	 `<option>Orange Juice</option>`
	`</datalist>`

`<dd>`	The `<dd>` element is used to mark up a description list definition (or value). This element should be used in conjunction with a `<dt>` element.
	
	`<dl>`
	 `<dt>Drinks</dt>`
	 `<dd>``Coffee`**`</dd>`**
	 `<dd>``Tea`**`</dd>`**
	 `<dd>``Orange Juice`**`</dd>`**
	`</dl>`

`<del>`	The `<del>` element is used to mark up content that has been removed from a document.
	
	`<h1>Upcoming Events</h1>`
	`<ul>`
	 `<li>`**`<del>`**`New Adventures - Nottingham`**`</del>`**`</li>`
	 `<li>Build Conf - Belfast</li>`
	`</ul>`

`<dfn>`	The `<dfn>` element is used to mark up a term that is being defined. `<p>The `**`<dfn>`**`Internet`**`</dfn>`**` is a vast computer network linking smaller computer networks worldwide.</p>`

`<div>`	The `<div>` element is a generic element used to group together other elements for layout or styling purposes.
	
	`<div>`
	 `<p>Paragraph one...</p>`
	 `<p>Paragraph two...</p>`
	`</div>`

Element	Definition
`<dl>`	The `<dl>` element is used to mark up a description list.

```
<dl>
  <dt>Author</dt>
  <dd>Matt West</dd>
  <dt>Technical Editor</dt>
  <dd>Nick Elliot</dd>
</dl>
```

Element	Definition
`<!DOCTYPE>`	The DOCTYPE is a required element that should appear on the first line of your HTML. The DOCTYPE declaration is used to specify which web standard the document conforms to. The HTML5 DOCTYPE is:

```
<!DOCTYPE html>
```

Element	Definition
`<dt>`	The `<dt>` element is used to mark up a term in a description list.

```
<dl>
  <dt>Author</dt>
  <dd>Matt West</dd>
</dl>
```

Element	Definition
`<em>`	The `<em>` element is used to place emphasis on a word or phrase. Text within an `<em>` element will usually be rendered in italics by the browser.

```
HTML5 <em>Rocks</em>!
```

Element	Definition
`<embed>`	The `<embed>` element is used to integrate an external application into your web page. This element is most commonly used for embedding a Flash application.

```
<embed src="flashapp.swf">
```

Element	Definition
`<fieldset>`	The `<fieldset>` element is used to group together one or more form fields.

```
<form method="post" action="#">
  <fieldset>
    <legend>Contact Information</legend>
    <p>
      <label for="name">Name:</label>
      <input type="text" name="name" id="name">
    </p>
    <p>
      <label for="email">Email:</label>
      <input type="email" name="email" id="email">
    </p>
  </fieldset>
</form>
```

continued

Element	Definition
`<figcaption>`	The `<figcaption>` element is used to add a caption to a `<figure>` element.

```
<figure>
 <img src="figure.jpg" alt="My Figure">
 <figcaption>
  This is my figure.
 </figcaption>
</figure>
```

Element	Definition
`<figure>`	The `<figure>` element is used to mark up a self-contained piece of content that is referenced from the main content of the page. These figures are usually images, diagrams, tables, or code listings. The use of a `<figcaption>` element is optional.

```
<figure>
 <code>
  function boo() {
   alert("boo!");
  }
 </code>
 <figcaption>A simple JavaScript function that displays an alert
to the user with the text "boo!".</figcaption>
</figure>
```

Element	Definition
`<footer>`	The `<footer>` element is used to mark up the footer section of a document (or the footer of a `<section>` or `<article>`). This element typically contains metadata about its parent section or page, such as copyright information.

```
<section>
 <h1>Section Title</h1>
 <p>Some content goes here...</p>
 <footer>
  Copyright Joe's Pizza Co. 2012
 <footer>
</section>
```

Element	Definition
`<form>`	The `<form>` element is used to mark up a collection of form-field elements that can be submitted to a server. The `action` attribute specifies a path to a file that will handle processing the form data, and the `method` attribute specifies how the data should be sent.

```
<form action="process.php" method="POST">
 <p>
  <label for="name">Name:</label>
  <input type="text" name="name" id="name">
 </p>
 <p>
  <input type="submit" value="Send">
 </p>
</form>
```

Element	Definition

`<h1>` – `<h6>`	The elements `<h1>`, `<h2>`, `<h3>`, `<h4>`, `<h5>`, and `<h6>` are used to mark up headings in your page. The number in the element name represents the heading's importance, with 1 being the most important and 6 being the least important.
	
	`<h1>Main Page Title</h1>`
	`<p>Some text content...</p>`
	`<h2>Subtitle</h2>`
	`<p>Some more text content...</p>`

`<head>`	The `<head>` element should contain a collection of metadata about the page, such as the page title, references to stylesheets, and the page keywords and description.
	
	`<!DOCTYPE html>`
	`<html>`
	`<head>`
	` <meta charset="utf-8">`
	` <title>HTML5 Foundations</title>`
	` <link rel="stylesheet" href="css/style.css">`
	`<head>`
	`<body></body>`
	`</html>`

`<header>`	The `<header>` element is used to mark up the header of a document or section. The header typically contains a heading element (`<h1>` – `<h6>`) and metadata about the section.
	
	`<article>`
	` <header>`
	`  <h1>About HTML5 Foundations</h1>`
	`  <p>Posted on 20 August 2012</p>`
	` </header>`
	` <p>`
	`  The section content...`
	` </p>`
	`</article>`

`<hgroup>`	The `<hgroup>` element is used to group together two or more heading elements. When the HTML5 outlining algorithm examines the page hierarchy, only the heading element with the most importance within the `<hgroup>` will be used.
	
	`<hgroup>`
	` <h1>Venture Deals</h1>`
	` <h2>Be Smarter Than Your Lawyer and Venture Capitalist</h2>`
	`</hgroup>`

continued

Element	Definition

`<html>`	The `<html>` element represents the root of a HTML document. Everything except the DOCTYPE declaration should be enclosed within the `<html>` element.
	
	`<!DOCTYPE html>`
	`<html>`
	`<head>`...`</head>`
	`<body>`...`</body>`
	`</html>`

`<iframe>`	The `<iframe>` element is used to nest a web page within another web page. The `src` attribute specifies the path to the resource that should be loaded into the iframe. `<iframe width="500" height="500" src="http://google.com">`
`<img>`	The `<img>` element is used to embed an image within a web page. The `src` attribute specifies the path to the image file, and the `alt` attribute specifies text that may be displayed if the image cannot be loaded. `<img src="logo.png" alt="The Joe's Pizza Co. Logo">`
`<input>`	The `<input>` element is used to create a form control that can usually be edited by the user. The `type` attribute specifies the type of `<input>` element that should be created. Possible types include: `text`, `email`, `tel`, `datetime`, and `submit` (to name but a few). `<input type="text">`
`<ins>`	The `<ins>` element is used to mark up an addition to a document. `<p>This text has been here for ages. <ins>This text was just added.</ins></p>`

`<label>`	The `<label>` element is used to mark up a label for a form control. The `for` attribute should contain the ID of the form control that is to be associated with the label.
	
	`<label for="name">Name:</label>`
	`<input type="text" id="name">`

`<legend>`	The `<legend>` element is used to create a caption for a `<fieldset>` element.
	
	`<fieldset>`
	 `<legend>Contact Information</legend>`
	 `<p>`
	  `<label for="name">Name:</label>`
	  `<input type="text" id="name">`
	 `</p>`
	`</fieldset>`

Element	Definition

`<li>`	The `<li>` element is used to mark up a list item.
	
	`<ul>`
	`<li>Item One</li>`
	`<li>Item Two</li>`
	`<li>Item Three</li>`
	`</ul>`

`<link>`	The `<link>` element is used to link other resources (such as stylesheets) to a document. A path to the resource is specified in the `href` attribute. The `rel` attribute specifies the type of resource. `<link rel="stylesheet" href="style.css">`

`<meta>`	The `<meta>` element is used to specify metadata for a document, such as the character encoding, keywords, or page description.
	
	`<head>`
	`<meta charset="utf-8">`
	`<title>HTML5 Foundations</title>`
	
	`<meta name="keywords" content="html5,web design,treehouse">`
	`<meta name="description" content="A book to help you get started with website design.">`
	`</head>`

`<meter>`	The `<meter>` element is used to display data relative to a scale. You can use the `min`, `max`, `low`, `high`, `optimum`, and `value` attributes to specify data points on the scale. `<meter min="-20" low="5" max="30" high="20" optimum="15" value="-10"></meter>`

`<nav>`	The `<nav>` element is used to define an area on the page that contains links to other pages or sections within the same document. The `<nav>` element should be used only for primary navigation links, like the main site navigation.
	
	`<nav>`
	`<ul>`
	`<li><a href="about.html">About</a></li>`
	`<li><a href="services.html">Services</a></li>`
	`<li><a href="contact.html">Contact</a></li>`
	`</ul>`
	`</nav>`

`<noscript>`	The `<noscript>` element is used to specify some content that should be displayed if JavaScript is not available in the user's web browser. `<noscript>Please enable JavaScript to use this website.</noscript>`

continued

Element	Definition
`<object>`	The `<object>` element represents an external resource that can be processed by a plug-in. Many developers use the `<object>` element in combination with `<embed>` to embed a Flash application or video into a web page.

```
<object width="560" height="315">
 <param name="movie" value="http://www.youtube.com/v/
HbcGxFeK8zo?version=3&amp;hl=en_US"></param>
 <param name="allowFullScreen" value="true"></param>
 <param name="allowscriptaccess" value="always"></param>
 <embed src="http://www.youtube.com/v/
HbcGxFeK8zo?version=3&amp;hl=en_US"
type="application/x-shockwave-flash" width="560" height="315"
allowscriptaccess="always" allowfullscreen="true"></embed>
</object>
```

Element	Definition
`<ol>`	The `<ol>` element is used to mark up an ordered list. This list may contain 0 or more `<li>` elements (list items). Web browsers will display numbers next to each of the list items by default, however this behavior can be changed using CSS.

```
<ol>
 <li>Item One</li>
 <li>Item Two</li>
 <li>Item Three</li>
</ol>
```

Element	Definition
`<optgroup>`	The `<optgroup>` element is used to mark up a group of `<option>` elements with a common label. When the options are displayed in a select menu, they will be grouped under the common label.

```
<select name="country" id="country">
 <optgroup label="Africa">
  <option>Egypt</option>
  <option>South Africa</option>
  <option>Tanzania</option>
 </optgroup>
 <optgroup label="Europe">
  <option>France</option>
  <option>Germany</option>
  <option>United Kingdom</option>
 </optgroup>
</select>
```

Element	Definition
`<option>`	The `<option>` element is used to mark up an option to be displayed in a `<select>` or `<datalist>`. By default, the option value is the text contained between the element tags; however, you can change this by explicitly specifying a value using the `value` attribute.

```
<select name="color">
 <option>Red</option>
 <option>Green</option>
 <option>Blue</option>
</select>
```

Element	Definition
`<output>`	The `<output>` element is used to display the result of a calculation. ```<form>

 <label for="speed">Speed (MPH)</label>
 <input type="range" name="speed-mph" id="speed" min="0"
max="200">
0
</form>``` |
| `<p>` | The `<p>` element is used to mark up a paragraph of text.

```<p>
 Design is the conscious effort to impose a meaningful order.
</p>``` |
| `<param>` | The `<param>` element is used to define parameters for plug-ins and should be contained within an `<object>` element. This element uses `name` and `value` attributes to establish a key-value pair to be used by the plug-in.

```<param name="allowFullScreen" value="true"></param>``` |
| `<pre>` | The `<pre>` element is used to mark up a block of preformatted text.

```<pre>
 This text does not use line breaks.
 However, as this is within a pre element, this second line will
still be displayed as a separate line in the browser.
</pre>``` |
| `<progress>` | The `<progress>` element is used to visually display a value that changes over time, such as the percentage of a file that has been downloaded.

```<progress max="100" value="23">``` |
| `<q>` | The `<q>` element is used to mark up a quotation used within flowing text.

```<p>
 Shakespeare once wrote <q>to be or not to be, that is the ques-
tion</q>.
</p>``` |
| `<s>` | The `<s>` element is used to mark up content that is no longer accurate or relevant. Content placed within an `<s>` element will usually be rendered with strikethrough.

```<p>
 Price: <s>£5.99</s> Now only £2.99.
</p>``` |

Element	Definition
`<script>`	The `<script>` element is used to add JavaScript code to a web page. You can also use the optional `src` attribute to load JavaScript from an external file. `<script src="script.js"></script>`

`<section>`	The `<section>` element is used to mark up a block of related content, such as chapters in a book. Each `<section>` can optionally contain a `<header>` and `<footer>` element.
	
	`<section>`
	 `<header>`
	  `<h1>Chapter 1</h1>`
	 `</header>`
	 `<p>`
	  `The section text would go here.`
	 `</p>`
	 `<footer>`
	  `By Matt West.`
	 `</footer>`
	`</section>`

`<select>`	The `<select>` element is used for creating a form control that consists of a set of options displayed in a drop-down menu.
	
	`<select name="color">`
	 `<option>Red</option>`
	 `<option>Green</option>`
	 `<option>Blue</option>`
	`</select>`

`<small>`	The `<small>` element is used for marking up the "fine print." This is content such as legal disclaimers and copyright information. This element should not be used to mark up the content of an entire page (such as a privacy policy). `<small>Copyright 2012 Matt West. All Rights Reserved.</small>`

`<source>`	The `<source>` element is used to specify a media resource for media elements such as `<video>` and `<audio>`. Developers can specify a number of `<source>` elements for a single media element.
	
	`<video width="400" height="225" poster="img/poster.png"`
	`id="myVideo">`
	 `<source src="videos/mikethefrog.webm" type="video/webm">`
	 `<source src="videos/mikethefrog.ogv" type="video/ogv">`
	 `<source src="videos/mikethefrog.mp4" type="video/mp4">`
	`</video>`

Element	Definition
`<span>`	The `<span>` element can be used to group a passage of text so that it can be targeted with CSS or JavaScript. The element itself has no semantic meaning. `Mike The Frog is highly skilled in `**`<span class="nonsense">`**`HTMLJavaPress`**`</span>`**`.`

`<strong>`	The `<strong>` element is used to mark up important text. This text will usually be rendered in bold by default.
	
	`<p>`
	 `<strong>``Do not cross the bridge`**`</strong>`**`, as the support structure has been weakened.`
	`</p>`

`<table>`	The `<table>` element is used to mark up tabular data.
	Tables should never be used for creating page layouts.
	
	`<table>`
	 `<tr>`
	  `<th>Subject</th>`
	  `<th>Result</th>`
	 `</tr>`
	 `<tr>`
	  `<td>English</td>`
	  `<td>B</td>`
	 `</tr>`
	 `<tr>`
	  `<td>Math</td>`
	  `<td>A</td>`
	 `</tr>`
	 `<tr>`
	  `<td>Science</td>`
	  `<td>C</td>`
	 `</tr>`
	`</table>`

continued

Element	Definition
`<tbody>`	The `<tbody>` element should contain the rows that present the table data.

```
<table>
 <thead>
  <tr>
   <th>Subject</th>
   <th>Result</th>
  </tr>
 </thead>
 <tbody>
  <tr>
   <td>English</td>
   <td>B</td>
  </tr>
  <tr>
   <td>Math</td>
   <td>A</td>
  </tr>
  <tr>
   <td>Science</td>
   <td>C</td>
  </tr>
 </tbody>
</table>
```

Element	Definition
`<td>`	The `<td>` element is used to mark up a data cell in a table row.

```
<td>This is a table cell.</td>
```

Element	Definition
`<textarea>`	The `<textarea>` element is used to create a form control that supports the input of multiple lines of text.

```
<label for="message">
<textarea name="message" id="message" rows="50" cols="50">
</textarea>
```

Element	Definition
`<tfoot>`	The `<tfoot>` element should contain a block of rows that consist of column summaries. You should place the `<tfoot>` element between the `<thead>` and `<tbody>` elements.

```
<table>
 <thead>
  <tr>
   <th>Subject</th>
   <th>Result</th>
  </tr>
 </thead>
 <tfoot>
  <tr>
   <td>Footer 1</td>
   <td>Footer 2</td>
  </tr>
 </tfoot>
 <tbody>
  ...
 </tbody>
</table>
```

Element	Definition
`<th>`	The `<th>` element is used to define a table heading. This heading could refer to either a column or a row.

```
<thead>
 <tr>
  <th>Subject</th>
  <th>Result</th>
 </tr>
</thead>
```

Element	Definition
`<thead>`	The `<thead>` element is used to group a block of rows that contain table headings.

```
<thead>
 <tr>
  <th>Subject</th>
  <th>Result</th>
 </tr>
</thead>
```

Element	Definition
`<time>`	The `<time>` element allows you to write human-readable dates that will be displayed to the user and also provide a machine-readable date to be used by computer programs. Machine-readable dates are specified using the `date-time` attribute.

```
<time datetime="2012-08-28">Next Tuesday</time>
```

continued

Element	Definition
`<title>`	The `<title>` element is used to set the title of the web page. This will be displayed at the very top of your browser window and/or in the browser tab. `<title>HTML5 Foundations</title>`

`<tr>`	The `<tr>` element is used to mark up a row in a table.
	
	`<table>`
	`  <tr>`
	`    <td>This is row number one</td>`
	`  </tr>`
	`  <tr>`
	`    <td>This is row number two</td>`
	`  </tr>`
	`</table>`

`<track>`	The `<track>` element is used to link a subtitle's file to a media element such as `<video>` or `<audio>`.
	
	`<video src="mikethefrog.webm">`
	`  <track src="subtitles.vtt" kind="subtitles" srclang="en" label="English">`
	`</video>`

`<ul>`	The `<ul>` element is used to create an unordered list that contains 0 or more `<li>` elements. The order of the items in an unordered list is not significant.
	
	`<ul>`
	`  <li>A List Item</li>`
	`  <li>Another List Item</li>`
	`</ul>`

`<video>`	The `<video>` element is used to embed a video file within a web page. A path to the video file can be specified either using the `src` attribute or by using a `<source>` element. Multiple `<source>` elements can be used to provide additional versions of a video file. `<video src="mikethefrog.webm"></video>`
`<wbr>`	The `<wbr>` (word break) element is used to signal a place where a line break may occur. This is particularly useful when you have a long string of characters with no spaces; it gives you control over where the browser will create a line break should the content not fit on a single line. `supercalifragilistic<wbr>expialidocious`

appendix c
Where to Go from Here

NOW THAT YOU have finished this book, you are probably eager to go out and learn more about web development. In this appendix, I list some books and online resources that you might find useful for advancing your knowledge of web development.

Books

Here are four books that I have personally found to be useful.

- ***Hardboiled Web Design*** by Andy Clarke (Five Simple Steps, 2010; ISBN: 978-1-907828-00-3)

  Andy Clarke is a pretty influential (and sometimes controversial) figure within the industry. In his book *Hardboiled Web Design*, Andy explores some of the new features introduced in HTML5 and takes an in-depth look into how CSS3 can be used to enhance your websites. Andy also discusses some of the day-to-day challenges that designers and developers face when creating websites, and offers up his opinions on how to deal with these. The artwork within this book is stunning, so if for no other reason, you should get a copy just to please your eyes.

- ***Introducing HTML5*** **(Second Edition)** by Bruce Lawson and Remy Sharp (New Riders, 2012; ISBN: 978-0-321-78442-1)

  In *Introducing HTML5* Bruce Lawson and Remy Sharp take you on a fully comprehensive exploration of all that HTML5 has to offer. This book is fantastic for those who want to learn about some of the more advanced technologies introduced in

HTML5, such as WebSockets, Drag & Drop, and Web Workers. The friendly writing style and occasional banter between Bruce and Remy make this book a really enjoyable read.

- **_HTML and CSS: Design and Build Websites_** by Jon Duckett (John Wiley & Sons, Inc., 2011; ISBN: 978-1-118-00818-8)

  In _HTML and CSS: Design and Build Websites_, Jon Duckett does a fantastic job of marrying together HTML and CSS. The design and layout of the each of the pages chops up the content into jargon-free, bite-sized chunks that can be easily digested by all.

- **_CSS3 Foundations_** by Ian Lunn (John Wiley & Sons, Inc., 2013; ISBN: 978-1-118-35654-8)

  In _CSS3 Foundations_, Ian Lunn uses a practical, project-driven approach to teach readers how to create stunning websites using the fantastic new features of CSS3. You will learn everything from the basics of CSS, such as how to style text and create basic page layouts, to more advanced CSS3 techniques, like how to add animations to elements. CSS3 Foundations is also part of the new Treehouse Series and has been designed to build upon the skills that you learned in this book.

Websites and Blogs

There are a lot of web development websites and blogs out there. Some are more useful than others. Here is a list of my favorites (in no particular order.)

- **A List Apart** (http://www.alistapart.com)— A List Apart (ALA) publishes articles from some of the best-known figures in the industry. The articles that you will find on ALA are unlike those found anywhere else. This is where new ideas are explored and shared.

- **Treehouse Blog** (http://blog.teamtreehouse.com/)—The Treehouse Blog is great place to find new tips and tricks that you can use to advance your skills as a web developer.

- **Mozilla Developer Network** (https://developer.mozilla.org)—The Mozilla Developer Network (MDN) is one of the best online resources for developer documentation surrounding HTML5, CSS3, and JavaScript.

- **HTML5Rocks** (http://html5rocks.com)—The HTML5Rocks website/blog has a number of great tutorials that you can use to learn about more advanced HTML5 and CSS3 features, such as IndexedDB and WebSockets.

- **HTML5 Doctor** (http://html5doctor.com)—The HTML5 Doctor blog contains a wide range of posts related to every aspect of HTML5. The "Ask the HTML5 Doctor" section can also be useful if you ever get really stuck.

- **.net** (http://www.netmagazine.com)—The .net website is great for keeping up-to-date on the latest goings on within the industry. I also recommend that you subscribe to the magazine. It's always packed full of fantastic articles, and tutorials that will help you to develop your skills as a web developer.

You can also find my personal blog at http://codingskyscrapers.com.

Index

Event schema, 180–184
events, 211

F

fallback content, 243–244, 246, 301
`familyName` property, 185
`faxNumber` property, 174
features sections, 39–40
fields, 120, 123, 134–137
`<fieldset>` element, 134–137, 343
`<figcaption>` element, 97–100, 344
`<figure>` element, 97–100, 344
figures, 97–98
file browsers, 133
`file` input type, 133
filenames, defining, 59
files
    converting, 238–240
    JavaScript, 213–214
    uploading, 132–134
fill colors, 304, 317–320
`fill()` function, 310, 315
`fillRect()` function, 304–305, 317
`fillStyle` property, 304–305, 317, 319, 326
`fillText()` function, 306–309
`final-expression` parameter, 223
`findNearest` function, 293–294, 296
Firebug for Firefox, 11–12
Firefogg converter, 239–240
Firefox (Mozilla). *See* Mozilla Firefox
`font` property, 306
`foo` variable, 218
`<footer>` element, 41–42, 344
footers, 26, 66–69, 92–93
`for` attribute, 193–194, 346
`for` loops, 222–224, 269
form data encoding, 114
`<form>` element
    `action` attribute, 112–113
    general discussion, 344
    `method` attribute, 113–115
    overview, 110–112
formatting, 157, 165, 238–239
forms
    accessibility, 193–197
    adding HTML5, 142–144
    adding message box with `<textarea>`
        element, 123–125
    attributes, 152–153
    `<datalist>` element, 154
    drop-down menus, 127–132
    `<form>` element, 110–115
    grouping input fields with `<fieldset>` and
        `<legend>` elements, 134–137
    input types, 144–152

`<input>` and `<label>` elements, 115–123
    overview, 109–110, 141–142
    saving customer data, 270–275
    Submit button, 125–127
    updating site navigation and Sitemap page, 137–139
    uploading files, 132–134
    validating data, 157–166
functions, 211, 218–220
future-proofing code, 20

G

games, 224–225
gedit, 11
`gender` property, 185
Geolocation API
    calculating distance between two sets of GPS
        coordinates, 291–295
    finding nearest restaurant, 295–298
    overview, 285–286
    users' locations, 286–291
`geolocation` interface, 286
`geolocation` property, 287
`GeoPosition` object, 286, 288
GET method, 113–115
`getContext` method, 302
`getCurrentPosition()` function, 286, 288
`getElementById()` function, 229–230, 232
`getElementsByClassName()` function, 230
`getElementsByTagName()` function, 231
getfirebug.com, 12
`getItem()` function, 267–268, 273
`givenName` property, 185
global attributes, 69–71
GNOME desktop environment, 191
Google
    marking up events data, 180
    microdata in search results, 172
    Rich Snippets Tool, 178
    Rome demo, 211
    The Wilderness Downtown demo, 211
Google Chrome
    audio formats, 239
    compatibility with Microsoft IE, 23
    debugging code with developer tools, 228–229
    general discussion, 9
    testing About page, 263–264
    video formats, 238
GPS coordinates, calculating distances
    between, 291–295
gradients, 317–320
grayscale, 204–205
greater-than sign (>), 15
grouping content
    with `<header>` element, 103
    input fields, 134–137

<option> elements, 348
options, 132
<span> element, 351
<thead> element, 353
guess variable, 225–226
guessing game, 224–225

H

<h1> element, 53–55
<h2> element, 53–55
<h3> element, 53–54
<h4> element, 53–54
<h5> element, 53–54
<h6> element, 53–54
hacks, 22
Hardboiled Web Design, 355
Haversine formula, 291–293
haversine() function, 293
<head> element, 14–15, 17–18, 43–45, 345
<header> element, 33–35, 42, 103, 345
headers, 26, 92–93, 199–202
heading elements, 53–55, 345
headings, 53–56, 74–75
height attribute, 16, 84, 300
height parameter, 304–305
Hello World! program, 212–213
help link type, 60
<hgroup> element, 74–75, 345
hidden attribute, 70
hidden input type, 123
high attribute, 336–337
hints, displaying with placeholder attribute, 153
home pages
    headings and <hgroup> element, 74–75
    main feature section, 74–75
    naming, 13
    overview, 73
    special offers, 78–79
    templates, 27–28, 29–30
    text, 75–78
home text sections, 39–40
Hoskins, Jim, 113
href attribute, 47, 57–58, 170, 347
HTML and CSS: Design and Build Websites, 356
HTML codes, 69
<html> element, 14–16, 346
HTML5 (Hyper Text Markup Language 5)
    cross-browser compatibility, 23–24
    elements, 14–19
    general discussion, 7–8
    overview, 7
    tools, 8–13
    web pages, 13–14, 20–22
HTML5 Doctor, 356
HTML5Rocks, 280, 356

HTMLMediaElement interface, 247
human-readable dates, 353
hyperlinks. *See* links

I

id attribute, 69, 116, 300
IDs, selecting elements by, 229–230
IE. *See* Microsoft IE
IE7 compatibility mode, 23
if statements, 221–222, 273–274, 296
if/else statements, 260, 287
<iframe> element, 346
Image objects, 328–329
image parameter, 328
image property, 170, 173
images
    accessibility, 202
    Canvas API, 327–331
    embedding in Locations page, 83–84
    maps, 85, 87
    poster, 244–246
    product, 99–100
<img> element
    adding product images, 99–100
    attributes, 16
    describing image in alt attribute for
        accessibility, 202
    embedding images, 82–83
    general discussion, 346
    LocalBusiness schema, 170
in-band subtitles, 261
index parameter, 269
IndexedDB API, 280
infinite loops, 224
initialization parameter, 222
initializing variables, 216
inline scripts, 212–213
innerHTML property, 232
input fields, 134–137
input types, 144–152
<input> element
    assigning labels, 193–194
    attributes, 119–120
    <datalist> element and, 342
    general discussion, 346
    input types, 120–123
    overview, 115–119
    saving user data from Bookings page, 272
    selecting multiple files, 133
    updating value of field, 232
<ins> element, 334–335, 346
inserts, text, 334
Internet Explorer. *See* Microsoft IE
Introducing HTML5, 355–356
iOS keyboard, 144–146

`itemid` attribute, 171
`itemprop` attribute, 169–171
`itemref` attribute, 171–172
`itemscope` attribute, 169
`itemtype` attribute, 169

J

JavaScript
    decision making, 221–222
    DOM, 226–233
    event listeners, 220–221
    functions, 218–219
    general discussion, 210–212
    libraries, 233–236
    loop structures, 222–226
    overview, 209
    `<script>` element, 212–214
    simple program, 215
    users' locations, 286–287
    variables, 216–218
JavaScript Foundations course, 210, 236
jerky playback, 256
jQuery library
    executing code on page load, 234–235
    overview, 233–234
    selecting elements, 235–236
jQuery object, 235
JSON (JavaScript Object Notation), 275–276
JSON object
    overview, 276
    `parse()` function, 277
    `stringify()` function, 276–277
`JSON.parse()` function, 277
`jsonPerson` variable, 276–277

K

`key()` function, 269
`key` parameter, 267–268
keyboards, customized software, 144–146
key/value pairs, 114, 266–270
keywords, 44–45
`kind` attribute, 262

L

`label` attribute, 262
`<label>` element
    general discussion, 193–194, 346
    input types, 120–123
    `<input>` element attributes, 119–120
    overview, 115–119
landmark roles, WAI-ARIA, 193
`lang` attribute, 16–17, 71
language codes, 16–17

`lat` parameter, 293
`latitude` property, 286, 288
Lawson, Bruce, 355–356
layers, 303
layout templates
    `<article>` element, 42–43
    content page, 30
    `<div>` element, 31–33
    `<footer>` element, 41–42
    `<header>` element, 33–35
    home page, 29–30
    `<nav>` element, 35–36
    overview, 25–27, 29
    for pages, 27–29
    `<section>` elements, 36–41
    sitemap, 27
legal disclaimers, 67–69, 350
legal requirements, accessibility, 190
`<legend>` element, 134–137, 346
length
    restricting, 162
    validating, 157, 165
`length` property, 270
less-than sign (<), 15
`<li>` element, 347, 348, 354
libraries, JavaScript, 233–236
`license` link type, 60
line breaks, 336, 341, 354
`lineLength` variable, 311
`lineTo()` function, 310, 312
`lineWidth` property, 310
`lineY` variable, 311–312
`<link>` element, 47, 347
links
    `<a>` element, 57–58
    accessibility, 202–203
    attributes, 58–60
    legal information and, 67–69
    overview, 57
    types, 60–61
    updating site navigation and sitemap for, 138
Linux, Orca screen reader for, 191–192
List Apart, A (ALA), 356
list items, 347–348
listening for events. *See* event listeners
lists
    ordered, 62–63, 348
    overview, 61
    unordered, 61–62, 354
local development servers, 263–264
LocalBusiness schema
    marking up business locations, 175
    `name` property, 171–172
    overview, 170, 172–174
    using microdata in restaurant website, 175–180

LocalStorage API
    arrays in, 279–280
    `clear()` function, 269–270
    `getItem()` function, 267–268
    `key()` function, 269
    `length` property, 270
    objects in, 278–279
    overview, 266–267
    `removeItem()` function, 268
    saving user data from Bookings page, 270–275
    SessionStorage API versus, 280
    `setItem()` function, 267
    storing objects and arrays, 275–280
`localStorage` object, 267–271
`location` property, Event schema, 181
locations
    calculating distances between two sets of GPS coordinates, 293–295
    drop-down menus, 129–130
    finding nearest, 295–298
    of users, 286–291
Locations pages
    complete, 297–298
    content, 84–86
    displaying distance labels, 295
    embedding images, 83–84
    marking up locations, 175–180
    modified to highlight location closest to user, 285–286
    overview, 83
    permissions, 290
    updating, 292
logos, 34–35, 53–57
`lon` parameter, 293
`longitude` property, 286, 288
`loop` attribute, 247
loop structures, 222–226
`low` attribute, 336–337
Lunn, Ian, 46

M

M4A (AAC codec) format, 239
machine-readable dates, 102, 353
main feature sections, 74–75
`manufacturer` property, 186
map images, 85, 87
`map` property, 174
marking up text
    `<address>` element, 335
    defining terms, 335–336
    emphasizing text, 333–334
    indicating importance, 333
    line breaks, 336
    `<meter>` element, 336–337
    overview, 333

progress bars, 338
    `<span>` element, 335
    strikethrough style, 334
    text inserts, 334
markup
    semantic, 193
    testing accessibility, 203–204
matching patterns, 163–164
`Math` library, JavaScript, 225
`max` attribute, 153, 157–159, 336, 338
`maxlength` attribute, 157–159
MDN (Mozilla Developer Network), 356
media
    converting files, 238–240
    Mute button, 259–261
    overview, 237–239, 247–249
    Pause button, 251–253
    Play button, 249–251
    seeking with slider, 253–257
    video, 240–247, 261–264
    Volume control, 257–259
Menu pages
    figures and captions, 97–98
    overview, 89
    product images, 99–100
    tables, 90–97
menus, drop-down
    `<option>` element, 128, 131–132
    overview, 127
    for restaurant locations, 129–130
message boxes, 123–125
`<meta>` element, 43–45, 172, 186, 347
metadata, 43–45, 103, 347
`<meter>` element, 336–337, 347
`method` attribute
    `<form>` element and, 110, 344
    GET method, 113–114
    overview, 113
    POST method, 115
methods. *See* functions
microdata
    Event schema, 180–184
    `itemid` attribute, 171
    `itemprop` attribute, 169–171
    `itemref` attribute, 171–172
    `itemscope` attribute, 169
    `itemtype` attribute, 169
    LocalBusiness schema, 172–180
    overview, 168
    Person schema, 184–186
    Product schema, 186–187
    schema.org, 168
Microsoft IE (Internet Explorer)
    audio formats, 239
    bug preventing from using poster image, 246
    compatibility with Google Chrome, 23

Microsoft IE (Internet Explorer) *(continued)*
 developer tools, 13
 general discussion, 9
 IE7 compatibility mode, 23
 video formats, 238
Microsoft NVDA screen reader for Windows, 191–192
MIME types, 134
`min` attribute, 153, 157–159, 336
`model` property, 186
`month` input type, 150–151
`mousedown` events, 256
`mouseup` events, 256
`moveTo()` function, 310, 312
Mozilla, 210
Mozilla Developer Network (MDN), 356
Mozilla Firefox
 audio formats, 239
 Canvas API documentation, 311
 developer docs for Canvas API, 331
 Firefogg converter, 239–240
 general discussion, 9
 video formats, 238
MP3 format, 239
MP4 format, 238–240
multimedia. *See* media
`multiple` attribute, 131, 133
Mute button, 259–261
`muteBtn` variable, 260
`muted` attribute, 247
`muted` property, 259–260

N
`name` attribute, 43, 119–120, 231
`name` parameter, 216
`name` property, 171–173, 186
native support, 238
`<nav>` element, 35–36, 347
navigation
 links, 57–61
 lists, 61–63
 overview, 57
 page layout, 26
 site, 137–139
`navigator` object, 287
`nearest` class, 296–297
nesting elements, 19
network information, 289
New Exciting Web Technologies (NEWT), 8
News pages, 100–105
`next` link type, 60
nodes, 226–228
`nofollow` link type, 60
`<noscript>` element, 347
Notepad++, 11
`null` values, 273–274

`null` variables, 216–218
`number` input type, 146, 153
NVDA screen reader for Windows (Microsoft), 191–192

O
`<object>` element, 348
objects, 211, 275–280
off-by-one bug, 224
offer text, 323–325
`offerTextX` variable, 323–324
offline access, 266
OGG (Vorbis codec) format, 239
OGV format, 238–240
`<ol>` element, 61–62, 348
online advertisements. *See* advertisements
`onload` event, 213, 328–330
`openingHours` property, 170–171, 174
Opera
 audio formats, 239
 browser, 9
 Dragonfly developer tools, 12
 general discussion, 9
 guide to WAI-ARIA landmark roles, 193
 video formats, 238
 Web Forms 2.0 specification and, 142
operators, 222
`<optgroup>` element, 132, 348
`optimum` attribute, 336–337
`<option>` element
 allowing multiple selections, 131
 general discussion, 348
 grouping options, 132
 linking to `<datalist>` element, 154
 overview, 131
 `<select>` element and, 128
 setting default option, 131
 `value` attribute, 131
Orca screen reader (Linux), 191–192
ordered lists, 62–63, 348
Organization items, 187
origin points, 303
out-of-band subtitles, 262
`<output>` element, 349
Outside of Society, 211

P
`<p>` element, 18–19, 170, 336, 349
pages. *See also* layout templates; templates
 About, 80–83
 content, 26
 displaying elements, 32–34, 37
 executing code upon loading, 234–235
 extending `<head>` element with metadata, 43–45
 hierarchies, 54–55
 home, 73–79

V

validating code, 20–22
validating data
    Bookings form, 157–160
    matching patterns, 163–164
    overview, 157
    regular expressions, 164–165
    requiring data from user, 160–161
    restricting, 162–163
validator.w3.org, 21–22
`value` attribute, 120–123, 131, 336–338
`value` parameter, 267
`value` property, 273
values, 16
`var` keyword, 216
variables, 232
    general discussion, 211
    `null` and `undefined`, 216–218
video
    accessibility, 261–264
    adding to About page with `<video>`
        element, 240–247
    controls, 242–243
    converting files, 239–240
    file formats, 238
    online, 3–4
`<video>` element, 170, 240–247, 354
visual design, 204–205
Voice Over screen reader (Apple), 191–192
void elements, 15
Volume control, 257–259
`volume` property, 257–259
`volumeControl` variable, 258
Vorbis codec (OGG) format, 239

W

W3C (World Wide Web Consortium), 20, 142,
    190, 281, 339
WAI-ARIA landmark roles, 193
Water/Ocean demo (Outside of Society), 211
WAV format, 239
WAVE (Web Accessibility Evaluation Tool), 203–204
`<wbr>` element, 354
web browsers
    Apple Safari, 9
    checking for support of LocalStorage API, 271

cross-browser compatibility, 23–24
detecting support for GeoLocation API, 287
Google Chrome, 9
handling inconsistencies with jQuery library, 236
Microsoft Internet Explorer, 9
Mozilla Firefox, 9
Opera, 9
overview, 8
storage limits, 281
video formats, 238
Web Content Accessibility Guidelines (WCAG), 190
web forms. *See* forms
Web Forms 2.0 specification, 142
Web Inspector Developer Tools, 12–13
web page templates. *See* templates
web pages. *See* pages
web standards, 20
Web Storage Support Test tool, 281
WebAIM, 203
WebM format, 238–240
websites, 210, 356
WebStorage specification, 281
`week` input type, 150–151
WHATWG (Web Hypertext Application Technology
    Working Group), 20, 339
`while` loops, 224–226
`width` attribute, 16, 84, 300
`width` parameter, 304–305
Wilderness Downtown demo, The (Google), 211
`window.onload` event, 213, 233–234
wireframes, 27–28
word breaks, 354
words, reserved, 216
World Wide Web Consortium (W3C), 20, 142, 190,
    281, 339

X

`x` coordinates, Canvas API, 303–305
XAMPP, 264

Y

`y` coordinates, Canvas API, 303–305
YouTube, 240